The Relationship Paradigm

The Relationship Paradigm

Human Being Beyond Individualism

Godfrey T. Barrett-Lennard

First published 2013 by
PALGRAVE MACMILLAN

Palgrave Macmillan in the UK is an imprint of Macmillan Publishers Limited,
registered in England, company number 785998, of Houndmills, Basingstoke,
Hampshire RG21 6XS.

Palgrave Macmillan in the US is a division of St Martin's Press LLC,
175 Fifth Avenue, New York, NY 10010.

Palgrave Macmillan is the global academic imprint of the above companies
and has companies and representatives throughout the world.

Palgrave® and Macmillan® are registered trademarks in the United States,
the United Kingdom, Europe and other countries

ISBN: 978–1–137–32972–1

This book is printed on paper suitable for recycling and made from fully
managed and sustained forest sources. Logging, pulping and manufacturing
processes are expected to conform to the environmental regulations of the
country of origin.

A catalogue record for this book is available from the British Library.

A catalog record for this book is available from the Library of Congress.

Contents

Part III: Unfolding the Worlds of Relationship

Part IV: Research and the New Paradigm

Preface

This book advances fresh thought about the human condition viewed as an interwoven tapestry of relationship on many levels. These include twosomes, families, friendships, face-to-face groups and teams, communities, organizations and ethnic and national associations. Couples tend to be nested relationally within families, families within communities, and communities within nations. People also live in associative relation with other species and are themselves creatures adapted to the earth's biosphere and its properties. Lives begin in relationships, and recognition of their centrality is a counterbalance to the inheritance of individualist thinking that has permeated Western culture. A relationship-centred view highlights the profound interdependency of life while also recognizing that each person's subjectively experienced world is distinctive and a precious part of being human.

To me as author this book is one whole, but readers will naturally differ in the features they especially resonate to and will give greater and lesser attention to its varied parts. It comes out of a journey of nearly six decades from the start of my doctoral studies and research, particularly inspired then by Carl Rogers' work at the University of Chicago. If I could really say in a few words what this book is about, there would be no need to read it. Here are some hints (complemented by the chapter contents table):

- The content is about relationship, in as much depth and width as I can present in a single readable volume. In the depth dimension it searches into the basic nature and pervasive presence and working of relationship in human life. In 'width' it encompasses worlds of relation that range from the voices within our complex plural selves through interpersonal and other domains on up to relationships within and between nations.
- Humans are understood as fundamentally relational in their/our nature. People can be very lonely (as explored within Chapter 3) although, and partly because, we live in relation in our inner lives as well as outwardly. The book's approach challenges and complements traditional emphases in the helping arts and sciences – and in the culture.
- Its main roots are in humanistic psychology and counselling, broadly, but its content extends further afield in the social and human sciences, and into relations with our animal relatives and the working of systems in nature. Arbitrary disciplinary boundaries tend to dissolve in the thought presented.
- Out of concern to understand movement, change and continuity, I am drawn quite often to looking back to how a system (even a nation) was born

with its own directional code and impetus. Part of my belief is that this temporal dimension is vital to comprehending the way things are, where they are heading and how they might change or become transformed.

- The book also reflects deep concern with qualities of subjective or 'lived' human experience while at the same time searching into the working and interplay of relationship systems. A subtle consciousness and ramifying feeling-life are pivotal aspects of our human complexity of being. This dynamic complexity, in its working, is a variety of system. Seeing each relationship as a complex whole, generally not enclosed but interacting with other systems, also helps to empower the thought unfolded here.

- The adventure of this book focuses more on gaining and presenting fresh understandings than on showing how to do things. Practice principles and illustrations appear in various places, and real events are carefully described, although the work is not designed as a training manual. It offers a foundation to build on for further inquiry and practice development over a broad sphere. I have sought to make the *thinking* so clear that readers can go beyond what I spell out to see further implications and new possibilities in their own work and living.

All this said, the book comes out of my life journey as experienced and thought about in its different phases and contexts. In saying a little about 'my' journey I do so as passenger and driver combined, and from a complexity of being in common with the reader, although our particulars vary. The life I call mine began in Australia and continued here through my mid-twenties with my life partner and our first child. Then, in Chicago, my world unfolded in a new phase that included doctoral research on the therapeutic relationship. My research interest soon widened to include a range of other helping and life relationships. The methodology has been used by other investigators ever since. Back in Australia, in 1963 I began serious involvement with intensive groups and later published theory and research in this area. Another move a few years later, to Canada, led on to a broader interest in human relations and the working of systems. It became clear to me that relationships also live profoundly in the consciousness of participants – and even in affected others.

Difficult experiences in the 1970s helped to trigger added foci of interest, including community and organizational life (each a chapter area in this book). It also occurred to me that personal therapy, which I still practised and set much store by, had a shadow side. Even while helpful to individuals it was a kind of fire-fighting endeavour with little impact on modifying societal forces and systems that could grind on people or generate stress and tension in relationships. Finally settled again (from 1983) on earlier home ground and again practising therapy as a main activity I was increasingly interested in the lived worlds of relationship of my clients, and wrote about this. Though not an activist in personal style, perhaps I could make more difference through my writing. It became 'now or never' to complete the book *Carl Rogers' helping system* that had lingered on from its serious beginning in Canada. Rogers' work had been hugely valuable to me, but I could see clearly that my own view of relationship and systemic processes was taking a further direction. While still interested in how one person (or group) was responding to another, my sights were on the emergent new whole of relationship itself, with its own properties distinct from personality.

That first book, subtitled 'journey and substance', was and is a large and satisfying contribution to the burgeoning person-centred movement. But I soon wanted to go further and began to work on another volume, which became two books (published in 2003 and 2005), the later one under the main title *Relationship at the centre*. But even that did not go far enough. Along with other work and writing I began to conceive of the present volume as a potentially comprehensive development of ideas in which relationship would be 'at the centre' in a more complete sense. But was I up to another book, I asked myself? I also wondered how others would take the more novel perspective I was bent on articulating. At first I kept the plan close to my chest. However, the work developed its own momentum, I began to be confident that I could bring it to fruition and it became more important to me than any other project.

In fact, I couldn't have written this book at an earlier stage: To begin with, I didn't know enough; and I needed a lot of time to think and learn more, and develop my route through the territory of the book. And even for me it was a step into the unknown – none of it was already written, much remained to be worked out, and the work I'm best known for wasn't central to it. The enabling stance of Rogers' approach has helped to seed the departures in thinking reflected in this book. Even the term 'person-centred' however applies more to the attitude, values and outlook infusing the book than to the most familiar content of that approach.

Viewing relationship and interdependence as being at the core of human life departs from the traditional thoughtways of Western culture and most prevailing tendencies in the human sciences and helping arts. Human personality and its variations, attitudes, needs, learning capacities, personal difficulties and deviance –and their interconnections – have in one way or another been the predominant focus of an essentially individual psychology. Other human sciences, including counselling, have grown out of the same culture. In the approach of this book the human self is seen as generated and developed largely through relationship. Aside from strong interest in the self and fresh thought on *inner* relations, the person *as individual* is to one side of the searching spotlight on relationship. My long involvement and thought in clinical/counselling practice shows through in various places, and I believe the book will be useful to practitioners concerned with change, personal or systemic. However, I do not present recipes, the book does not aspire to be a 'how-to-do-it' manual, and my central concern is with something I see as more basic: the anchorage of ideas through a roving search for deeper understanding.

Understanding that keeps developing, informed by questing thought and complemented by skills of practice – practice that is at once a servant of this thought and that flows back to further inform it – are foundations in my view for effective action. My experience with others, as a searcher-practitioner, scholar and participant-observer over the territory of this book, has helped to inform it. One main dimension is the working out of ideas through to what I venture to think is a distinctive paradigm, one that offers a freeing vision for new thought, research and approaches to the protection and healing of relationships on multiple levels.

The first three chapters of this book probably are the most accessible to any interested reader. The ideas gradually become more complex though I do have long practice as a writer and seek to convey nuanced meaning in uncomplicated language. While possibly of surprising scope, the chapters are all thematically connected, and the work could be studied as a whole. I expect, however, that most readers will proceed (perhaps after the early chapters) to parts of most immediate relevance to their interests. Some chapters (9 and 10, for example) could be foci of study in their own right, although the cross-referencing and interconnections of idea are most likely to lead you as reader on into other chapters. It would be a pity to miss the short final chapter, which sums up understandings and elements of the paradigm outcome of this book. The *word* 'paradigm' was not in my original *title*, and I owe the present form to my attuned publisher's editor.

If much of this work has a conversational flavour it reflects a sense of relationship with fellow readers and others I have imagined speaking with as I wrote. If you wish to speak back to me I would *welcome* it. I have an email address at Murdoch University, but am mostly at home at gt_barrett-lennard@iinet.net.au. If this does not work at a later time other family members, including my sons John (nearby) or Lance (in Vancouver), and counsellor daughter Judi Barrett-Lennard, can be reached via the internet. Let one of us know if you also would like a postal address for me. My wife Helen, alas, died early in 2012, and I dedicate this book to her memory as a gallant, treasured life partner and mother.

Bon voyage

Godfrey Barrett-Lennard

Part I

Human Relationship: Nature and Domain

1
The Idea and Variety of Human Relationships

What is a human relationship in its basic nature? Does the way that people behave together constitute their relationship, or, is it centrally about the feelings each one has with and about the other? You, the reader, no doubt have observed many relationships. Do you think (or agree) that they have a kind of chemistry with its own qualities that cannot be predicted just from knowing each member separately? Further, do relationships only develop in interpersonal face-to-face situations? Or, do they arise also between groups, communities, even nations? On another level, is it meaningful to speak of relations within our own complex selves (think of inner arguments as a possible illustration). These are a small sample of the questions you or I might raise in this basic realm of human existence. One broad observation is that relationships vary greatly in kind, quality and people-dimension, and there is much to be understood about them. What follows is the opening of a full-scale effort to advance that understanding.

This chapter in the first part is concerned with the basic nature of human relationships or, more exactly, with how we might best view and think about that nature. Two connecting issues are then considered. One of these is to explore the inner life of relationships as their participants experience them. A further aspect is to begin to sketch out the very broad domain and reach of human relationships. Leaving aside inner relations, they are seen as ranging in structure from one-on-one all the way up to international and other big-system relations. And, they can be distinguished qualitatively as in the simple illustration that follows (*not* a test, but an invitation to connect from your own experience) adapted from the detailed exploration in Chapter 6:

Think of two differing relationships that you know from the inside or as a close observer. Try rating them (your own personal sense) somewhere on the line between the following pairs of contrasting qualities. You could identify and plot one relationship as 'A' and the other as 'B'. There is no score, but it might interest you to see if/where they are alike, where they differ most, and where it's 'hard to say'. If you wish, add to the broad *relationship* qualities; or plot additional relationships.

Harmonious	____|____|____|____|____|____	Discordant/conflictual
Intense	____|____|____|____|____|____	Subdued/flat
Radiating warmth	____|____|____|____|____|____	No warmth/icy
Vibrant/energetic	____|____|____|____|____|____	Lethargic/inert
Competitive	____|____|____|____|____|____	Collaborative
Struggling/stuck	____|____|____|____|____|____	Flowing/evolving
Responsive	____|____|____|____|____|____	Reactive

On the Basic Nature of Human Relationships

Relationship traditionally implies connection and exchange between individuals or groups, each aware of the other in an association that matters to them in some way (positively or otherwise). Implied is the assumption that life, consciousness and human agency all reside in the participants not in relationships, which serve to satisfy needs of the members. However, relationships often engage people very strongly as a source of meaning and vehicle of self-expression. They are a major force in people's lives. Thus, it also can be said that relationships are a further level or kind of life that specifically comes into being through association. This life expresses itself and speaks through the participants and can also have a presence and distinct quality to concerned outside others. These two views of relationship – (1) as a structure and process of in-between activity and (2) as an emergent entity with its own character and life – warrant unfolding to reveal more of their core meanings and assumptions.

Relationships as Vital Bridges Between Lives

Linkage or connection of some kind seems basic to any idea of relationship. In a widely implied view, the link is a joining bridge between persons who also stand apart in their being. The relationship opens the way between these islands of conscious life and meaning. There typically are exchanges of feelings, stories, ideas and intentions, physical actions, and of gifts or other objects – any of which may be desired and valued, or unwanted and reacted to. In this view, each participant lives an individual life, and relationship is a major avenue for the expression of this separate and needful life. In personal relationships, each member is a felt presence to the other. It is an association and sometimes a partnership *between people* whose lives intersect and have meaning, often utility and sometimes threat to each other. In relations between groups and larger systems, each *group* is a consequential presence to the other in widely varied ways and there may be flow of interchange between them.

From this familiar standpoint it would seem obvious that the mentioned features are in keeping with what relationship is essentially about. We are separate beings (or groups of people) who have needs or concerns that involve one another for their satisfaction, and who are associated by choice or circumstance. Relational engagements that arise from circumstance can be very strong, as between children in families. Relationships that are self-chosen, perhaps with considerable investment of self, can nevertheless be transient. If there come to be disturbing features and little satisfaction for either or both parties then distancing is likely and the relationship may effectively end (see, e.g., Miller & Stiver, 1997, on *strategies of disconnection*).

This position implies a transactional or exchange view of relationship, in keeping with the dominant individualist mindset of Western culture. An even broader assumption is that people stand or fall by their own merit and actions, and have full responsibility for their relationships (Barrett-Lennard, 2007a). They give, receive, judge, compete and do lots of other things in relation. Where a relationship is faltering, stressed or conflictual it is the two (or more) parties who are causing and enduring this stress or conflict. Individuals feel the emotional impact; other kinds of effect are basically their doing and it is they who are responsible for any kind of resolution. The relationship itself is not a force in its own right, even though damaging consequences might flow from conflict or breakdown. Any healing processes occur in individuals and apply only indirectly to the relationship. Although this perspective has much familiar meaning some of its assumptions are open to serious question.

Relationships as Emergent Expressions and Forms of Life

An alternative view recognizes relationship as itself having or partaking of life. A literally new human life starts from complex interchange, usually in an intimate relationship. In fertilization a fresh sorting of chromosomes from the two parents occurs. A human embryo then progressively forms within the mother's body. At some point, evidently starting before birth, there is a dawning of consciousness in this new being that is not yet aware of itself as another life. Infants gradually learn that they are separate from their parent, though dependently connected, and each acquires their identity through this and other relationships. Thus, in the forming of a new life, relationship comes before individuality. Later relationships emerge from the conjunction of formed though still evolving people.

A person is an enormously complex whole arising from the coming together of a great range of component entities, the intricate brain and nervous system being the most complex and integrative subsystem within this emerging whole of a complete person – who possesses properties (notably including consciousness) not possessed by any parts. Effectively, a human life is a more encompassing and higher order system than the components that it arises from and integrates (see Chapter 2). Similarly, a relationship is an emergent live whole on a further level, with its own properties. It is not simply an additive combination of its parts, not of the same kind as a personality but of another order (Barrett-Lennard, 2007a, 2009). Kriz (1985/1989) speaks of self-organizing processes as fundamental to the understanding and working of complex systems. A whole person can be seen as a self-organizing system. Many underlying structures and subsystems are essential for this life, but none of these wholly programs it. The whole has its own flexible 'program'. Similarly, an emergent *relationship* has this self-organizing quality.

This alternative view acknowledges that we are basically co-existent beings. A disposition to relate is wired into our make-up. In most formed relationships each person has a consciousness of 'we' as well as 'I'. This we-consciousness (Barrett-Lennard, 1993) is often reflected in dialogue and typically experienced in inner reflection. Interactive behaviour in relationships, however, often occurs without individual intention, even when either or both partners would wish it to have a different quality. A configuration of relationship process comes into action, which partners cannot simply turn on and off at will. They have helped to determine their 'we' process, but also are influenced by it. Their relational pattern will, in addition, influence and be influenced by other relationships.

Formed relationships normally are not static; they continue to evolve depending partly on the participants' stages in life and their experience outside the relationship in focus. Children as young as three or four often form a variety of significant relationships, some necessarily dependent and others where dependence is not such a marked feature – as perhaps with grandparents or playschool carers. Older children may bond strongly with non-family peers as well as within their families. The context of family systems, culture, school and models of relationship in the young person's world all play a part. People tend to have a web of relationships that naturally influence forming new relations.

The Lifetime and Inheritance of Relationships

As mentioned, some relationships begin at the birth of a child, or before birth in the case of a pregnant mother and the stirring baby within. They also, it seems, begin between unborn twins (Castiello et al., 2010; see also Piontelli, 2002). They can last through the overlapping lifetimes of the participants, or even longer as further noted. They develop and change, in interaction with the changing consciousness of participant members and the influence of external relational and other systems. Relationships that benefit from and contribute to the fruition of participants may develop a 'co-actualizing' quality (Motschnig-Pitrik & Barrett-Lennard, 2010). Given that life processes are always on the go, and that the contexts of encounter with others are so diverse, relationships vary greatly in effective longevity as well as in kind and quality (see next section). Moreover, any close relationship or one that is distinctively important to the participants tends to remain in memory long after that relationship is externally active.

Thus, even after the life of a participant ends, relationships may live on strongly in the thoughts and feelings of a surviving member, with images replayed, interior conversations, continued engagement with a person's meanings and values and perhaps even a sense of the other's presence. And even when both or all members of the original relationship in focus are no longer alive their observed and felt relation can live on in others who were affected by and witness to it. This appears to hold not only in family and other intimate contexts, but also in some relations between groups and communities or even nation states. Furthermore, strong echoes of such relationships may recur in the next and further generations. Thus, even though relationships do not have characteristics that are passed on genetically, both individual and group memories can provide the vehicle for significant inheritance. This thought invites attention to ways that relationships vary in their working.

Relationship Differences in Experience

Immediate experience in and inward reference to a personal relationship mostly focuses on 'you' or 'me', or one of us toward or in response to the other. Our inner images centre on the parties to the relationship and include feeling or thought messages, one to the other. These might convey 'how I'm feeling with you', 'this is what *I* think [said as an invitation or a challenge]', 'you're telling me...', 'I remember when...', '*you* are making *me* upset', 'let's you and me do X____'. Communication in relation may also advise or instruct the other, check out an understanding of them, and variously criticize or ask for the other's help (see Goodman & Easterly, 1988). Most exchanges fit our tendency to perceive agency as located in individual people (and in individual groups). An engagement process is seen as being in 'my' hands, or in 'yours', or with some share to each one. How the *relationship itself* is working, and what its qualities or problems are, is seldom considered – and usually quite absent in the heat of conflict.

Although a relationship does not literally speak, it expresses itself. Its process voice can be heard by or visible to the attuned observer and sometimes to the participant who is listening for it. As most of us have felt or observed, relationship qualities vary widely. In examples already implied, they range from being stuck in a repeating pattern to being in free unfolding motion; from having a strongly cohesive quality to being disjointed or fragmented; from having a lively intensity to being subdued and muted; from a reactive jumpiness to a flowing responsive quality; from having a strongly sharing quality to a quite withholding ambience; and from being high to distinctly low in energy.

Immediate feelings of participants within relationships cover an even greater gamut. Level of trust and felt safety is an important variable. The warmth of feeling of either party toward the other is a vital aspect in personal relationships. Relations between groups can also be more or less respecting and regardful. The extent to which this regard is conditional on the other party meeting some expectation or desired quality, or whether it is conveyed without judgement of the other, has crucial bearing on the emerging relationship. As the reader may know, Carl Rogers distinguished unconditional positive regard on the part of the helper toward his/her client as a primary ingredient in therapeutic relationships (Rogers, 1959). This did *not* imply acceptance of all *behaviours*, but a profound and genuine receptivity to the felt experience and meanings of the other person. The not uncommon experience of being judged and found wanting by the other tends to inhibit open expression and felt security, as well as reducing any immediate warmth for the judging other. The aspects of level of regard and of the degree to which this regard is unconditional can be separately defined and even measured in relationships, as in my own work (see Chapter 11 and Barrett-Lennard, 2003, chapter 8).

Compassion and empathy are not identical processes though often linked in expression. Compassion implies a strongly felt concern for the experience and perhaps suffering and circumstance of the other. Empathy implies an inner resonance and recognition of the felt experience and meaning of another person. Although it involves activation within the listener of a related quality of felt experience, this is not carried to the extent of identifying with the other and losing track of what is distinctive about *their* experience. A tendency to respond empathically also implies the broader linkage of being a sensitive, involved part of the human world of felt experience and meaning. Communicated empathic understanding can simultaneously connect and release the other from an inner burden. For this and related awareness processes to happen within a relationship the parties need also to experience each other as open and truly the way they are presenting themselves. A simulated portrayal of this quality may briefly have similar effect but, since transparency is part of such genuineness, even skilled simulation is unlikely to work for long (see, e.g., Rogers, 1961, part 2, and sources in Bohart & Greenberg, 1997).

Nearly all felt attitudes can vary in degree or strength, and mostly they have opposites (examples are given in Chapters 3, 4 and 6). Emotional response is in our make-up and part of being alive. Although anger, contempt and other negative feelings can hurt others, their complete suppression or denial in a relationship keeps its surface temperature at a critically low level. Relationships with little participant feeling in them are barely alive. Individuals discover themselves in relationships and may find that self-change and relationship enrichment go hand in hand. Discovery learning of how to express negative emotion in ways that do not injure and may even enhance particular relationships can be a vital sphere of change. Similarly, conveying immediate positive emotion in natural expressive ways that are also perceptive of the other happens in (and is part of) enriched relationships.

These various attributes all have bearing on whether a relationship in its overall process state has a growthful actualizing quality. Very positive states of this kind, especially in personal relationships, have been distinguished and closely described (Motschnig-Pitrik & Barrett-Lennard, 2010). Relationships commonly begin by two or more people coming into each other's experienced presence. While most personal relationships have a developmental potential, a small minority only are thought to reach an optimal or co-actualizing quality – understandably so 'in that relationship development, like actualization, tends not to be a smooth and linear process but one with peaks and valleys and sometimes plateaus of repetition or sameness' (ibid., p. 376). And, the aforementioned qualities of mutual feeling, attitude and empathic attunement that 'help to grow' a fruitful relationship may be too weakly or unreliably present for this to happen.

Across the span of anyone's variety of engagements with others the relational chemistry and quality of association naturally varies. Altogether, people (though women more than men) devote a large part of their communication to reactions and issues relating to their felt experience with others. Such discourse, however, mostly points to individual experience, including desires, reactions to and perceptions of the other. It seems that participants seldom refer directly to their own emergent relationship itself, that is, to their 'we' process as distinct from how 'you react to me', or 'me to you'. This lack of reference to their interactive whole is plausibly a big part of the reason why such conversations often go round in circles, bearing little fruit of a problem-solving kind. The participants in an individualist culture may not know how to think about and address their relational bond as such – a matter I will come back to. Here I will turn to the overall domain of relationships in human life.

The Full Spectrum of Human Relationships – A Preview

People are relationally engaged in their inner lives and in a wide variety of small and large systems of association. Besides interpersonal relationships within and outside families, there are relational bonds with groups, communities and even larger systems, and these groups and systems have widely varying patterns of association with each other. Relationships are both wholes *and* parts. As well as having their own identity, they are encompassed or 'nested' within larger relational systems. The two-way influence between the nested and encompassing systems can, of course, be stronger or more visible in one direction than in the other. Families are a small-scale example of a 'container system' that both influences and is influenced by the twosomes (and triads, etc.) within it. This interdependent relation between the embracing system and its constituent relationships applies on many levels – as, for example, in the case of an organizational system and work teams or departments within it (Chapter 8).

Families live within larger groups and communities of distinctive culture, which naturally influence the family mores and how members relate to one another. This cultural ethos flows into the kinds and qualities of relationship that form but does not govern them, for the constituent relationships have their own returning influence. Family size has an obvious bearing on the diversity of family relationships. Each member experiences each other member in a two-person relation, and is likely to be the third person (if a child) in a relation with the parents as a twosome and also as one of a duo interacting with a single other member. Many configurations are possible and the array and interaction of relationships in a multi-child family is a complex total system (Barrett-Lennard, 1984; 2003, chapter 7). All of the relationships contribute to qualities of the family whole and are influenced by it.

Communities clearly are of many kinds, based for example on place of living, ethnic or religious affiliation, or being in the same vocation. Members may be on a convergent path in an educational or training context, sharing a recreational or hobby interest, or belonging to the same religious or social group. The term 'community' is at times misapplied to aggregates of people having something in common but with little actual interconnection. A *community of relationship* can start with people finding themselves linked by contacts, location and/or a similarity of paths. Out of the intersection of their lives relationships and networks of association grow and develop into a more or less cohesive communal whole. Communities are sometimes transient (for example, if they emerge in a situation of shared emergency or acute danger) and may be temporary in a fast-changing external context, or long lasting. They may contain a high density and cohesion of relationships, or be of looser form where members do feel an affiliation with the larger whole but have first-hand contact with relatively few others.

One defining quality of a community is that members are effectively within reach of one another, even if dispersed among a larger population. They can communicate in a common language, usually with elements distinctive to the community, and tend to have attitudes or sensibilities in common. There is a measure of interdependence and a boundary (even if somewhat fluid) to their community. Together, these features imply that members share the experience of being part of something larger together that they identify with (Barrett-Lennard, 2005, pp. 84–85). Communities can of course be active and well functioning or divided and struggling. Whether healthy or not, communities worthy of the name are conceived as human relationship life forms, with a 'consciousness' that is evolved and mediated through the preserved history and consciousness of their members (ibid., p. 85). Chapter 7 closely explores the ways in which communities form and flourish, processes by which they decline and dissolve or recover, and their vital role in the larger spectrum of human relationships.

A big proportion of human experience in nearly all contemporary societies also takes place within and in relation to organizations. Most people work in such systems. They are complex containers and generators of relationship, person-to-person, and between sub-organizations and their included groups. Organizational systems interact in consequential ways with other systems of similar and differing kind. Of their nature, in 'developed' or developing cultures, most organizations produce goods or provide services in strong competition with other providing systems. Quality of life within organizations often is not a priority or else it is supported in the interests of maintaining motivation and stability within the system. Stress in face-to-face relationships appears to be common in workplaces within large organizations. There is much potential, also, for interpersonal and group relationships to form and at times to flourish and be strongly valued by participants – especially in organizations in which the well-being of members and their relationships *is* a system-wide concern. Chapter 8 of this book closely explores these and related topics.

Whole nation states typically encompass a huge array of diverse organizations, communities and smaller systems, each of which is internally complex. Clearly, the relation of such major national wholes with each other may be enormously consequential for their inhabitants. The European Union is a leading example of a group of nations now strongly affiliated with, on balance, hugely positive effect on their international relations. Historically, their relationships in various combinations involved selective alliances and periodic extremities of warring conflict, including the enormity of suffering and savaging of relationships in the two world wars of the last century. Chapter 9 explores numerous other examples of the many-sided destruction and gross distortion of relationships in warring conflict. In peace or war, each person whose self-identification stems partly from membership in a national or similar whole has a significant relation with that whole. The constituent governmental and related systems are also parties to relationships with citizens in many contexts. The contained organizations, communities and smaller groups have direct or indirect relations with the whole and with each other.

This glimpsing view of the spectrum of interwoven human relationships from interpersonal to big-system levels is developed much further in later chapters. Chapter 6, in particular, reaches to form a systematic picture or working taxonomy of the whole domain of relationships. The role of relationship stress and distress in human disturbance also leads to a fresh envisioning of 'psychopathology' (Chapter 4). Community in its central relationship dimensions, and large organizations as major containers of relationship, are the mentioned foci of two other chapters. Chapter 9 searches into the drivers of international and inter-ethnic conflict and the formidable issue of healing relations between large people-systems who have been at war. Chapter 10 opens into view the great variety, working and impact on participant lives of human–animal relationships.

In Conclusion: Defining Relationship

A basic premise of this book is that a relationship is not an additive or simple combination of its members, but a phenomenon of a different order and kind. This view recognizes that people form and evolve through relationship, live interactively on diverse levels and in many different patterns, and are relationally engaged in their inner lives. We are physically separate but *co*-existent beings. Our DNA was forged contextually over eons of time and culminates for each life in a reconfigured combination occurring through an intimacy of relation. Beyond and building on this genetic inheritance, people acquire their identities largely through engagement with others in their own lives. Relevant associations are not only within their families and in other face-to-face relations but extend to the varied groups, communities and cultures that they are part of. Each of us lives in and through a complex multi-level web of relationships.

It seems fitting to end this chapter with a concise working definition of relationship. Aspects of this outline will come into fuller view over the course of this book, and a distinctively arranged outline of qualities also appears in Chapter 6. Terms such as 'participant', person-system or 'living system' can refer in what follows to a single person or a family, group or larger interactive system:

1. A relationship includes two or more participants engaged in an emergent transpersonal process in which the members are integral components in the resulting distinctive whole.
2. The resulting relationship whole can be viewed as a dynamic living system within which each component person helps to elicit the contributing process of other member-persons in the influential whole system.
3. Relationship in its varied forms and inner representations is where human living primarily happens. Relationships not only serve individual and group needs but are themselves primary expressions of human life.
4. The participants within a relationship are involved and living in other relationship systems and they carry contributing influence from one system to the other.
5. Participants come into a new relationship with interests and attitudes born outside it. However, these are not imported unchanged into the fresh context since this relationship comes from a new combination and has its own emergent life.
6. Generally, relationships are dynamically nested within larger *relational* wholes – family systems and face-to-face groups, organizations, communities and subcultures, these dwelling in still-larger national and transnational systems.
7. A relationship 'we' (to its members) has its own presence and derived consciousness. This 'we/us' consciousness expresses itself through the participants but comes out of the emergent relational whole.

8. Each formed relationship can be said to evoke in a participant an expression and configuration of self that is (more or less) distinct to the context of that relationship.

The last part of the next chapter offers criteria of poorly and well-functioning relationships. The earlier parts concentrate on the remarkable biological underpinning of human consciousness, the emergent formation of self and the interdependence of this complex self and the varied relationships it engages in and that help to form it.

2

Intricate Relations Within the Person-Organism

As organisms humans are made up of a great many interacting parts that need to work together in intricate synergy. Furthermore our very complex consciousness is not just a unitary whole but is multi-patterned. Different modalities of self emerge when a person engages in different kinds of relationship (see Chapters 3 and 11). Thus, the sphere of inner relations seems a natural place to start the main study of this book. Here, I will plunge in at once to use the language of living systems.

The Human Organism as a Union of Living Systems

Living organisms are complex, open, interactive systems that normally seek to maintain themselves and reproduce their kind. Far from being self-contained or 'closed', living systems absolutely require an environment with properties and resources compatible with their own properties and needs. It is no wonder that this is the case since in contemporary understanding living beings are evolved creatures of their natural environments. The human organism, besides its fit and relation with the outer world, contains on the inside a myriad of part-processes that work and flow together in an enormously intricate dynamic whole. These parts are themselves complex and distinctive systems that require each other for their complementary and interwoven functions in the whole. The whole is naturally self-organizing in its environment, partly due to a feature present and complete from the very beginning of a life: the remarkable building plan coded in the organism's genetic DNA structure.

The complexity of a person-organism is, first of all, evident in the great variety of component physical systems. Standout features are our brain and nervous system, the heart and intricately detailed circulation system, lungs and respiratory system, skeletal structure and muscle systems, the less visible but ramifying and influential endocrine system, the digestive gastrointestinal system, the liver factory, and many others – including the system of encoded genetic blueprints present in each cell. These varied high-precision systems each contain a great number of distinctively organized and specialized cells, each cell a living mini-system with many component parts (Kolb & Whishaw, 2005, chapter 3; Raven et al., 2008, part 2). Interdependence is a fundamental principle. One illustration, given by Mader (2002, p. 198), is the way that the kidney and whole urinary system contribute to the needed environment and functioning of no fewer than 10 other main systems in the body.

The brain is the outcome of an enormously long evolutionary journey. One fruit of this journey is an overall architecture of major complementary regions. The most distinctively developed (in humans) and enveloping cerebrum, with its several major lobes and other differentiating features, includes the cerebral cortex. This extensive but thin outer layer, with its incredible density of neurons – perhaps 10 billion in all (Raven et al., 2008, p. 887) – includes areas closely linked to human consciousness. Much of the brain is also occupied with crucial regulating and other 'autonomic' functions largely outside awareness. Fanning out from the brain is the hugely intricate system of sensory and motor nerves. A human eye alone contains over 100 million light-sensitive retinal receptors and a myriad of connecting ganglia and other nerve cells with paths to the brain (ibid., pp. 912–914). The enteric nervous system resident in the human gut is a partially autonomous and even more extensive and complex subsystem than the eye and visual system (Furness, 2006; Wikipedia: 'Gut flora').

Altogether the human brain is estimated to include upwards of 100 *billion* neurons and an even larger number of supporting cells of several kinds (Kolb & Whishaw, 2005, pp. 77ff.; Rains, 2002, pp. 21–22). Each neuron grows dozens or scores of forming and reforming dendrites that fan out a bit like the delta of a major river. These discharge or receive electro-chemical signals to and from the dendrites of other neurons. These connections and the many assemblies and networks they are part of make for a literally astronomical number and scope of anatomically based process elements. This vast foundation and its dynamic working – seen in whole-brain activity via scanning technology, and in clusters and individual neurons via use of minute probes (e.g., Doidge, 2008, p. 50) – provides the huge potential for our most elaborately differentiated and varied consciousness, memory-storage and behavioural repertoire. One of the presumed underlying principles I see is that complexity of structure permits complexity of function.

Throughout nature we find that when things combine into a larger unity new properties emerge. In a simple example, liquid water results from the fusion of oxygen and hydrogen gases. Similarly, human consciousness is seen as an emergent property arising from the exquisite complexity of our organism, especially the brain (see Deacon, 2007, on emergence). One implied property of the latter is its enormous capacity for learning. This includes the learning of who one is, as a distinct though complex self. For a child, let's say, much received feeling and other communication in relationships carries messages about how the child is seen and regarded, which flow into the child's forming sense of identity. The child's spontaneous expression, assertion and testing of self also give rise to feedback over a very wide possible range. No particular view of self is inborn; rather, this comes through experience. What is inborn includes an impressionable nature and huge capacity to learn from experience, a need to 'map' experienced reality and develop some navigational framework and, in particular, a propensity to come to an awareness of self through experience and engagement with others.

The incredibly complex human brain is always dynamically active, busy with 'housekeeping' chores mostly outside consciousness (regulating our heart action, breathing and digestive processes, and a host of others), generating nonconscious responsive-adaptive behaviour (Wilson, 2002), and processing conscious mental activity and action. Recent research implies that the brain is highly responsive in details of its working to new experience and learning. A primary way that this happens is by the continued development and other modification of neural (synaptic) connections and circuits. The brain even has substantial capacity to recover from damage or avert deterioration (Doidge, 2008). Awareness of self and patterns of self-engagement must of course involve brain function. Current research and understanding would imply that self-awareness and its working necessarily involve very complex and detailed patterns of neural organization that keep on adjusting through new experience.

The Emergent Multi-Self

In childhood, and almost certainly in adolescence and adulthood, people experience very diverse relational contexts: in their families, with school friends and members of their peer culture, with close mates and also antagonists or enemies, and with teachers, bosses, workmates and others. Relationships with intimate partners and with young children of one's own usually follow. Most contexts carry direct or implied – and at times powerful – messages about how the person is seen or judged by the other. In positive vein, some engagements convey permission or active encouragement for spontaneous and adventurous self-expression. Such varied and important contexts of relationship with their diverse feedback necessarily will foster complex images of self. Specifically, they can be expected to give rise to contextually differing modalities of self. I refer to these differing modes as 'contextual subselves'.

Extensive writing, both in literary works and in the human sciences (e.g., Barrett-Lennard, 2005, pp. 6–11; Rowan & Cooper, 1999), as well as much everyday and clinical observation (see next chapter), speaks to a plural quality of self. Empirical research has begun to yield systematic evidence of self-diversity (presented in Chapter 11 and Barrett-Lennard, 2008). I see this diversity as part of the normal human condition, usually taking adaptive forms though sometimes a socially 'dysfunctional' way of coping (see Chapters 3 and 6). There appears to be an inbuilt desire for the positive regard of others, which unfolds to include also a need for self regard (Rogers, 1959). These needs help to lay the ground for development of a diverse or plural self since received regard from others often is conditional – rejecting or unresponsive toward one aspect of the person's way of being and responsive and accepting in the case of another manifestation of self. Below is an illustration of diverse potentially desired qualities in a relationship for readers to personally try out:

Think of two or three significant and *different* relationships in your own life and, for each relationship, select the qualities that best fit your sense of how the other prefers or wants *you* to be. You will be able to see if and where one relationship context invites a different choice and combination of qualities than does another.

Competitive, plays to win	*Cooperative, joins as equal*
Controlled and cool	*Spontaneous/open*
Risks him or herself	*Plays safe, looks before s/he leaps*
Imaginative/shares dreams	*Thinks logically/uses reason*
Proud, expects to be looked up to	*Deferent, knows his/her place*
Expects to lead, take charge	*Follows easily, prefers others to go first*
Seeks perfection/exact skill	*Ploughs on and gets through things*
Shares feelings, is transparent	*Not emotional; feelings don't spill over*
Intelligent, quick, in front	*Solid, middle of the road, fits in*
Energetic, spirited, feisty	*Low key, relaxed, easy going*
Vigilant, appraises critically	*Accepting and accommodating*
Gentle, considerate, supportive	*Assertive, expects others to shape up*

Young individuals differ greatly in the extremity or strength of conditional attitudes they experience in relationships with parents, teachers and others in the course of their development. And, for the same person, how diverse the experienced conditional attitudes are from one pivotal relationship to another will affect the diversity of their expectations and modalities of self. That such variation typically occurs seems to this author to be no longer in doubt, as further documented in the next chapter and Chapter 11. When a person enters a new relationship the self-mode that comes into action will depend in part on similarities between this new context of relationship and the one(s) through which the activated pattern of self had earlier formed. This expectation has some resemblance to earlier thought on transference processes, but the emphases on naturally occurring plurality of self and continuous interaction between self and relationship are major points of difference. A new association (say, with a friend *or* a person in authority) will not be identical to any in the past, and may moderate the triggered self-mode for the future. Through fruitful therapy, or a quite new quality of relationship, this moderation may be so substantial that the activated self-mode is transformed.

If a person were to be nurtured in an exceptionally homogenous attitudinal environment the consistency of relationship would work to limit diversity of self. A lack of significantly varied experience and self-adaptation may not equip a person well to live in a very diverse relational world. There can, it is thought, be too little variation in an individual's pattern of self-being. To be versatile in the sphere of human relations means to be able to cope or flourish in a variable relational environment. In this view, therefore, the well-equipped person would have a developed repertoire of experience-based resource modes suited to the great variety of engagements involved in a complex environment and world of relationships. The implied need for complex diversity of self-being leads me to re-examine the issue of how to think about personal or psychological health; what it can mean to be a well- or optimally functioning human being.

Wholeness and Health of Persons and Relationships

The human organism, as discussed, contains a vast community of cells. Each cell is a living entity and vital contributor to the organ, body system, part of the brain or other functional component of which it is a member element. Each group or subsystem of cells has a crucial and distinctive role in the greater community of the complete organism. Without this division of labour by specialist components working together the organism could not survive. Diversity is seen as a principle of life, reflected from the start of each human organism by the crossover of genetic information from the two parents to form a unique new combination. Without the resulting diversity the larger group would weaken and could die out. Neither the individual organism nor the group can afford to be seamless and uniform, just as it cannot exist as a collection of parts that do not fit together and merge in jointly creating a larger living whole with its own properties.

Conceptions of human psychological wellness, positive mental health or optimal development and actualization have tended to hinge on the idea of inner unity, integration, congruence, self-consistency or being all-of-one-piece (e.g., Jahoda, 1958, pp. 35–41; Wyatt, 2001). In the thought advanced here such notions as traditionally portrayed are seriously limited. A person requires a certain plurality of being, to be healthy and function well. Yet, as noted, it is possible for a person to be diverse and variable in a way that is distinctly unhealthy. What does a quality of wholeness – of being at the same time both 'many and one' – imply in this thought? One approach to answering this question is to think of the whole person as being like a well-functioning group. In such a group the members all communicate and get on, and each one contributes something distinctive that complements other people's contributions. The member interaction itself generates new potentials and the group as a whole develops a transpersonal identity and capacity. The inner diversity, communication and mutual knowing of group members all contribute as it faces outward and selectively calls on member resources that are most relevant to the situation presented. Similarly, and at best, a person responds in a given relational context with a mode of self-being that is already attuned to that context but also has the strength of the whole behind it.

A further basic issue regarding wellness requires no analogy. Given that people live, in great measure, in and through relationships that develop their own life, health is not simply an individual property. Rather, the well-being of selves and relationships interweave in a complex reciprocity of influence. A person could be healthy in one important relationship and not well functioning in another relational context. Thus, it is seldom possible to say that a person is healthy or unhealthy in a completely general sense. Psychosocial health needs to be seen within and relative to a context, even in the cases of people diagnosed as psychotic (see Chapter 4).

In an example of the influence of relational context, a psychiatric hospital client code-named Loretta was interviewed in very different style by three therapists. With one highly receptive clinician who responded with acute empathic understanding and human warmth she expressed herself fluently, without evident pathology and with progression in the dialogue and the client's feeling. With another therapist who directly challenged her thought and pushed her to confront irrational features that she needed to change, the client brought the Devil into her explanation and then took on the role of defendant in a broader and vigorous counter argument with the therapist. She showed herself to be mentally acute if deviant in her vision of 'forces' at work, and there appeared to be no progression in her own processing or the relationship (Barrett-Lennard, 2007b, p. 132; Raskin, 1996).

There is nothing especially novel in the idea that a healthy quality of personal functioning generally hinges on context quite as much as anything inherent in the person who is in focus. Counsellors who work with couples and families tend to draw on a systemic way of thinking. Almost certainly, they would have vivid experience of couples where the partners function very poorly (and painfully so) in communication with each other but appear to be basically healthy and resourceful individuals who do well in other relationships. While it is possible for a person to become so demoralized and depressed that they lose confidence to engage in almost any immediate relationship it is my view that in nearly all cases such a person can come to life in some relational context – if not with another adult then perhaps with a young child or a highly responsive animal friend or even in a natural setting that nourishes them. And in working with a therapist the evidence is that the quality of the helping relationship is a potentially decisive feature in the person's movement to greater health, within and with others (Barrett-Lennard, 1998, chapter 13).

Clearly, relationships can vary greatly from extremes of 'ill-health' to those of exceptionally positive quality. One approach to a definition of positive wellness or a 'fully functioning' quality of relationship is to envision its opposite or what it is not like, and then to portray corresponding qualities of distinctly well-functioning relationships. The six items that follow are potential features of dysfunctional relationships. Not all features would apply in every such case.

1.   Destructive extremes of conflict that deeply stress, hurt and work to alienate members from each other.
2.   Being stuck in a highly repetitive pattern of interaction, which to a point shields participants but does not nourish them.
3.   Verbal exchange that regularly carries little direct expression of owned feeling or inner meaning.
4.   A quality of struggle to maintain separate positions in the relationship, thus with no holistic quality or sense of an encompassing mutually experienced 'we'.
5.   Interaction that largely ignores the self-identity and distinctive experience or personhood of the other and works to distance members from each other.
6.   An extremely brittle or 'knife-edge' quality. One variant of this quality rests on tacit agreement not to rock the precarious boat. Any fresh fracture leaves the relationship as or more brittle than before.

A view of well-functioning relationships has features that parallel the first set, but are transformed in positive expression, and there are two broad additions. For a given person, these qualities may apply in some of their relationships, but not apply in others that enjoin differing modalities of self.

1.   *Well-functioning relationships* are open to expression of differences. Conflict is not eliminated, but it does not leave festering wounds and may further mutual understanding.
2.   Communication occurs spontaneously over a wide range of content and effectively feeds and nourishes the relationship.
3.   Exchanges have an expressive richness through sharing of implicitly owned feeling, observation, thoughts and meaning.
4.   There is a collaborative, interdependent quality with a strong sense of 'we'.
5.   Sharing exchanges occur within an ambience of mutual respect for each other's diverse self and experience that also supports freshness in the relation.
6.   The relationship moves responsively and adaptively, holding together with a natural cohesion not susceptible to fracture.
7.   In formal view, the relationship is an open, adaptive living system; a system in dynamic motion through the between-member processes and feedback from outside sources.
8.   These qualities of process are enhancing and growthful in kind, jointly for the participants and their relationship. 'Co-actualization' is a new name for strong expression of this overall quality (Motschnig-Pitrik & Barrett-Lennard, 2010).

Conclusion

A person might be confused by their own variability, supposing perhaps that their identity should be manifest in a single consistent self that always faces the world in the same way. This assumption does not take into account the enormous complexity of the human brain and the extraordinary range of human capacity and consciousness that results. The remarkable thing is *not* that a person is variable but that s/he is *a* person; that such a vast and improbable assembly could ever work as one whole. This whole is not autonomous, of course. It cannot live separately from a life-supporting environment and is always in some needed relation with other people, with systems in nature (such as an oxygenated atmosphere in a suitable temperature range) and with other species (see Chapter 10).

From the remarkable whole of the human organism, the consciousness that emerges includes a subtle and variable awareness and expression of self. This variability arises partly from differing attitudes experienced in formative relationships, attitudes that encourage or discourage the self in particular directions. New relationships selectively call on formed modalities of self that may then be affirmed or modified through this fresh experience. Some engagements of self can be considered healthy and others relatively unhealthy. Health or wellness of functioning is not ingrained (not cemented in individual personality – see Chapter 6), but is that of a *person-in-context*. Relationships that engage the same person with different others can, self-evidently, vary greatly in their qualities.

The differing modalities of self can amount to inflexible alternative configurations or, alternatively, to working patterns transparent in the person's awareness and open to refinement through continuing experience. In this latter case the person is not always the same, but is primed by formative experience for responsively distinctive engagement in different kinds of relationship. 'Relations' within the person are of great importance for personal wellness and fluency of engagement with others. In effect, varying inner voices may argue and deny one another or make for enrichment and versatility of the whole. The knitted-together working of the diverse self and its life of relationship is further explored in the chapter that follows.

3

The Diverse Self In and From Relationship

In dialogue we commonly acknowledge ourselves with use of the first person pronoun 'I': I think, I feel, I believe, I suggest, I want, I hope, etc. Self-reference as 'me' often conveys something about the speaker's receiving or wanting self (e.g., 'he frightened me', 'do this for me', 'it is difficult for me'). 'Myself' and 'not myself' used in similar contexts are highly self-referential. But what is this self or owned inner being we speak of? Is it our whole personality and make-up, is it what distinguishes us as individuals from other people's selves, or is it just the Me that we are conscious of or, more exactly, the concept we have of who and how we are either in general or in a particular relational context? The self-in-context alternative comes closest to my usage in this book. Given that anyone's self is multi-faceted, a single overall picture of what we are like is at best a generalization. According to who we are with or, even more specifically, in what circumstances, we might well describe ourselves somewhat differently from our sense of what we are like in another context. I will point to some research that backs up the view that indeed we are 'many' as well as 'one', after speaking first of other kinds of evidence.

The Reality of Self-Diversity: Five Kinds of Evidence

1. Evidence from Everyday Experience and Conversation

References to being 'not myself', 'a different person', 'in two minds', 'letting myself down', or to having 'fallen apart', 'turned into jelly', 'pulled myself together', 'slipped back', 'come to my senses', or that 'I don't know what came over me' and other such expressions all reflect an acute awareness of personal complexity and variation. Any genuine expression of being surprised by one's own behaviour or felt reaction suggests that the speaker assumes a familiar self or pattern of being and senses another side of his/her make-up, one that is 'not really like me', 'out of character' or 'not true to who I am'. It may well be, however, that the speaker's surprise and discomfort with this alien or rejected self is a reaction when they are in particular company. In a very different rela-

22

tional context, the same self-behaviour might pass unnoticed or even seem positive. Of course, it can at times be a struggle to decipher and deal with the outer world and this can be mixed up with the tension of competing inner voices. It is these different voices and action patterns that particularly reflect and contribute evidence of *self*-diversity.

Great numbers of people participate vicariously in sporting contests, seeming to lose or transcend their everyday selves in the presence of skilled athlete heroes in action with their teams and opponents. In many cases the pattern change is so marked that it seems clear that a different configuration of self has come into play. So too in some racing carnivals, musical or theatre performances and other situations that arouse and engage people deeply. This self-to-self shift can be greater still for the players or performers themselves who enter into their expressive roles and engage in a particular potent expression of self with others. The evident transitions from one self-mode to another usually occur spontaneously in response to the contexts in which they occur. On reflection, the person might be quite aware that they 'changed gears' in a way that is natural to them and that accords with our complex nature as humans.

Men and women can be warriors in armed combat – fierce, dangerous, prepared to overpower or kill a threatening enemy – yet also tender with a loved partner or with their own child. Neither of these almost diametrically opposed action patterns need be inauthentic or false in the person's being. Rather, they can be dramatic examples of self-diversity. We would be much more limited creatures if capable only of one way of being. Some of our diversity can be understood as learning to be fine-tuned to the individuality of situations and how best to engage and express ourselves. But, variations often go further than this implies and can be better described as shifting from one mode or configuration of self to another.

2. *Evidence of Self-Diversity in Serious Literary Writing*

In formally accepting the Nobel Prize in Literature, William Faulkner focused on the rendering of personal complexity and conflict as the core element of literary art. Young writers of today, he said, have 'forgotten the problems *of the human heart in conflict with itself* which alone can make good writing because that is worth writing about, worth the agony and the sweat' (Nobel Prize 1949: William Faulkner, italics added). This core value fortunately was not lost and has evolved in its expressions. In one later example and in the words of a prominent reviewer, the Australian author Peter Carey's *Oscar and Lucinda* [Carey, 1988] 'are two of the most perfectly realised characters in modern fiction'. In particular, the character and core relationships of Oscar in this Booker Prize-winning novel come to embodied life with a subtlety and evocative realism that reflect the complexity of human consciousness and the interplay and influence of relationship both within and outside immediate awareness.

A century ago in a British context, Arnold Bennett's people-centred writing included his classical novel *The Old Wives' Tale* (Bennett, 1908). The book traces the lives, settings and relationships of the two central characters over half a century, from girlhood to death. One striking feature is the interior conversation of the two women. The distinctive plural voices of Constance and Sophie are developed in compelling depth. The interlocking nature of self and qualities of relationship is an implicit major feature, revealed in extensive self-conversation, withheld and expressed feeling, and in the different life choices of the sisters.

In Dostoevsky's *Crime and Punishment* (1866) the alienated young man (Raskolnikov) at the centre of this remarkable narrative conceives of and makes himself carry out the murder of an elderly woman pawnbroker, as he sees it, for the sake of his family and to prove to himself that he can stand outside the rules and 'morality' of his world – although afterwards in a developing agony of anxiety and then of inner conflict. The intensity of the book hinges on the sustained and passionate self-talk which, together with interactive communication, exceeds all other text and largely carries the story. Raskolnikov speaks, argues and cries out inwardly, and seeks and hides in strained dialogue with others, in long passages of evocative and mesmerizing writing.

The impact of culture and environment on sense of self, especially when there are transformative shifts in life context, is wonderfully illustrated in David Malouf's subtle and powerful novel *Remembering Babylon* (1993). The central character, Gemmy, worked as a small child in poverty in a sawpit in London and then, with his first sense of belonging, as 'Willet's boy' – in the business of rat catching. At age about 11 he ran far through the night from a fire he had started in Willet's abode and found himself when he awoke on a ship at sea – where he entered a further phase of deprivation. Some two years later, at the dawning of his adolescence and evidently deemed by some of the crew to be a frustrating and serious liability, he was dropped overboard off the isolated Queensland coast and washed up, alive, on the shore. There he was found and rescued by a group of native aborigines who allowed him to follow and attach himself to their band. He became attuned and knowing of their world and grew among them to mid-twenties idiosyncratic manhood. Great development in implied selfhood naturally occurred, but without complete severance from his former identity and blurry past memories.

Gemmy learned of a coastal settlement of white people near his tribal area, observed them unseen and finally approached a group of children and was then drawn into an affiliation with their family. Although soon accepted into felt relationships with this family and a few others, and on a journey of development from the impoverished 'British' childhood self of his earlier life, Gemmy's aboriginal linkage became disturbing to some other members of the white community. Their threats and abuse divided the community, and Gemmy's fragile membership became unbearable to him, his other self remained a living part of him, and he disappeared to rejoin the black tribal community. One can speculate that his inner selves never made peace because there was no peace between his relationships with the black and white communities in which these selves evolved. Many other literary works help to illuminate the working of self and relationship in human life (Barrett-Lennard, 2005, pp. 7–8), which parallels documentation from therapy.

3. Evidence of Self-Diversity from Transcripts and Case Studies of Clients in Therapy

In a self at odds with itself differing subself patterns and voices sit in uneasy or opposed relation and the client person may be anxious, depressed and/or stuck in trying to fend off part of his/her own self-being, as illustrated in my last book (2005, pp. 8–11). The therapy journey of one (implicitly) self-diverse client was studied in detail by Rogers (1954) as part of the classic client-centred research on therapy outcome. Rogers' 91-page report is an exceptionally wide-ranging study of a single therapy case. For the client, 'Mrs Oak', finding words to express herself was a difficult trial-and-error process, and she struggled to put the jigsaw puzzle (her term) pieces of her felt experience and meaning into some sort of coherent whole. She had entered therapy from a context of very disturbed relationships with her husband and daughter, and an implied crisis of meaning in her life. In the given interview excerpts and therapist's commentary, most of her discourse involved self searching and exploration, with a great deal of uncertainty and fluctuation in focus.

From the picture given, Mrs Oak was a very wounded and vulnerable yet determined person, profoundly lacking confidence at the start in her own voice and capacities, and handicapped in connecting felt experience with communicative expression. It seems clear that the growing bond with her therapist became strong and healing in quality, and very important to both. In effect, the client's overt focus was mainly on the relationship with herself and the discovery that she was and could be a self with agency and ability in relationship. Self-evidently, she lived a distinctive self with her therapist, she had been almost another person with her daughter and she could not give of herself as a sexual being with her husband, from whom she later separated. Little or no information is given about relationships with her parents, other family members or friends. At the time of this study, even though the client's self was systematically studied from several different vantage points (actual or ideal, as perceived in the past, as seen by the client or by others, etc.), the idea that a person's experience of self naturally differed according to the relational context was not in the purview of client-centred thought. The emphasis was on increased awareness and acceptance of all aspects of self and on thus achieving an integration and wholeness through therapy.

One of the clients Rogers interviewed much later, in the 1970s, was code-named 'Sylvia'. In the transcript of their published fifth session (Farber et al., 1996, pp. 261–276) Sylvia implies four modes of self-being: a firm parent mode with her children, a distinctly different mode in her relationship with Rogers, a third kind with black men – to whom she found herself very strongly attracted – and evidently another mode with her conditionally regarding parents. With Rogers, she allows herself to be dependent (her word), vulnerable and comforted. Her parents' attitudes included clear disapproval of her interest and attraction to black men, a part source of her inner conflict. (A post-Rogerian understanding of the dynamics of this conflict is briefly discussed in my 2005 book, p. 10.) The diverse self of a former client of my own also is illustrative. The unfolding of her therapy and our relation is reported elsewhere (Barrett-Lennard, 2009) and the account here is a fresh encapsulation.

> Sophie (to give her a new name) was at war inside herself and haunted by experiences in relationship, especially in her family. She also felt knotted, stuck and revolted by a bad, almost alien entity inside herself. On the 'outside' she was an attractive and in many ways resourceful young woman. In the self that she mostly spoke to me from she was in an agony of frustration and despair over the dark, sneaky-bad and alien identity she harboured within her outwardly acceptable self. With her parents, especially her father, she held herself stiffly, guarded and with no spontaneity – by implication, in another mode of self-being. She also felt despoiled by her earlier relation with another family member, with its own very disturbing memories. Her way of being with me, though quite constricted at the start, gradually became more focused and expressive in her path of exploration of self and relationship. Sophie's problems, as she saw them, were embedded within her though rooted in past relationships and with crippling effect on most present associations. She had been largely 'frozen' in the past with men, and felt handicapped and impotent in that side of her life.
>
> Sophie's and my relationship, our forming 'we', was born out of where we each came from and was not an easy birth. Each of us was strongly motivated in distinctive ways and we were able to manage the challenges and come to a productive partnership. Early on, I came to realize that she very easily took my response as 'reading' her from the outside, or explaining her issue, not simply showing I was with her in taking in *her* feeling and meaning. She needed that sense of 'withness' with me, *before she could be sure herself that she was saying what she felt.* One of my own retrospective learnings is that *communicating back and forth is not merely an exchange of messages but always part of the relationship in which they happen. The messages are ripples in the flow or stream of this relationship, and have their meaning within this ongoing flow.* Among other things Sophie was anxious about whether I would take her seriously and 'hang in' there with her for the long haul – and it proved to be a several-year haul. Her relationship and feelings with me became an open topic now and again. She gradually saw herself in a different light, felt differently even in her family relationships, and experimented and spread her wings in increasingly context-sensitive and versatile ways. She did not become less complex but the change reflected more partnership within herself and in her relationships.

Some other therapist authors have articulated ideas about self-diversity, stemming from practice experience. David Mearns found that it is not unusual for a client in therapy to identify and even give names to differing inner personalities or subselves. The varied *configurations of self* (his term) can differ from each other in attitude and ways of coping, and even be constrained by differing moralities. They can live together somewhat like members of a family, differing in interrelation and influence. One of Mearns' examples (1999, p. 126) is the case of 'Derek', whose identified patterns included 'clever me', 'bully me', 'lost little boy', and 'me who knows what is right'. Mearns' understanding differs from mine in that he does not tie the emergence or activity of these patterns to different life relationships.

Gestalt therapist Erving Polster devoted a whole book (1995/2005) to a 'therapeutic exploration of self-diversity'. He emphasized that a person is 'host to a population of selves' (p. 41). To briefly illustrate, one of his clients displayed patterns of self that pivoted on appearing competent, being respected or admired, and being a person of determination. These characteristics matched images that other people had of him, but which he feared were phony. Underneath, he is described as feeling worthless and negatively stubborn. Through therapy the discrepancies greatly diminished, but remained a potential he watched. Polster evidently agrees that the forming of multiple patterns of self is a built-in part of our complex nature as humans.

4. Self-Diversity Indicated in Notable Observation-Informed Theoretical Writing

The idea of multiple relational selves as an expression of human complexity in a multi-voiced world does not come only from the field of psychotherapy. Especially since his 1991 book *The Saturated Self* came into prominence, Gergen has been a particularly visible and energetic advocate of this direction of thought. The human mind as he sees it develops through and is embedded in relationship. As expressed for instance in his later book, *Relational Being* (2009), 'our mental vocabulary is essentially a vocabulary of relationship' (p. 70). He proposes that 'mental discourse originates in relationship', 'functions in the service of relationship' and amounts to 'action within relationships' – also described as 'co-action' (ibid., pp. 70–76). More broadly, 'rational thought, intentions, experience, memory, and creativity are not prior to relational life, but are born within relationships... [They are] embodied actions that are fashioned and sustained within relationship' (ibid., p. 95). I resonate also to one of Gergen's chapter headings, 'Therapy as relational recovery', yet not to all of its content. He notes: 'It is not mind-repair that is ultimately at stake, from the relational perspective, but relational transformation'. This observation could suggest an either–or view, either 'mind-repair' or 'relational transformation', whereas each of these things can involve and imply the other.

William James' towering classical work (1890/1950) had already advanced far-reaching thought about the nature and scope of the human self (ibid., chapter 10). He gave close and pertinent attention to the complex 'social self', especially as manifest to others. 'Properly speaking,' he wrote, '*a man has as many social selves as there are individuals who recognize him* and carry an image of him in their mind' (ibid., p. 294). Since these images tend to fall into groups, he continues, 'we may practically say that he has as many different social selves as there are distinct *groups* of persons about whose opinion he cares' [and] 'he generally shows a different side of himself in each of these different groups'. He also notes that there may be a 'discordant splitting' of these several selves or there may be 'a harmonious division of labor, as where one tender to his children is stern to the soldiers or prisoners under his command' (ibid., p. 294). James' emphasis is on the social self as variously presented rather than inwardly experienced, but overlaps significantly with the perspective of this book in his recognition of self-diversity and implication that this is relationship dependent.

Another major contemporary contribution is to be found in Hermans' prolific work pivoting on his conception of the 'dialogical self' (see Hermans & Hermans-Konopka, 2010). The term 'dialogue' is used by these authors with a breadth of meaning that implies communication, self-engagement, interpenetration, and positioning both against and with others. The term 'society of the mind' is used to refer to a lived internalization of the person's social world with its diversity of voices. Thus inner and outer are interdependent and interwoven in the inherently dialogical self. The social world is represented internally and this internal representation feeds back into and has a part in that world in any engagement of the self. The diversity of the dialogical self, the Hermans argue, is normative in the globalized and multicultural world of today. This self in effect is also extended in time, drawing on traditional images, the modern individualist presumptions and a 'post-modern' self that is far more relativist and oriented toward constructed meaning.

The dialogical voices are often 'collective voices of the groups, communities, and cultures to which the individual person belongs', but 'speak through the mouth of the individual person' in the various ways that they identify themselves (ibid., p. 6). As taken within the person the I-voices are said to converge in a 'dialogical space' through which the person may 'reposition' in their attitudes and beliefs (ibid., p. 6). This inner dialogue is not just self-talk; the voices are engaged in interchange and are both private and collective. Both self and other are conceptually included in the dialogical self, and a blend of inner and outer messaging is naturally ongoing. Thus the self is both one and multiple and tends to be in dynamic motion. The Hermans' latest book (ibid.) runs to 386 pages and unfolds many more features of their thought system and its implications. There clearly are evident similarities between my view of the self and the more elaborated thought of Hubert Hermans and his colleagues, and there are distinctive features in each case. I give more emphasis to direct relationships in self-development and would hesitate to use the language of dialogue for interactive engagement with and between broader social systems.

The classic psychoanalytic view of unconscious processes as unseen drivers of emotion and behaviour implies an inner separation in the sense of one part of the motor of human behaviour lying beneath another. The more lateral notion of dissociation of personality into separate compartments of awareness and action (see next chapter) comes a little closer to the view I am presenting, but is also distinct from it. The concept that the human self is *normally* diverse and that the existence of distinctive subselves can be a major asset in human functioning as well as sometimes taking disabling forms is a more novel view (though not at odds with Hermans' thought, as I understand him). The wellness of any very complex systemic whole implies that *each* component or part system is functioning optimally in its distinctive way *and* is in effective communication or linkage with other component systems. In humans the powerhouse system of consciousness, as it develops through relationship, contributes hugely to the complexity of our species and to the relevance of personal therapies that are highly responsive to relationship issues lived by our clients.

5. *Evidence from Empirical Research Focusing on Self-Diversity*

Though the Hermans speak of 'a gap tween theory and research' (2010, p. 74) there has been a beginning. In a cited experiment, Baldwin & Holmes (1987) focused on the effect on young women participants of inwardly engaging with 'private audiences'. On coming out of the imagined presence of the other (e.g., an elderly family member *or* a young campus friend) the participants were exposed to a 'sexually permissive' piece of fiction. It was found that their enjoyment of this varied according to their preceding 'inner company'. The authors claimed that their 'results demonstrate the influence of internally represented significant relationships on the experience of self' (ibid., p. 1087). In a cited less rigorous but uncontrived clinical study the investigator studied 'burnout in people living at the interface of different cultures' (see Hermans & Hermans-Konopka, 2010, p. 69). In this illustrative case, the client's family moved, when she was a young child, from Turkey to a very liberal European setting. As a young woman she took part in the free local lifestyle, but carried the denied standards of her moralistic Turkish background within her. She entered therapy in severe dialogical self-conflict. There she gradually came to see each of the two worlds in much more multi-faceted and overlapping ways. Reportedly, she also found that her parents were less stuck in a denied past self than she had been, and welcomed the current close boyfriend she introduced them to. The opposites had become subjectively complementary (ibid., pp. 69–70).

The formal research most in line with the perspective of this book grows out of my own work and also is limited in extent so far. My focused interest in self-diversity study began in 2000 with a paper subtitled *Relations within the self –*

self within relationship (Barrett-Lennard, 2000/2007c). This framed the idea of self-identity forming through *varied crucial relationships*, each different relational context drawing self-formation in a distinctive direction. These contexts would typically include the parent–child relation, any relationships with siblings, with one's own child, with close friends, with teachers and with supervisors or 'bosses', with opponents or enemies, and in teams or other groups of special importance to the person. How much the resulting configurations of self-experience and behaviour varied, and whether they complemented each other or were sources of inner discord, would differ from one person to another.

At one extreme, the subself modes might be so compartmentalized that the person manifesting one mode of being would disown or be unaware of another mode that they nevertheless switched into in some circumstances. Each bounded mode would in this case tend to repeat a fixed pattern. At an opposite well-functioning pole the person generally would be quite aware of their diversity and each mode of self-being would be a congruent and adaptive expression of self. No mode would be simply repeating an exact pattern each time it was active, but would work as a dynamic resource that continued to evolve through fresh experience.

The method of investigation I used entailed the development and use of a self-descriptive questionnaire, the self to be described as experienced in a number of distinct relationship contexts. A useful source to draw on was the self-concept inventory used in classical studies of client-centred therapy outcome (Butler & Haigh, 1954; Ends & Page, 1959). This original instrument gave what amounted to a generalized picture of self. The new questionnaire, called the Contextual Selves Inventory (CSI), taps into the ways in which self is experienced during engagement in *each one* of the selected life relationships. Skipping over a first exploratory study, a compact 20-item form was answered by 70 participants in three different workshops I conducted (Barrett-Lennard, 2008). Participant self-descriptions generally supported the hypothesis that the way the self is viewed tends to be highly responsive to relational context. Detailed analyses of how individual items were answered, how they were inter-correlated and tended to cluster into subgroups or factors have contributed to further refinement of the CSI.

Respondents rate the CSI items on a scale of 1 (Never or not at all like me) to 7 (Very or always like me), as they feel and see themselves in the context of each one of a number of specified life relationships. Opposite each self-statement there are answer spaces arranged in columns on the answer sheet, one column for each relational context. The top of each column shows what that self-context is, for example, with the person's spouse/partner, their mother, father, sister or brother, etc. The reader might like to try this out for him/herself, using a simplified adaptation of the CSI, with 10 items borrowed from the present 24-item two-page instrument.

Select three or four different important relationships in your life, not all positive. Answer each self-statement to describe how you are, as you feel and see *yourself*, within each chosen relationship context. Picture yourself with the other person, bringing images to mind if you can. Then ask yourself 'How do I really feel about the way *I am*, when I'm engaged in that relation'. I suggest you simply use numbers 1 to 5 for your answers:

Use 1 to mean that the statement is *never or not at all like you* in that relation.
2 can mean that the statement is *usually or mostly not like you.*
Use 3 to mean that the statement is about *equally like and unlike you.*
4 can mean that the statement is *usually or mostly like you.*
Use 5 to mean that the statement is *very* (or nearly always) *like you* in that context.

This of course is not a test; simply an opportunity to think a bit more about yourself-in-relationship, for example, as you compare the columns of self-answers for each context.

Self-statements	In 'A' relationship	In 'B' relationship	In 'C' relationship	In 'D' relationship
I am full of life and good spirits				
I notice faults and am critical in my outlook				
I take initiative, raise issues, start things				
I look for alibis and excuses for myself if things go wrong				
I forgive easily – don't hold grudges or try to 'get even'				
It is pretty hard to be myself				
I am agreeable and tend to fit in with what others want				
I am inwardly on my guard				
I am imaginative and can share my dreams				
I put on a front when I'm uneasy, not showing how I feel				

Some participants report a quality of discovery as they envision and compare themselves in different personally important life contexts. I will speak further about research with the CSI, both done and envisaged, in Chapter 11. It is one promising approach in the study of self-diversity expressed in relationships. Inventive use of less structured qualitative methods of inquiry into people's experience of themselves in differing contexts would be valuable to use as well, and broader discussion of the self-relationship nexus in human life is called for.

The Yin and Yang of Self and Relationship

It would be possible to focus on relationship to the point that the idea of a personal distinctive self virtually disappears. If personal selves were to be viewed entirely as a socially constituted phenomenon (see discussions by Gergen, 1994, 2000, 2009; Gergen & Gergen, 1988) the whole idea of *a self* as an entity or process in its own right would at the least become problematic. It appears to me, however, that an argument that individual selves are illusory could be turned around and equally applied to the phenomenon of relationship. It might be argued, and indeed is sometimes implied, that human association exists (or could exist) simply in the service of autonomous selves. Neither extreme view is credible to me.

The concept of a personal self is a human construct. However, to jettison the idea of self would suggest that people have no individuality, although each one is a versatile whole conscious organism. Granted then that this immediate discourse on self and relationship is not about solid entities and is an enterprise in understanding phenomena that is reliant on the use of language, there is more to say in keeping with the metaphor of yin and yang. Given that the self or subselves develop in relationship, they are an outcome, an outcome also rooted in the active potential of the human organism. As well as being an outcome the resulting self feeds into the quality of further relationships – which as they develop also act back on the still (and perhaps always) formative self. If one thinks of self and relationship as living systems this mutuality of influence is just a part of how things work in the real world. No one component, nor the whole person, possesses autonomy; each, of their nature, is engaged with other human and non-human systems.

There can be no self without relationship, understood as the principal vehicle by which self-identity comes into being. Similarly, there can be no relationship without some connection or conjoining of separable entities – as is most evident in the forming of a new relationship. Thus, in their forming, self and relationship are intertwined. They are not the same order of system, but in general neither can exist without the other. There are exceptions, notably, in the case of an infant in whom a self cannot be said to have formed though the parent–child relationship is one of strong attachment. Also, relationships can be quite asymmetrical, as when one person feels attracted or in some way connected, but without reciprocated feeling by the other or even without the other's awareness of the first person. In this case the other has subjective presence for the first person, as also is true in vivid memory of an important relationship that the other party has abandoned or where they have died.

A consistent yin and yang of association between self and relationship leaves room for great variation in specific quality. A harshly conditional attitude from a parent or partner within a relationship influences the other person to attempt a guarding posture to avoid hurt and, behind this, an inner critic is likely to grow that in turn is judgemental of itself. Conditional attitudes can of course be mutual and, in any case, are expressed within a system in which nothing is completely independent in its process or without any returning effect. A distinct impression that a particular feature has a certain effect might truly reflect an important link but generally cannot reveal an exclusive causal relation for this is not how influence works in complex systems (see Chapter 5). Processes of self, relationship and their connection are crucially involved in the complex phenomenon of loneliness, to turn to next.

Loneliness and the Self

Loneliness has many faces and hangs over individuals, groups and even cultures as a major feature of diminished life quality. The nature and varieties of loneliness, its epidemic manifestations in mass culture, and ways in which societies might respond to this epidemic are issues of great social importance. Its varieties and groupings can be seen to pivot on three basic features: self-estrangement, interpersonal loneliness and the loneliness of alienation or non-belonging in any larger group or communal whole (Barrett-Lennard, 2001; 2005, chapter 8). In present perspective, the first and second of these groupings are so interrelated in their origins that they can be considered together as a single broad region.

Within this region, a quality of loneliness can result from subself separation to the point that a part or mode of self is lost from any clear awareness by the most dominant or frequently activated part. This way of being 'out of touch on the inside' seems to sap energy, confidence and vitality, and any sense of being at home with oneself. It may be such a 'low grade' and chronic detachment within the self and with others that the person is not aware of it except, perhaps, during special moments of self-reflection or exceptional contact with another person.

The literal loss or fracture of a person's sense of self, which may occur when the stresses of their relational and inner world are overwhelming, and the person closes down into a desperate shielding process often labelled 'acute schizophrenia', is a more extreme form of self and relational disconnection. The not uncommon experience of periodic weird dreams, or other episodes of temporarily slipping out of the 'trance of everyday consciousness', can help us if we think on it to feel more fellowship for people who are stuck in their nightmares. A person in such a nightmare may feel an outsider in a slippery, shifting world that eludes them, deeply uncertain of who s/he is, and very afraid of any relationship. All this is to be in a terribly lonely cut-off place. When a person's sense of self disintegrates, any self-to-self relationship can be mystifying at best and potentially a dangerous realm.

There is another kind of absence of any distinct sense of self, though its experiential quality and origins are quite different from the condition just mentioned. Some people appear to have never developed a feeling or sense of being a known and knowable person. In place of felt identity there seems to be a hollow space, and perhaps a kind of hunger that has never been filled; a hunger one might say from the outside, for identity, for selfhood, to be a 'me' with describable qualities in any given context and a sense of direction that carries over from one situation and time to another. Any urge to find purpose and meaning has little chance to germinate, let alone to take root and grow. People who are relatively 'self-less' have feelings but no friendships or sense of secure attachment to others. They can appear to live in an almost 'relationless' world, tossed on an ocean of superficial, transitory or seemingly indifferent response from others.

The loss or undoing of a foundation of personal life that had been rich with meaning is another source of loneliness. The dislocation of being in a totally different and unfamiliar living environment, or handicapped by injury and loss of capacities formerly taken for granted, or caught up in major political and social upheavals in the milieu of 'home' can all, understandably, trigger very cut-off lonely feelings. Traumatic losses or change are happening all the time to a great many people old and young, and may strike at some stage in the lives of most of us. A frequent feature in such loneliness is the rupture or loss of relationships that formerly were anchor points in the life of the self.

Interpersonal loneliness can arise from the loss of relationships, their chronic absence or the mentioned disturbances or collapse of the self. As a naturally bonding species, humans have built-in potential for deprivation. The human self is restricted in its development where a person has had no experience in relationships with siblings or other childhood contemporaries; little if any parenting where emotional attachment, responsibility and example are built-in; and/or an absence of contact with any unlike others. A person from such an 'empty' world not only experiences people as strangers at first meeting, but is themselves a stranger to the process of meeting and engagement. The result can be an unfilled hunger or aching loneliness for closeness of relationship, perhaps for a friend or a lover, for felt companionship, or a child to nurture. In the absence of self-to-self meetings significant new relationships cannot emerge, and at the extreme a person may be limited to functionary associations that do not exist for their own sake but just as a means to some outside end. Predominant experience of this 'ulterior' kind and little involvement in relationships that are their own reward can leave a person profoundly lonely.

As foreshadowed, there is a further potential level of relationship. Perhaps because of our tribal origins it appears to be in our nature to hunger for community, for a sense of belonging within and as part of a larger world than immediate family, friends and close group relations. Without this development and linkage of a communal identity, people feel no rootedness and sense of inclusion in a world of fellow humans who recognize them and assume mutual belonging. Without a sense of being fellow-members of a significantly acquainted and connected larger community, most people would not be motivated to invest in that wider community or milieu – even less so if they have no sense of agency in their lives. Alienation from the wider world 'leads easily to an exclusive concern with self or, at best, *with self plus a small life raft of immediate family or other personal allies.* Where this happens, loneliness on a community level perpetuates itself' (Barrett-Lennard, 2005, p. 108).[1]

Each of these levels and kinds of loneliness is a systemic process with potential to perpetuate itself. However, it is not a completely closed system and can change when qualitatively quite different experiences do happen and register in the person. In view of the nature and origins of loneliness, a crucial new experience always would involve other people (or, at the least, draw on the animate world of nature). To be crucial in meeting a person's lonely thirst for bonding connection or inclusion, the new experience would need to be relevant to the particular nature of the loneliness and the make-up and circumstances of the person. Further related discussion and thought is included in my previous book (ibid., pp. 108–112), and is extended in later sections of this one. It remains here to speak briefly about the life and association of the self in big organized modern systems.

The Relational Self in Big Systems

Any big system is host to a great many more relationships than there are members, since most people would have a range of associative links in the system and there are a multiplicity of relationships between groups and other subsystems. In a large nation state, personal selves and face-to-face relationships exist in a vast landscape of human association on many levels. Each person-self defines itself in some degree by its membership in the whole. The unequal association between a person and their country or national whole under its existing leadership may have great significance to them. At one extreme, it may be troubling, oppressive and a heavy weight on most of its members or, at another extreme, it may be a source of deep meaning or inspiration to them. Major industrial and commercial organizations are themselves very complex entities given the widely varying roles and diverse kinds of association of their constituent members and groups. In a competitive environment, member quality of life is seldom a leading organizational priority for its own sake (see Chapter 8). Whatever its nature, a big system gives and receives influence from the living selves of its members and their diversity of relationships.

---

[1] In his major work on *Polarities of experience* Blatt (2008) views 'relatedness' or involvement in relationships as a fundamental propensity and expression of human personality, one that may be undeveloped or dominant. Similarly, a focus on the other pole of definition and protection of self may be a central preoccupation or relatively undeveloped. This perspective would provide another starting point for an understanding of loneliness – and much else.

One principle in the study and portrayal of the human associative world is that any relationship is a system associated with other systems on the same level (or of the same generic kind) *and* is also nested in larger systems of association. A whole-family dynamic, for example, influences twosome relationships within the family, and the dyads influence each other and act back on the quality of the whole. Families exist in two-way relation with their ambient community or subculture. Closely linked work teams usually operate in parallel with other teams as well as in interactive relation with the larger organization of which they mutually are part, etc. Thus, person-selves typically live and evolve within an environment of relationships, in which systems of relation on a variety of levels carry influence to and from the centre of interpersonal life. Surrounded by this complexity it is hardly surprising that personal selves are complex and multi-configured.

Zooming out to an even broader view, a nation state that suffers 'civil' war, or war with another state or people, is a context not only for extreme personal suffering and loss of individual life but for stress-induced breakdown, destruction and distortion of relationships. War is itself a way of relating, usually, under the condition of extreme perceived threat or ambition by at least one of the protagonist people-systems or their leaders. Most people are greatly disempowered by societal or warring conflict, since the dangers they face are not within their control to prevent (Chapter 9). Recovering a sense of safety and ability to manage their lives comes through a changed quality of relationships, however this occurs.

Even a peacetime pluralistic civil society involves an ocean of relationships of widely varied kind and quality. Clearly, differing directions in the overall course of this or any society are possible. One envisioned *potential* is the gradual forging of an ethos, expressed through many channels, in which the qualitative development and well-being of the engaged human self in relationships and systems at all levels is a pervasive value in practice. There are some principles but no blueprint for this 'forging' movement, which, necessarily, would be an ongoing self-adjusting process. Further information and ideas in this whole sphere are explored in Chapter 9.

Conclusion

This chapter holds that self-diversity is a natural expression of our complex make-up and exposure to diverse others. Indications of the complex multi-configured nature of the human self are all around us, although increased systematic study is needed to decipher how this natural plurality of being works (Chapter 11). Human relationships are seen as engines of self-formation *and* as emergent from the association of selves. Thus a core proposition is that humans are both creatures of *and* co-creators of relationship. We overlap each other in features of consciousness though each person lives in a more or less differing orbit of relationships and is distinctive in the totality of his/her conscious being. Self and relationship are interdependent partners in human life. Troubled loneliness in some form is a very familiar human experience. The next chapter considers modes of acute human distress outside the norm yet not discontinuous in their working from familiar and 'normal' modes of being. Traditionally classed as varieties of psychopathology, these distress patterns do not require misplaced notions of sickness or disease for their understanding.

Part II

Human Distress and the Working of Systems

4

Psychopathology or Disturbed Relationship? On Suffering, Disorder and Being Well

Most of us have experienced painfully felt episodes in our own lives. Such pain or agony is a result of happenings, a consequence of being in the world, most notably, the world of relationship in its varied manifestations. Participants enter those relationships from a larger influential context, including predispositions acquired in other relationships, even with roots that extend to previous generations. In psychotherapy the participants bring human associations carried alive in felt inner experience. The client's world may include relational fear or longing, worries about personal behaviour and feeling, more severe modes of distress, and memories or fantasies of joyful or satisfying encounters that support hope for a better way ahead. Difficulties that propel clients into personal therapy are not truly dysfunctions of a separate personality but are understood here as expressions of relationship.

A person may be acutely lonely, anxious, depressed, fearful, or suffer other painful or debilitating process states that have complex origins in the person's lived experience with or involving other people. Loneliness can take varied forms, all of these forms arising from or affecting relationship life as already explored (Chapter 3). Troubling self-judgement and inner conflict are understood to have their grounding in relationships, especially those imbued with strongly conditional attitudes during self-development (Bozarth & Wilkins, 2001). Usually such conflict is associated with anxiety and it can lead to immobilizing depression. As well, fear of individuals or collectives of others also tends to produce anxiety. 'Paranoia' and obsessive-compulsive behaviours also seem to have an underpinning of fear, often unacknowledged and plausibly growing out of past or present felt danger to the relationally vulnerable self. If some working through of relationship trauma occurs in safety, and if present associations become more life-giving, distress and its symptoms can recede. Relationship distress can arise in many contexts – small and large system.

Contexts of Relationship Distress

Tension and Conflict in Couple and Family Relations

Family relationships often embody a high intensity and complexity of process – as most readers would know first hand. People who suffer extremes in those relationships may need assistance, explicit or informal, but seldom are *merely* victims since they also are participant influences in the family system. When a child, say, experiences strongly conditional attitudes in a dependent relation with a parent or other influential member, a very judgemental proclivity toward self can develop and then activate in further relational contexts. However, this highly judgemental relationship is not the child's whole world, and an inner battle of self-attitudes and desires is likely. This may unfold through other experience and emerge as a serious difficulty.

Extreme anxiety, deeply depressed feelings or other acute distress or withdrawal are acquired ways of responding rather than fixed endemic dysfunctions of personality. They also are considered here as propensities typically activated much more in some contexts than in others. They are process tendencies, not structural states. They have developed in relationship and its meanings to the person, are reflected in their mood and expectations, and contribute to their response in other relationships. As a participant in those systems the person's response is part of the process, but does not govern it. This view broadly accords with Murray Bowen's innovative systemic *and* experiential approach to family process, represented in a recent volume (Bregman & White, 2011) of valuable contributions. A related way of thinking is also advanced by McGoldrick & Carter (1999) in their account of interdependent self formation unfolding through the life cycle.

Although some partner relationships are quite oppressive to one or both parties, there typically is a complex systemic process going on. Simple attributions of individual personality-based cause and responsibility are not adequately reflective of this process and thus of little or even negative value. Participants may welcome non-judgemental recognition that their relationship is floundering or that it feels out of their control. Diagnostic labels applied to them individually are not only of very questionable validity, but easily deflect attention from the working of their relationship system and in this way are counter-productive. A core idea is that the partners may be reasonably healthy or well functioning, but a dysfunctional process between them remains possible since this is on a distinct further level than either one's individual make-up.

There are different ways that members can 'keep their eye on the ball' than to fixate on what their partner is doing or feeling that is wrong. One way that may help is to draw back and search for *evocative words or images* to describe *their twosome*. What does this entity look like, what is its action style or pattern that is not the same as either one and seems to have its own life? Having shifted focus the partners might each ask themselves: *'What am I doing that is feeding into this We or Us in its tense, blaming, exhausting and distressing process?'; 'I know that our troubled relationship is not all my doing, and not entirely his/her doing. It's something about Us that I wish we could find a way out of. Maybe if we both want to confront this elusive complex whole that is us, our twosome in action, and can watch out and not just fall into the same pattern while we work at it, we will get somewhere.'*

These expressions are one way of wording the direction of thought they convey, which a given couple might translate in a language that is more natural to them. It clearly is not easy to change a distressing relationship with its own momentum. Part of the challenge is to somehow be truly attentive both to the other *and* to oneself and at the same time begin to sense the third entity or 'voice' of the relational encounter process itself. Sometimes a helper who is adept and sensitive in their listening to each party and to the voice of their engagement may be necessary to help the partners discover how they are able, perhaps to their surprise, to be in touch with all three levels. This span of awareness need not be in focus all at the same moment yet still be interwoven *so that neither partner is neglectful of 'your experience', 'my feelings' and this third level of Us that comes out of You and Me together in our relationship process.*

Relationship Stresses in Community Disturbance or Collapse

Communities typically contain many families whose well-being is influenced by their community affiliation and who also feed into and help to co-determine the broader quality of community. Non-family relationships in the community, of course, would also receive and contribute to such influence. Communities in contemporary societies are rarely insulated from other bodies. They can come under all kinds of outside stresses or be eroded from within by multiple tensions or, sometimes, by a growing indifference. Extended stresses on communities (usually unintended and due to 'unseeing') from mining and other major commercial and economic developments, from the growth of cities, natural disasters, voluntary and forced relocations, and even the impact of climate change, are causing or threatening the extinction of communities, especially those based on geographically local settlement. Since felt belonging flows from a systemic relationship that extends beyond the family to the person's larger communal world, the lack of community affiliation is an impoverishment of relationship (Chapters 5 and 7).

Especially where significant community affiliation has existed but been lost this may stress the closest personal relationships and, in any case, leave the participants isolated in an environment that amounts to an aggregate of people – each in survivor mode or out for 'number one'. If the community is collapsing or torn by dissension within itself, the separated members may grieve for this loss as a kind of death; a grief that needs to be shared not just with another grieving 'refugee' but in relationships where the person feels deeply received but not reinforced in their pain and loss – so that they can build from their painful yearning into a recovered sense of wider human connection.

Communities, as mentioned before, are of many kinds and qualities. The community relationship may help to liberate and grow their members, it may provide important supports and safety, it might only be a refuge that members can survive in or, in the case of some cult groups, it may involve a quality of mind control that amounts to a communal prison (Chapter 7).

When the viability of a community that has been rich with meaning and relational support to its members is being overwhelmed by assault or changing circumstance the stress and dislocation for members is prone to be self-perpetuating. At first, members may pull together in defence. However, if this 'armoured' stance is ineffective a more disintegrative process can result. People may naturally regress into a survival mode, in which they no longer count on each other, their mutual empathy and bonding declines, they feel unsafe or frightened and look mainly to close kin or mates and to any possible outside institutional help. If an active defending posture does continue, formerly peaceful relations with other communities may shift to an aggressive-competitive quality as the embattled community tries to sustain itself.

Individuals or families usually can survive the collapse of an immediate and even core community _within a larger environment that provides support and options_. Put another way, there is usually an outer or larger society in which the community was nested and which provides another (less close) level of relationship. This outer supportive social environment and relation is not always available, of course. The larger context may even have produced the disintegration of the community. In this case, the former members are truly refugees that need supportive inclusion within an alternative humane body of people that do offer an inclusive societal and community relationship. Our world presently includes a huge number of such refugees, many of whom are escapees from very dangerous environments where there is no longer any supportive community for them or their families. Thus 'abandoned' they take great risks in trying to find a safe harbour _somewhere_. I see needs for safety and communal belonging as being conjoined in a larger urgency: most simply put, the imperative of being engaged in living relationships.

Relational Process in Severe Societal Upheaval and Conflict

As just implied, the desperate urgency of escaping refugees may arise not just from the collapse of their local community, but from the breakdown or convulsions of a whole society, especially where there is severe internal conflict or civil war (see Chapter 9). Few communities survive intact in this circumstance, except perhaps for a 'community' of people whose whole outlook or belief system is entrained in the posture and practice of combat against an enemy viewed as evil or godless. Relationship casualties have the potential to drain the wellsprings of life from a whole people. Each person, typically, participates in a range of individual and group relationships that linger in the memory and grief of survivors when those other lives are lost. The survivors from those relationships also are affiliated with others who then are indirectly afflicted by the first person's death.

Factional wars, attempts to annihilate whole communities, terrorist attacks and major dislocations of people within states are tragically frequent (and discussed with many examples in Chapter 9). The enormous resulting stresses, especially when sustained, can bring on a nightmare struggle for existence and destroy or warp relationships. The tragedy and count of individual deaths typically is the main content of information reported outside the zone of conflict. This quite inadequate account does not convey the inside experience that, for every such loss, there is a much wider grievous accompanying loss and fracture of relationships. Dyadic relationships, family systems and their interconnections and the savaging or destruction of communities are all casualties. Morale, livelihoods, hope and life meaning hinge on these bonds. Given subsequent trauma-sensitive enabling opportunity (mostly unavailable in practice), much healing and regrouping on the part of survivors can occur. Their memories of events of course remain – and need to, in the interests of increasing personal and communal wisdom. The consciousness of being a survivor, often accompanied by the guilt of 'Why me and not him/her/them', can evolve with effective help into a sense of having another chance in life and, from there, into a proactive engagement in other relationships, livelihoods and future-oriented development of family and community systems.

Re-envisioning 'Psychopathology'

The discrimination of handicapping and distressing difficulties via the usual distinctions of psychiatric/clinical (psychopathological) disorder is misleading. I already have argued that we always are 'in relationship' in our living. As actively conscious beings, people perceive and respond to stressful situations distinctively, and develop diverse ways of coping. Thus their endeavours to cope and manage, even in what Shlien (1961) has called 'an impossible life', take various forms that I acknowledge but do not portray as kinds of pathology or 'illness'.

Organic brain damage: If a deviant pattern of behaviour and experience has a distinct, known organic basis (Alzheimer's, say) then of itself it doesn't belong as a *psycho*pathological condition even in conventional usage. Human brains have a great deal in common but their complexity defies standardization in full detail (see Chapter 2). Apart from effects of clear-cut physical disease or damage, or occasional faulty 'wiring', our individual patterns are acquired, developed or modified through experience in some way. And they are affected by experience even where there *is* brain damage. Experiencing is a life process held to be ongoing continuously and is assumed to underlie distinct conscious perception, though the latter is a level of processing in which memory and former learning also play a big part (Rogers, 1959). Experience and perception, therefore, can be out of step (ibid.), and ordinary instances of this are common in everyday life – as, for example, when a person has a vague sense of something that they afterwards perceive and discriminate consciously (e.g., 'That's what was happening!'; 'Now I know what I was feeling!'). Perception as construal of experience always occurs in a context, whether features of that context are discriminated in awareness or not. And, this context is believed always to contain or be influenced by relationship, held in memory or immediately present.

Anxiety: An anxiety 'state', often so-called, is a most human process developed through experience. If a person is readily, often or nearly always anxious, this not only derives from the person's relationship history but also would vary in intensity and expression according to the immediate relational context. It is not a condition of a separate, encapsulated personality with a single pattern. Anxiety is a kind of fear, with or without the presence of immediate danger or threat as seen by observers. The person who is anxious has 'learned' that (some or most) human associations carry potential risk to the self. There is a past experience-based risk of judgemental criticism or slight, of making mistakes, of humiliation, of being attacked in some way, perhaps of having an accident that others cause or contribute to. Anxiety also can arise from fear of the self – fear of one part of the self by another part, thus involving an inner relation. Common observation would suggest that levels of anxiety vary according to the relational context, expected or immediate; they do not stay on a constant level. Non-human sources of danger can be (realistically) frightening, sometimes intensely, but the quality of fear is not the same as anxiety that develops through learning in association with others. In present perspective, anxiety is a naturally occurring response to kinds of present stress and past hurt or danger. When intense, the person is suffering and may decline in effective capacity, especially in contexts that heighten their anxiety.

'Depression':   Depressed or low mood that is sustained and seems relatively intractable is often called 'clinical' and deemed to be endogenous. This can be contrasted with reactive depression that is more short lasting, episodic or related to immediately grievous events. Guilt and despair at having failed are feelings rooted in relationship although triggered by an event where one 'should' (in one's own eyes) have managed differently or produced a different outcome. Such feelings understandably can unfold into generalized despondency or depression. Implicit or closely related features are the loss of confidence and hope. An opposite shift in psycho-relational therapy, for example, is a movement from 'woundedness to hope' (Barrett-Lennard, 1998, pp. 111–112) which, when it occurs, can be carried to other relationships. Depression is recognized as a huge public health problem (US Department of Health and Human Services, 1999). It is viewed here as a quality of felt experience, mood

and withdrawal generally induced by circumstance, especially in a person sensitized through relationships to feeling inadequate, hopeless or a failure. A person can seem to be 'stuck' in a depressed mood, in some self-reinforcing way. Presuming that the intimate 'yin and yang' of self and relationship (Chapter 3) can be re-aroused, the person is not stuck fast or irretrievably – even if at present feeling completely hopeless in their world.

As in the case of anxiety, depression and accompanying withdrawal and/or reactivity is not at a constant level in all situations. Both observation and theory imply to me that a significant lifting of depressed mood is almost always possible through a relational experience of a quite different nature than the context in which the person became depressed. Often, the process of reaching the *attempted coping process* of depressed withdrawal has been a long one for the client person; by the same token, confident emergence from it may only happen gradually and with sustained experience of healing effect. The releasing/healing engagement needs to involve the person deeply, whether through a life relationship or an effective relationally oriented therapy. When *'depression' is seen as a motivated coping endeavour* that includes emotional withdrawal or 'shutting down' to avoid more acute conflict and/or pain (and possibly also to signal that the person is in trouble) a helping response naturally is sensitive to this. The question 'What is depression good for' was posed by Blechner (2008, p. 572), who points out that 'all the human emotions evolved to serve useful purposes'. 'Sadness', he proposes, 'can signal that we have suffered a loss and will need to lay low for a while until we readjust'. In this perspective, no attempt is made to shock, drug or forcefully instruct the person out of their depression. Contact can of course be difficult during extremities of depression, especially if the person believes that no one else can truly care since they are 'weak' or unworthy failures.

'Paranoia':   Patterns ascribed to this class are transparently relational, usually involving an excessive (to the observer) mistrust and suspicion regarding the intentions and potentially harmful action of others, a particular other or a situation involving others indirectly. Plausibly, experience in relationships that involve unpredictably explosive or other threatening behaviour by a powerful other is one origin of this reaction. Extreme fear by a closely associated other may also feed into it. Calculated and humiliating bullying in a position from which there is no 'escape', even if it occurs intermittently yet is continuous as a menacing possibility, could induce a fearful mistrust, one that might build to a posture of anxious suspicion of other people's potentially harmful intentions. In terms of motivation such suspicion is understandable as a self-protective response, even if it seems 'unnecessary' or ineffective – an explanation that also fits its often variable nature.

In a relationship that becomes familiar as a context of transparent expression of non-judgemental and generally warm responsiveness, the same person's behaviour may not be 'paranoid'. Certainly this was true of a former client who came to me with a psychiatric diagnosis as paranoid schizophrenic, but never showed suspicion of my motives or concern and sustained a generally trusted marriage partnership. Human complexity is such that many people have a wary and mistrustful subself mode that applies in certain relational contexts, a mode that is bedfellow to other modalities of self that are not that way in other quite different relationship contexts. An empathic, genuinely regardful and unjudging helper would not directly challenge the person who does harbour troubled suspicions and fear. To the individual these may be all too real and their desire to protect the self is a natural reaction. If and as the client person experiences safety with a helper, they are able to share more of what they are up against in their experienced world, and a therapeutic exploration process can begin. Paranoia even if generalized is not cemented in an individual's basic make-up but most plausibly is an acquired pattern of cognitive-feeling response and behaviour by a complex vulnerable person struggling to manage lurking perceived danger or threat to self-identity.

'Obsessive-compulsive disorder' is another purportedly psychopathological condition. The OC process is likely to be accompanied by conscious apprehension, which is muted while the person is able to engage in the avoidant-compulsive behaviour. If circumstances prevent this behaviour, extreme discomfort, anxiety or fright is likely, although the interpersonal context at the time may mitigate this reaction. If the person is feeling received and safe in an immediate relationship, the urgency of their protective-compulsive routine usually diminishes. This pattern may originate from somewhat ambiguous but strong messages that the person understands as warnings of certain barely avoidable dangers, danger of contamination for example, that can be minimized by particular avoidant behaviours. The shock to a person's awareness if her/his world shifts and becomes more complicated, confusing or dangerous (though they desperately try to keep everything on track) can naturally leave them with disturbing memories and stress that may contribute to an OC pattern.

The link to relationship in an obsessional process may be diffuse or lost to consciousness, but if the individual gains a sense of security in their relational world their behaviour will be less driven and more open to the sufferer's own reflective and critical appraisal. Human complexity is such that more than one process can be expected: the OC dynamic and behaviour itself and, also, likely frustration and/or shame at being 'driven' and hampered by the compulsion. Again, this pattern is an acquired coping avoidant 'safety measure' (not a sickness). It may seem to have a life of its own, but turn out to be intricately connected with the person's life experiences. A discovered connection or new meaning to that experience may help to make the 'compulsion' more understandable to the person and bring increased capacity for choice.

Schizophrenia: Diagnostic judgements of 'thought-disordered' schizophrenia come typically from observation in professional encounters that maintain relational distance in terms of the inner thought of the diagnostician. For a person who is deeply apprehensive in most relationships, who experiences a moving target of feeling and thought inwardly – thus without a sense of identity that stays put – this (stress) context makes coherent articulation even more difficult. The clinician's appraisal is fraught with potential failure to reckon with the impact of the immediate and 'strange' (for the client/patient) diagnostic inter- view or testing process and a tendency to over-generalize from 'peculiarities' of communication amplified by the immediate relational context. As mentioned earlier (Chapter 3), I regard 'acute schizophrenia' as a desperate shielding attempt to cope in the face of fear of relational intrusion by others and a radi- cally altered or chaotic inner world, one that may no longer include a coherent known 'me' or 'I'. A helper may need to quietly signal genuine but non-intru- sive interest and availability until the other gains sufficient courage or sense of safety to begin a usually cautious but sometimes torrential sharing process (Rogers, 1967). Or, where the other is so shielded and separate as to seem with- out awareness of the helper's human presence, that presence might gradually be brought to the client's attention by the physical mirroring way of respond- ing described by Prouty (1994).

When contact and sharing exploration begins, it may be possible for the client's movement to gradually build on itself. Accounts by Rogers (1967), Shlien (1961) and Cholden (1956), among others, bear testimony to the view just mentioned. There is also support for the understanding that 'schizophrenia' is not a single unified syndrome but has many faces and grades of severity, viewed here as patterns of response to (acute) human distress (Sanders, 2007; also Sullivan, 1961). Symptoms associated with this classification also vary for the same person according to the relational context, even with therapist others – as seen, for example, in the case of Loretta, interviewed by three therapists of contrasting orientation (see Barrett-Lennard, 2007b, p. 132; Raskin, 1996). People diagnosed as schizophrenic may be acutely distressed *or* suffering on levels out of sight to most others, but not afflicted by or host to any disease (see, e.g., Sanders, 2007). Unsurprisingly, on close acquaintance each such person is distinct within themselves and in their relational worlds.

Thus, practice would stay differently and better grounded if diagnosticians and therapists simply provided, as necessary, a qualitative description without diagnostic labelling or a language of illness. The description may point to any of various possible features related, for example, to contact difficulties, distress- ing feeling, mood or thought processes, immediate crises and deviant percep- tions, extreme coping strategies, and evident need for special assistance or care. At best such appraisal would occur before the person became 'settled' and rein- forced (partly by specialist judgement of 'mental illness') in this initially desperate coping mode or, better still, before it became extreme and isolating.

'Dissociation':   The natural diversity of the human self-system means that some subself modes can distinctly differ from others and still make for a well-

functioning whole. Difficulties arise if, during active engagement in a principal mode of self, a person is scarcely aware of slipping at times into a distinctly different self-mode. The extreme case of a person who lives in modalities of self that are cut off from each other in consciousness has given rise to the identification of 'dissociative disorder' (with various subtypes: Barlow & Durand, 1995, pp. 223–235). It is thought that the detail and horror of an extreme trauma may somehow become encapsulated in a subconscious self-system. This seems to have been the case in a client, 'Mary', whose therapy experience and process is reported by both members of a therapy dyad (Morris, 2007; Turner, 2007). Although these reports are powerful statements within the authors' frames of reference, they leave me with questions and an opportunity to point briefly to a somewhat differing interpretation that illustrates another perspective related to 'dissociation'.

The reports indicate that Mary's father had sexually and physically abused her, sometimes violently, as a little girl, implying an extreme and traumatic deficiency in the father–daughter relationship. Her fear was intense, to the point of terror when she also was pushed and locked in a cupboard by her father. Yet there are hints that she wanted to somehow please or appease him and win a different response. In mentioning an episode of intense anger toward her therapist Mary alleged that he had rejected her just like her father had done. Thus, Mary's feelings toward her father seem to have been more relationally complex than solely a fear response to his abuse and violence. Evidently she was an only child, with no sibling relationships (certainly none are noted) and the only family member with whom she reported having a close loving relationship was a grandmother – specifically, not her mother. Her situation and experience with her mother or father after they separated is not mentioned, and there is no indication of client knowledge of other relationships in her father's life (had he been abused, for example, or did he have any other intimate relation?). Given her early childhood trauma and adult neediness, one might expect the client to relate easily to any encouraged idea of a split-off and submerged 'Young Mary' self – mostly experienced and treated as being like another person.

Mary was a student training in a related professional field and her report reflects an intellectual as well as personal interest in broader meanings of her trauma and its unfolding in therapy (she wanted to record her therapy journey and also asked her therapist to do so). The core focus of Mary's therapy as reported was on her inner life, especially including the Adult Mary/Young Mary division and dynamic. Her relational world, past and present, also could have been a major dimension of her therapy – certainly one I would have been highly responsive to as her therapist. When she began to speak of the trauma with her father but could not yet face the horror of it I can imagine empathically sensing that terror or fear in her and saying something like 'Just now it scares the living daylight out of you to contemplate going back there to feel what you went through or say how it sits inside you'. *If* this was sensitivity on target, I am imagining a somewhat different, though still long uphill, therapy journey.

Had I been Mary's therapist in this case, the idea of the forming self of Mary's childhood being somehow preserved and trapped inside her (see Warner, 2000) would still have come to the fore *if* it emerged as her independent sense. More likely, I believe, the trauma episode and memories would have turned out to be a crucial contributing factor in an available subself mode carried into the present. One of the other interesting elements to me in these courageous accounts is the idea of a third client entity referred to as a 'wise observer' (Turner, 2007) – a cognitive-reflective 'executive' awareness process (my term) also behind Mary's choice to go into therapy and stick it out.

Other categories and patterns of distress could be discussed but those mentioned illustrate the approach and way of thinking that I find persuasive. In a word, highly stressful experience can induce extremities of coping response in which experiential wholeness and capacity in relationships are seriously reduced, but the metaphors (for that is what they are) of 'mental illness' and psychopathology are heuristically unsound and misleading. Jacobs & Cohen (2010) present a distinctively argued related view. Based on their analysis and the perspective of the *Diagnostic and statistical manual of mental disorders* (DSM; American Psychiatric Association, 2000) these authors propose that

> separating people's feelings and actions from their own unique circumstances and context amounts to a moral, not scientific enterprise. *The study of how people fare in living should abandon the concept of mental disorder and related terms.* (Jacobs & Cohen, 2010, pp. 312–313, italics added)

The reports of Mary (Morris, 2007; Turner, 2007) distinguish 'parts' of self. Since in my view differing subsystems naturally evolve within the overall self-system, I trip on the language of 'parts' (though Warner's [2000] observations make a case for the term in childhood trauma), which suggests to me a literal segmentation of personality. Even in the case where subself configurations are compartmentalized and effectively shut off from each other, they are alternative modalities of being of the person, especially ways of being in relation. These modalities are in this sense dis-associated, but a diagnosis of 'dissociation' is fraught with potential to imply a literal structural splitting of personality in which context and relationship no longer play a part.

Although these discussed (and other) kinds of disturbed function in human coping occur, the metaphors of sickness or pathology are unnecessary, misleading and limiting to advances in thought (see also Milton et al., 2010). Logically, pathology or an illness are either present or not present. To implicitly equate being well with an absence of 'pathology' is faulty and inadequate in more than one way. One of these ways is that it leaves no incentive to search into the meaning and processes of positive wellness – my next focus.

A Modified Perspective on Wellness

As earlier noted, wellness is not simply an individual property but interacts with and applies to relationships on many levels. This is consistent with the idea that a person could function well (thus be 'healthy') in one important relationship and be poorly functioning in another. The (more or less) diverse ways of being that are reflected in each person's repertoire of self-modes engage selectively according to the context. Conceptions of psychosocial well-being emerge through human association and thought. An example is the author's proposed criteria of a well-functioning relationship offered on page 20. The participants in such a relationship need not be paragons of health in all respects but clearly would have the active potential for a well-functioning mode of being that can be expressed through positive relationships.

Psychosocial 'wellness' always manifests in a context. Although such a quality may seem to radiate from within, it is visible only in its expression not as an enclosed property of personality. A person-self evidently needs a responsive environment, especially of its own kind, to flourish in. Further, an immediate relationship, as discussed, resides in some interdependent relation with larger systems. Thus, the 'health' of these more inclusive systems is at the least indirectly relevant to the well-being of individuals in their included personal relationships. What being healthy or well functioning is understood to *mean* on a psychosocial level also is influenced by the cultural context. Although there is no absolute marker or definition, considered working concepts open to further refinement are needed guideposts.

The section of Chapter 2 headed 'Wholeness and Health of Persons and Relationships' (pp. 18–20) introduces the thought being extended here. It includes mention of Jahoda's still-interesting inquiry (1958) into 'positive mental health', which broke new ground at the time in reaching beyond the already much-travelled domain of mental disorder or ill-health to speak carefully about personal wellness. There is natural overlap with distinctions advanced and refined by Maslow (1970), Rogers (1959; 1961, chapters 8 and 9; 1964), and Allport (1955), among others. These distinctions emphasize self-actualizing and growth processes as contrasted with 'deficiency' or survival-based motivational processes. Rogers already was framing his conception of the 'fully-functioning person', published (Rogers, 1961, pp. 183–196) along with subsequent developments in his thought. These included his concept of personal process as ranging from a fixed self-perpetuating and repetitive mode of functioning to an open, highly engaged, continually renewing and strongly developmental mode – briefly, as he put it, from a condition of stasis or fixity to one of flowing process (ibid., pp. 125–159). (Measuring scales flowing from this conception – including *Manner of Relating* by E.T. Gendlin – appear in Rogers et al., 1967.)

My 1998 book offers (p. 180), in sequel with and embracing related features of Rogers' thought, a summary of the characteristics of 'well or optimally functioning persons'. This approaches a more classically personality-centred view than I hold now, though I have taken elements from that summary in a fresh outline that gives more emphasis to the person in context. The propositions to offer here fall in five process clusters that are separately distinguished in the interest of clear portrayal, but conceived to interpenetrate and work together in the engaged *well-functioning person*. A brief conclusion to this chapter follows their presentation.

- **Cluster one**: *Interwoven inner–outer process:* Feeling, symbolic consciousness and meaning freely *interweave* in the person's inner processing. S/he operates on an information-rich basis. Listening well both to others and inwardly is linked to progressive enrichment of meaning and engagement.
- **Cluster two**: *Identity in relation:* The person's organization and view of their personal identity is a multi-faceted dynamic whole that works as an implicit guidance system. This whole is distinctive in its 'many in one' configurations that continue to develop – sometimes through unsettling crises that lead on to self-transcending shifts, as further noted. Such people tend to be 'easy in their own skins' within relationship and not judgemental in stance toward themselves and others. Their valuing attitude toward self is intrinsic, not a reactive need to regard self as superior to others.
- **Cluster three**: *Active agency:* The person is active, initiating and conscious of agency, not passive in stance. S/he tends to be curious, exploratory, inquiring and interested in further knowing. In drawing on skills and knowledge from others, the person does so in their own way. These qualities apply over a wide range of natural endowment.
- **Cluster four**: *Self-transcending process:* The person does not operate according to a fixed 'program' but in a live actualizing and generally fluent process. Their personal path is oriented more to process quality and progressive becoming than a pre-planned life structure. This also implies openness to relational and inner discovery and unfolding. Capacity for 'creative synthesis' has been advanced as a primary element in psychological well-being (Gaylin, 2001).
- **Cluster five**: *Congruency in relationship:* The person is generally present and authentic in relationships. Different but congruent modes of self-being are called into play in different contexts. S/he tends to be interested in others whether similar or differing from her/himself, and this active experiencing of the other tends to be mutually enriching.

Conclusion

Personal healing is seen here as centring not on change in personality, but on movement in the ways a person is living and relating in his/her world of association with others. This primary world not only includes people who are physically present but also those in the person's feelings, thought and memory, and in the ambient presence and impress of communal culture. Relationships with a therapist or other helper fall within the emergent process forms of human life. 'Individual' therapy is something of a misnomer since clients always bring their lived worlds of relationship within them. Beneficial therapy does not respond to the client as if s/he were just distorted or trapped from within, or one who only needs to learn another way of processing their experience. Rather, the client is actively encountered in relationship by the therapist in a sharing/inquiry process that is naturally inclusive of the relational worlds they bring within them (Barrett-Lennard, 2009).

The next chapter turns to key issues applying to the whole approach of this book in seeking to confront the systemic complexity of human life and relationship. This further step grapples with the issue of 'causation' and systemic change when one endeavours to think in a truly interactive and non-linear way.

5

How Does Influence Work in Complex Relational Systems?

I speak of 'systems' freely in this chapter. To refer to persons and personal rela-tionships as systems may at first seem an impersonal object-like designation, though each of us is a complex system as well as being an experiencing subject. These are complementary not opposing views. Of course, I would not say to a person '*You* are a complex dynamic system', unless I wanted to confuse or risked insulting them. But in speaking more generally and with no implication of denying selfhood (which is part of being our kind of system) this view emphasizes our non-mechanical complexity. It also positions us as sharing this general quality with most other life forms and any natural phenomena that are dynamically complex.

Dynamic systems are powered with energy – both energy that is used in keeping the system going and energy expressed (or released) through engage-ment with other systems. The human organism in particular expends energy continually, if not in overt behaviour then in streams of activity going on inter-nally. There is no 'off' switch to this activity while life continues. An extraordi-nary synchrony of regulating and interactive processes is involved in maintaining life and 'working order'. These processes underlie and include the person-organism's active conscious engagement with its world. Subsystems on various levels cooperate in 'fuelling' and powering humans for thinking and feeling and physical activity in an essentially self-organizing process. Seen from the systems side, human relationship systems encompass participant individu-als as their necessary components.

'Cause', Influence and Contingent Events in Human and Other Systems

Relationships require energy and are seen as being fuelled through their constituent members in the multi-level process of association. As an active energy system a relationship, effectively, goes out to meet its environment of other people and relationships, with varied and complex sharing of influence in the resulting process. The overall process is more like a dynamic network or web of interacting elements than a simple mechanism in which each part has a constant function in the whole. System complexity generally involves a 'network of interdependencies' (Grisogono et al., 2010, p. 39). Effectively, there are many potential pathways through such a network, these pathways cross-linked and influencing each other (ibid.).[2] Thus, the usual linear-type models of causation just don't apply to the way it works. How then can we approach understanding 'influence' in complex human relationship and other systems?

Many complex systems are nominally hierarchical. The smaller component parts are functional units that combine in turn into larger subsystems and so on up to the whole system under consideration – as in most organizations (see Chapter 8). Influence processes in this case can be 'top-down', where overall aims or policy directives are passed 'down' to primary working groups. Influence can also be 'bottom-up', even in the same systems, since each component or subsystem has its own properties and necessary contribution in the working of the whole (see Ellis, 2007, pp. 114–122). Ellis, among others, also notes that human systems generally have certain outcome objectives or goals (many inanimate systems also work to achieve and regulate an outcome) and feedback information and processes are commonly a recognized source of influence. Furthermore, 'Multiple layers of causality are always in operation in complex systems' (ibid., p. 123).

Complex systems may have numerous collateral branches and components of different function that are not just hierarchical. Nor is the language of 'cause' very appropriate when many interacting influences may be working at the same time. In practice, the notion of contingency may often be preferable, that is, the idea that two or more things can be associated with some regularity without an assumption that either one is causing the other. The 'things' in this case might be an input to a system and a particular output behaviour or class of responses. From a careful study of such contingencies it may be possible to make if–then predictions that are reliable enough for certain practical purposes. Change the context within which the particular contingency of events has been observed and it could disappear. This can even occur in the small system of personal therapy:

Consider a therapist–client dyadic relationship with an anxious client seeking relief. Suppose a lessening of anxiety is in fact occurring, but then there is a change in the client's life situation. S/he loses her job or someone very close has a bad accident or falls seriously ill, and her/his anxiety level suddenly rises again. As a result, the gain initially felt is lost, and the distracted client leaves

---

2   A given example follows: 'The firing of a particular neuron in a brain is influenced by the input signals received from many other neurons, and its own firing in turn influences the probability of firing for many other downstream neurons, including some of those *that provide its own inputs*' (Grisogono et al., 2010, p. 7, italics added). This intricate 'causally circular' process may not be feasible to track and in many cases is linked to emergent processes on a higher level, that is, in consciousness (see also Deacon, 2007).

therapy, but (let's say) agrees to a follow-up. This inquiry, a little later, suggests that the client (though anxious) has gained more confidence in being able to recover and manage her/his life stresses. The client's work in therapy and some re-visioning through the crisis are understood to have contributed to this broader change. This would imply that the therapy relation, itself a complex system, was not acting alone or with one kind of outcome.

In another example, a work team may succeed in a demanding task on one occasion and fail another time, by the same criteria and with the same group of members (as is familiar in sporting teams, for example). If the team is viewed as a human system, explanation is not difficult. Each person checks into the group from a wider life context in motion, the members' feelings and communication resume from their experience now, and there may be new messages from the larger system within which the team operates. Each iteration of the task is in some respects a new beginning: the many process steps from this beginning through the team members' fresh interaction and joint activity lead on to the task outcome. The process flows along non-identical paths to somewhat differing ends. Thus the same outcomes are not always achieved.

Clearly, the lack of a linear cause and effect relation does not imply absence of influential connection. Indeed, the systemic nature of a complex phenomenon specifically implies the likelihood of manifold connections and crosscurrents of influence. In an example from another familiar field, the measurable components of weather include air temperature, humidity, presence or absence of rain or snow, the air pressure and wind (direction and speed), land surface features such as vegetation, elevation and slope and the temperature and other conditions of adjacent water bodies (see, e.g., Trenberth et al., 2000, pp. 4–13). Cloud formation – generally an essential precursor to rain – is by itself a very intricate process. None of these variables act alone on any other feature; all are affected in the short or longer term by other components, which then can act back in complex feedback circuits. For example, high air temperature, high humidity and low pressure may 'produce' rain, especially in air flowing on an upward slope. Rain then reduces the air temperature and, especially if the wind direction also changes, the rain may stop.

In the example just given, and in spite of the diverse interactive influences, many observations and careful deduction can lead to a working understanding that allows a useful level of prediction of outcomes – such as later temperature or rainfall. The 'outcomes' of interest, which as they happen also become influences within the system, depend of course on the concerns of the observer. In the broader context of global climate change, it is not the increase (two degrees, say, in the context of much larger daily and seasonal changes) in average temperature that is itself crucial but all the factors that interactively combine to contribute to this temperature change. Deforestation and increase in CO_2 emissions are just two of these, and crucial associated effects include change in rainfall patterns and food production, the shrinkage of sea ice that then reduces its moderating influence on temperature and change in ocean water levels and quality (see, e.g., Prinn et al., 2008). Feedback effects in a complex system have the potential to trigger change that builds on itself in an escalating process, as is evidently happening on a global climate level and is discernible in many other contexts: disease epidemics, financial system crises, grasshopper and 'cane toad' plagues, unhindered growth of powerful organizations, and manifold examples in ecological systems in nature.

The evolution of our whole planet also is instructive. At first, the new-formed earth was molten right to its surface. As it slowly cooled and crusted, water vapour could condense and oceans gradually formed, but there was no free oxygen in the atmosphere or sea. The earliest life did not require it, but interacted with its aquatic environment to produce chemical changes that released oxygen. Finally, as this primitive microbial life multiplied across the planet it evolved into new forms that used and relied on oxygen. Its blooming profusion and other plant life contributed to a radically changed atmosphere and led to our biosphere. Now, almost everywhere on the earth, and especially inhabiting the oceans, tiny life forms in enormous quantity are a recognized crucial link in maintaining the climate and conditions for all advanced life (Allaby, 1989; Brown, 2007; Dupré, 2008).

Complex systems generally require constancy or equilibrium in some vital respect in order to work well and exist over time. Thus they often have regulating subsystems (involving feedback processes) that constitute a crucial path of activity within the system. This is especially true of living systems and includes the familiar mammalian examples of temperature regulation and oxygen and sugar balance in the blood. Our own and most life systems are reliant on a context of other self-regulating systems, ultimately including atmospheric oxygen levels and limited temperature ranges in the planetary biosphere. Social and interpersonal relationships are also subject to regulatory constraints (at least 'soft' and sometimes 'harsh') from family, group, community and law enforcement systems.

Relationship systems as living entities are never literally static, although some appear just to fluctuate and repeat themselves without really shifting. Important member needs might be satisfied by the status quo and put at risk by change. Even where change is desired, participants may be at loss about how to achieve it, or they may try an oversimplified approach that does not work and leaves them feeling defeated and powerless. Family traditions, cultural mores and other 'external' factors can all constrain or discourage change. How *do* complex systems like a marriage or an established parent–child or close group relationship change voluntarily? Given that a formed relationship has its own momentum and life, the context is not simply a you-and-me situation and what each one wants. Thus, it seems crucial that participants reckon with this complexity and realize that they have contributed to the phenomenon of the relationship itself, to their 'we' with its own character and direction that they cannot simply bypass. Even in a personal dyad, the challenge of change clearly is not just a one-person matter.

In informal expression, the relationship is a 'we' distinct from the 'I' of each participant, a 'we' that may not 'want' to change, but prefers or tends to hang on to its own identity. Participants may not be used to thinking this way and yet might ask and try to sense 'What is it that keeps us, as a unit or twosome, on our present course?' As they come to see more clearly the way they work *together*, the questions may naturally shift to 'Can we really change this? Do we both want to?' Even if one or other feels weak and afraid of the other one's power and intention their *relationship* is co-determined. Thus, change may require, to start with, that participants develop a sense of their twosome as having its own nature distinct from either one. They may then find it possible to attend and 'listen' to this 'us'. If this happens, attributing full responsibility to the other or to self would not be convincing any more but seen, instead, as contributing to the difficulty.

My purpose in this encapsulation is to suggest how a therapy process might profitably start in thought and action, not to fully illustrate the process. For readers interested in theory-informed couple or family therapy, sources (some already mentioned) that could prove valuable to the discerning reader include Becvar & Becvar (2009), Bregman & White (2011), Gaylin (2001), McGoldrick (1998), O'Leary (2011) and Walker & Rosen (2004).

Process and Influence Within Relationships and Between Them

Since communication is such a basic ingredient process in human relationships, a shared language to convey felt embodied meanings plays a crucial role. Many of us have the working belief that a personal relationship thrives on each person's genuine openness of expression, regardful attentive listening and a mutuality of empathic awareness. Viewed from another angle, a thriving personal relationship enables or supports these qualities. Empathy can be both a contributing influence and an effect of overall relationship quality. Both as influence and effect it presumably stems from what participants bring to a relationship and what then emerges and develops there. Where empathy and the other mentioned qualities are on a low level (however this happens), the result could be considered an impoverished relationship. Yet, the relation may still last and even carry attitudes of loyalty, its familiarity may be of considerable importance to participants and they may take comfort over the idea that things can only improve. In any case, many interacting influences rather than any single cause are involved in the active continuance or troubling decline of a relationship.

Suffering and injury in interpersonal relationships has no simple origin. Even the assumption that one or other participant is individually to blame for difficulties, whether acute or lasting, is rarely justified. Although influence might be quite unevenly shared, no one participant has an exclusive or wholly governing influence on the *relationship* that emerges. If members can experience their relation as itself having life and influence and being like a third feeling voice that each one needs to find a way to listen to and understand, then their difficulties together are seen in a new light. Blame of the other (or even of self) is likely to recede and may open the way to a problem-solving process. Shortly after framing this observation, I heard a radio interview between two men from unrelated families, a father and a grandfather. The father had lost a son, killed almost at random by the other's grandson in a youth gang. After angry and intense grieving the father came to regard the young murderer (age 14) as a victim too, and he and the grandparent teamed up to initiate a substantial movement together to promote change in the afflicted societal/community systems underlying similar violent tragedies.

Influence from 'outside' a particular relationship may, of course, have great and possibly damaging impact on that relation. I put the word outside in quotation marks because the broader orbits of the partners involve other relationships, including one or more larger systems that surround and impact on their relation. Contextual influences are always present from such sources, whether of small effect, positively supportive, or with the effect of stressing and undermining the relationship in focus. Family systems provide a case in point where (for example) the disapproval of parents or jealousy among siblings is carried outside their nuclear family to impact strongly on the marriage or partner relationship of one of those siblings. In another example, the family as whole, the parent couple and particular members within it are all in interactive relation with varied outside systems in areas such as education, employment or welfare.

The interaction of relationships, each one a complex system, may have a discernible pattern to the attuned observer while also introducing a further level of complexity. In the domain of international affairs, the relation (for example) between the United States and Israel has been used in seeking to influence the relation between Israel and the Palestinians – often without visible benefit, though at times it may have averted more deterioration and conflict. Divisions within each camp, vigilant Israeli concerns in relation to the wider Arab world, the dark shadows of history on both sides, and of course the working of local political/economic systems and leadership ambitions are a sample of interacting factors likely to have worked against improvement in relations. Relational systems as well as individuals often compete for ascendancy or other apparent advantage. Bringing about change in the way particular systems relate clearly needs to take into account their inner working and the fears or disadvantage some component groups are likely to see when the status quo is altered, even to reduce tensions. Even in warring conflict each system includes people whose perceived interests, possibly their life meaning, are embedded in the circumstances or process of the conflict. Chapter 9 includes a searching exploration of related issues, studded with examples.

Relational System Stability, Shifts and Prediction

Stability of a system is not the same thing as being stuck and unchanging. Stability implies a balance between tendencies toward continued development (or runaway change), and a counter-tendency to protect and conserve a system as it is. Active stabilization implies processes that keep the system on an even keel and restore equilibrium when it is disturbed. Thus a 'stable' system is not stationary. It might be in repetitive motion or it may be evolving and growing organically – with a strongly self-organizing quality. It may be favourable for formed human relationship systems to be in a dynamically stable (as distinct from static) quality of functioning. This sentence includes the words 'may be' and 'formed' to suggest that this state is not always desirable or applicable, as further considered.

States of marked imbalance or disturbance to the usual flow of a relationship or other living system sometimes trigger emergent, pattern-changing or self-transcending growth. Even a serious crisis may lead on to such change, especially if it occurs in a larger context in which options and support are experienced. Safe association in the wider reference group or system in which the crisis occurs may be necessary for the outcome to be productive. Separations and divorce of couples, for example, where family and other close relationships in the former partners' lives are preserved and the wider reference culture remains supportively open to them carry potential for the mentioned growth-developmental effects. In an unsatisfactory relationship, as felt by one or both parties who desire nevertheless to persevere together, 'risky' disclosures coupled with concern for the other as well as self and the emergent 'we' may jolt the relationship into a different and more fruitful process. Of course, 'confrontations' do not always work this way. Much depends on their intent and authenticity, and how they are followed up in the relational dialogue.

Given the inherent complexity of human systems the interior processes involved in balance or stability can defy precise determination. Yet, some generally indicative features might be discerned and the overall motion of the system in a known larger context fairly well gauged. The context often includes a further relationship that naturally influences the immediate working, say, of a particular couple relationship. The immediate effect of a sharply disparaging communication by one party on the feeling and response of the other may be fairly predictable to a perceptive observer, even if not anticipated by the participants. Predictability implies stability or sameness, and this quality may apply to a relationship under tension as well as to one that is more relaxed and free flowing. It seems that in stressed systems of nearly any kind some inputs can trigger a sudden new inner path to an explosive 'output' response. I will briefly offer diverse examples.

The first case to mention involved a massive grid system of electric power generation and supply, with a host of subsystems connected in a web of pathways. In the event in focus, an initially small-scale failure during a heat wave triggered events in other subsystems and, before long, a great cascading sequence of failures. The failures and blackout spread across the whole Northeastern United States and also Ontario, affecting over 50 million people (US-Canada Power System Outage Task Force 4/2004; Wikipedia, 2010). There are many generating systems in the grid, lots of switching responses had occurred automatically, there were human errors, some high-voltage lines failed and finally there was a total systemic collapse. Big-system efficiencies had helped to foster a whole with unforeseen vulnerabilities. In the final Task Force report on this crisis event, 'inadequate system understanding' is signposted as the number one overall cause of the breakdown.

In cases opposite to the above, in which component systems are largely sealed off from each other, for example in the context of a centrally controlled totalitarian political state, extreme hazards may apply to certain subsystems of people forcibly cut off from and virtually invisible to most others in the populace – as happened for instance to the Jewish people in Nazi Germany. People can of course also be 'out of touch on the inside' (Barrett-Lennard, 2001) as in the very different example of those with the desperate coping strategy of chambered subselves or 'multiple personality'. With different inner voices or subsystems of consciousness virtually out of contact with each other, there is great cost to the quality of life and relationships of the person.

To take a quite different example of systemic process, the onset of World War I involved a violent tsunami-like shift in the working of a great system of interlinked nations. The systemic mix of factors potentiating the war included a network of defence alliances, strongly nationalist sentiments, the imperialist and/or militarist stance of some major nations and the triggering assassination of a prominent royal leader. The resulting explosion began with Austria-Hungary declaring war on Serbia (a Serbian nationalist had shot their Archduke Franz Ferdinand), then Germany went to allied Serbia's defence, France was drawn into war with Germany, which also involved Belgium, which then helped to bring (ally) Britain into the war, and affiliated empire colonies and nations followed. The eruption and spread of war was a runaway process in an unstable larger system, and wound up embroiling over 50 countries. The human decisions (reluctant by most leaders) for the resort to war grew partly from simplified linear thinking. It was supposed that individual alliances would be protective, but how the whole interconnected super-system of nations would react if war broke out was not anticipated, at least in time to stop the momentum of events. Most governments thought the war would be over in a few months; none predicted the vast death toll and enormity of human suffering, or the draining of national economies, or the social and political after-effects of the war – which included potentiating World War II (see, e.g., Henig, 2002; Joll & Martel, 2007; Kelly, M. in About.com).

One lesson to be taken from these and other convulsions flowing from unpredicted system reaction processes is the crucial need to develop and apply ways of thinking that, far from being causally reductionist, assume systemic complexity from the start. Expecting and looking for chain reactions can be a useful step, but the web of process in systems often is more complex than billiard ball sequences and its envisioning requires a mindset that seems rarely to be brought to bear in practice. Arguably, it needs to become a matter of course to think of the working of any extensive system as a complex dynamic network with a diversity of interacting influences and pathways. Indeed, a viable future for humankind may depend on this kind of stance and how well we humans learn to 'read' the complexity within, among and around us.

Vehicles to this learning would include fluently systematic and deeply reflective observation – coupled with empathic attunement to people in the case of human relationship systems. For large human and non-human systems, this process would, I propose, entail close study of the constituent elements and their interconnections and how they work in the fabric of the whole, *in many cases of similar kind or structure*. This general approach already has led to major fields of knowledge, for example in the case of astronomy. Even in that field, however, with the powerful principle of gravity supported by additional knowledge such as the known spectral shifts in light from rapidly advancing or receding bodies, the mathematics of connecting and predicting events is extremely complex. A huge amount of observation, producing gradual increase and periodic marked shifts in understanding, has been cumulating for a long time. I think there are lessons in this for the human sciences, since both spheres confront the challenge of understanding the working of complex systems. Astronomy appears to be much further ahead in its capacity for prediction than, say, the behavioural or social sciences – and without controlled experiments!

Another (potentially overlapping) approach in learning to read complex systems involves experimenting with models growing out of observation and combined with careful steps of inference. The simplest models seem to be of the if–then variety, with a number of ingredients on the 'if' side and outcomes of interest on the 'then' side. More elaborate and adequate models would, in my view, include an envisioning of paths of interactive process between *if* and *then*, and then applying specific variations in component features or connections in the system model. A 'pathway' has a direction and internal route: it is not just a generalized arousal of the whole system. An initial model could be tested using actual data from available closely documented cases. Another test would use early information from an immediate new case to predict the ensuing process and outcome features. Finally, the further refined and tested model would contribute to policies and working structures to avert related destructive system events. Each new case could lead to some further refinement of the understanding. This analysis has particular relevance for large-scale events that tend to recur, such as the collapse of a financial system or the build-up of tensions leading to war. Another (imagined) event, smaller in scale and more engaging in kind, is an illustration of systemic disturbance and its resolution within a family:

The members of a family learn, let's say, that a distant relative wants to visit and stay in their home with them for an unspecified period. This relative is perceived as having very different tastes and political and religious views than those held within the family. One of the children faces having to give up his room and double with another child who also resents this. The slender family budget will be stretched further and the relative is expected to want to borrow the family car or be driven around. He is on the wife's side of the family and the husband particularly resents the pending invasion as he sees it, so that tension between the couple builds. They try not to show this to the children, who are immediately aware of it anyway. The latter complain angrily about all the expected constraints on various levels. The parents, feeling their own conflict, are also very anxious about being seriously embarrassed with the visitor over their children's behaviour. Latent tensions within the family come to a head and the parents' anxiety escalates. The oldest child (age 15) threatens to move out. The family is in a painful crisis over a pending visitor. Their relationships are buffeted and strained, and everyone will have experienced the vulnerability of their family collective. How might the whole dynamic and impact have taken a different course?

If the parents and even the oldest child were to experience their family as a network of interacting personalities and relationships, including their own, and be open to understanding this whole 'organism' and its parts as far as they possibly could, this would be a very different starting point. This openness could lead to free discussion among all family members about how they were taking this news and affecting each other with their reactions, and how they thought to solve it – not ruling out the option of discouraging the visitor from coming. Such exploration would be expected to increase mutual awareness of relational feelings within the family more broadly. Potentially, trust would have increased, with an accompanying sense of being in shared control of the situation – opening the way to problem-solving dialogue. Options not seen at first would come to view, some members might even feel that it would be interesting to have first-hand exposure to the very different outlook, a roster of taking turns in doing things with the visitor might be envisaged and more than one kind of TV and room rearrangement could become apparent, etc. Some members may now feel for the visitor at least in the sense of wondering and wanting to know more of what it was in his life that triggered his travel plans and what he was seeking in coming to visit. Some feedback to the effect that this pending visit had been a matter of intense dialogue in the family might now seem to be rather easily conveyed.

The example just given refers of course to a situation that is imagined in its specifics and the course of its unfolding along two possible paths. Further paths might be enumerated. Other examples of crisis system events that could evolve along very different paths include potentially catastrophic bushfires, the outbreak of a dangerous new disease, and the assault on a community from an invasive industrial development or a natural disaster. Alternate ways that these and other complex emergencies 'work' and can unfold invite increased understanding that is both wide-angle in terms of the whole context it takes account of *and* in-depth in terms of specific processes and their interconnections. Being able to predict how a human or other system is likely to respond to particular kinds of activation, and the inner paths to alternate outcomes, can be of life and death importance.

Conclusion

It is almost a truism that nothing in nature or human affairs is wholly separate and autonomous from all other features. There is always linkage to be found and, often, a tissue of interconnection. In a given case, the challenge is to discover the order in this complex interrelatedness – without which we do not really understand the phenomenon. Because a search for direct sole causes is out of keeping with relational and other natural systems this approach is usually misguided and its 'findings' may be quite misleading or even destructive in their application. Given that influence is distributed and interactive in complex systems and that their working is often so hugely consequential, there is great need for research that assumes this complexity from the start. This implies a generally naturalistic approach and concern to visualize the whole system in its dynamic working and response to other systems and events. Where investigations are triggered by a need to examine particular features (such as qualities of attitude, behaviour or feeling) these elements of special interest need to be viewed in context, not as though they had separated existence and impact. As implied, this way of understanding complex process also has direct relevance for almost any enabling practice with people (see Kriz, 2008).

The ideas in this chapter flow into my inquiry and thought through the two further parts of this book. The opening chapter in the major Part III that follows is a change of pace in its original, systematic examination of ways *to distinguish relationships* in and beyond the face-to-face interpersonal realm.

Part III
Unfolding the Worlds of Relationship

6

Distinguishing Kinds of Relationship: An Ordering Scheme

The vast span of human association includes relations between relationship systems. The feuding families of the two lovers in Shakespeare's *Romeo and Juliet* are an instance of relationship between small systems. Whole communities and nations can be entities in relationship. Relations between human and non-human individuals and species also are of vital importance in human life. This chapter visualizes the order in this great spectrum of relation, though with relatively more attention to small systems than to big ones. It offers an answer to the question of how to identify and compare particular relationships using a versatile common framework, a framework that is both helpful in practice study and invites wider research. The chapter begins by further picturing the overall province of relationships, thus to set the stage for what then follows.

Process and Structure in Little to Very Large Relationship Systems

There is a huge range in the *mix* of member qualities, in relationships. The varied elements of make-up all feed into the relationship that emerges. To start with, the number of people involved and the structure and context of their interchange has a major impact on what is possible or likely. And, there is a huge range of different qualities of relationship. Very large systems are multi-layered and involve extremely complex patterns of communication and experienced association. The discussion that follows is arranged under three broad headings according to the scale of the relationship – interpersonal to international.

Interpersonal and Small-Group Relations

Interpersonal relationships alone include many different structures, besides all the qualitative variation. The settings generally include face-to-face contact, although direct communication at a distance sometimes leads to significant personal relationships. The varied possible contexts may foster close or intense association (notably in the case of couples and families) or more casual and scripted encounters. Many different structures occur even within families. Besides the parent couple, with all its wide qualitative variation, there are parent-with-child dyads and (often) sibling twosomes. A child's relation with his/her parent duo, who may often respond jointly or in each other's presence to the child, is distinct in its dynamics from the one-on-one parent–child twosomes. There can be recurring and distinctive 'kids with parents' (e.g., 2×2) processes, and varied other configurations nested in the whole-family relational system, as described in detail elsewhere (Barrett-Lennard, 1984; 2003, pp. 77–92; 2005, pp. 65–82). Each member has an experience-based vision of 'my family' and relationship with this whole.

Close small friendship and other groups that come together informally, and gangs, teams and experiential learning-encounter or therapy groups, typically include a network of interpersonal relationships that include twosomes, trios and other combinations. Any of these micro-relationships may function differently in the presence of the group, where the same participants are linked also with other members. In the flow of communication in an internally active group the focus tends to move from one pair (or larger subset) to another and in some moments a member is communicating to the whole group, implying an individual–group relationship. Some relationships among group members naturally will be closer than others in understanding or warmth. Thus a small group even of six or seven people can be interpersonally a very complex relational microcosm (Barrett-Lennard, 1979; 2003, pp. 68–74).

Almost everyone is a member of formally constituted face-to-face groups – as in schools, workplaces, sporting teams, organized club groups, professional, personal development or therapy groups and in hobby and other groups sharing special interests. Such groups typically include a designated leader or convener and there may be a further hierarchy of responsibility among the members. Relationships clearly grow also from affinities of feeling, ideas and style among the members. The potential complexity of relationships increases exponentially with the size of the group (Barrett-Lennard, 2003, pp. 68–74). There are, for example, six different pairings in a family of four, 28 possible pairs in a group of eight people, and 120 in a group of 16 (the formula is $n(n-1)/2$, where n is the number of members). Large organizations containing many face-to-face associations, subgroups that communicate with each other and larger branches or divisions, are a very different species of human relationship system.

Relationship Modalities in Organizations and Communities

Although the formal structure of an organization doesn't govern qualities of the included relationships it has great bearing on how members are interconnected.

Any large organization is likely to contain a huge variety of relationships both personal and role-related. Many different tasks and functions typically are involved in creating the products or services of the organization, and there are other activities designed to support the system itself. Generally, its basic producing 'work' is done by team groups of members who are in face-to-face contact. Friendships and competitive relationships develop within these groups and extend to associations with some members of other subgroups. Coalitions or alliances that are not part of the formal structure are commonplace. Within the basic working subgroups each person would have at least a casual fellow-worker relationship with each other member. And each one usually is in a relation that has an authority dimension, with the team or group leader or spokesperson. This 'foreperson' has working relationships with the leaders of other groups and typically there is at least one person who they in turn report to at the next level 'up' in the overall system.

In contemporary organizations of a more egalitarian kind a group member might easily have significant associations with particular members outside their own work group. In many organizations, including universities, there are specialist or professional (faculty) members and administrative and supporting staff with different responsibility. The contributions of the latter may be based as much or more than those of faculty members on who they get to know in various administrative and support contexts and the quality of relationships they form with those other members. Often these associations provide 'short-cuts' that can be crucial for the working efficiency of the organization. Many constituent relationships have a personal-informal dimension valued for its own sake even if not of great depth. Other relationships pivot on communication about tasks or plans and policies, and these may be shallow on a personal level. Overall, the organization pivots on a great range and variety of relationships that involve everyone in diverse contexts. Such whole systems often are in strong competition with other systems of similar aim and this competing quality tends to carry down within the system and influence all but the most personal-for-their-own-sake relationships in the organization (see Chapter 8).

Relationships with fellow workers, bosses, administrators and the system itself clearly range all the way from ones that flourish and benefit members in their lives outside the organization, to others that are strained, stressful or have personally demoralizing or 'withering' effects. People also have relationships with organizations that they depend on from an 'outside' position, say, as clients or customers of banks, supermarkets, entertainment and hospitality systems, and government departments. For individuals, it can be a very asymmetrical and impersonal association that they struggle to manage. Even so, their association with some directly known rank and file members of the other system can have a personally appreciated quality unlike that which the organization itself is felt to stand for.

Groups and branches within an organization have interactive relations that may be distinctly felt by their respective members. And the whole organization exists in interface with other organizations both of similar type (e.g., both might be mining companies) and of quite different kind (e.g., industrial versus government, or company versus trade union). These associations involve human systems operating in relationship with other human systems. Their association is a form or level of human relationship.

Communities are bonded largely by the feelings and circumstances of members. What members are drawn to and the relational and practical needs a community serves are crucial factors. Usually, communities do not form for the purpose of producing something or providing a service and/or profit to outsiders (as in most organizations) but come into being more for their own sake as centres of belonging that are important in reflecting and contributing to the felt identity of their participants. Thus, they are mostly 'looser' in their structure than organizations are (see Chapters 7 and 8). Traditional communities, however, can have important practical functions that include their own protection as a group, but these functions are interwoven with their members' sense of who they are, and by the quality of looking to each other and feeling a distinctive communal outlook and affiliation. Relationships within communities tend to develop more organically than is typically true of organizations. Where people have leadership roles in communities they tend to be elected to those positions, not installed by a Board, shareholders or other agency.

There is a tribal sense in some contemporary communities based, for example, on a combination of class and kinship or some deep quality of alliance and affiliation passed through generations. Communities of common residence and similarity of circumstance, especially in small towns or villages where the population is relatively stable, are a long-standing form. Communities based on significant common interest or belief system, or common attachment to a distinctive neighbourhood, or connected by similar strong lifestyle preferences, have vital importance to those involved. Communities sometimes arise by happenstance as might occur, for example, when a sizable group of people are thrown together on their own resources in a shared crisis, or through the trial-and-error discovery of an associative context which draws those involved to feel at home and supported in their way of being. Individuals, especially in a fast-moving mobile society, may feel significant attachment to more than one community, or more than one in turn. Thus, relationships within and between communities are diverse in kind and widely different in quality.

Relationship Origins and Configurations in Nation States

A nation state containing an extensive and complex system of people who are interconnected in multiple ways is effectively an encompassing relationship system. Sizable nations contain a vast array of relational subsystems, big and small, that interact with each other, both in direct ways and indirectly through relations with subsystems that are in direct contact. It is interesting to envision different ways that nation states come into being, since the formation process would have a major bearing on the nature and quality of relationships among individuals and groups both at that initial stage and as a legacy for the future.

In one kind of birth, a nation evolves organically from an initially small community that has the space, natural resources and internal energy to keep on growing. It is not likely to be an evenly flowing process, given a diversity of players, the transitions to new arrangements as the system enlarges and external influences. As a forming nation expands to a dimension where members have no direct contact with most others, it is necessary for the whole to differentiate into a variety of subsystems of varied function and identity, these in turn connected through an overall coordinating and/or governing system. This unfolding growth can lead to a well-integrated whole in which members feel bonds of relation and belonging not only with their families and small groups but with the larger communal subsystems and organizations united within a known and cultivated whole – the nation itself. In this case, the various subsystems will tend to be complementary rather than competitive.

A second way that nations form is through the forceful joining into one large group of formerly separate and substantial collectives of people, under a single ruling government and often a dominant leader. This would make for top-down development and organization of subsystems, and many of the inter-level relations would have a prescribed quality. An imposed conjunction of different ethnic or other groupings each with its own identity and ethos (as, for example, in the former Yugoslavia) would leave the assembled nation prone to underlying tensions and fears around loss of identity that may surface in conflict. A developmental or healing process could in principle occur, but require a shift by the central authority toward actively fostering the natural diversity and a different quality of relation between the diverse component systems. Such change from forced joining under an authoritarian system to a more benign and democratic one may take a long time and, of course, it may not happen at all.

In *a third kind of emergence*, a nation begins from a large, subjugated faction of people breaking free from an existing larger nation or empire, to form an independent state with its own ethos and sense of identity, laws, and system of government. Most of its citizens would be connected at the start by their common resistance to their former regime and a shared hunger for the strongly desired independence. This origin could make for a generally positive quality of personal, intergroup and inter-level relationships in the new polity. However, in practice, the breakaway founding collective might well have included one or more minorities obliged to be part of the new whole but still with equal or stronger attachment to what was left behind. In this second case some groups may continue in uneasy relation with the majority until and unless their difference and relative autonomy came to be respected and secure.

The process just mentioned can have much in common in its ethos and working with the further (*fourth*) *case of a nation born* not from division of a larger whole, but *from revolutionary overthrow of an existing order and substitution of another*, incorporating essentially the same population and spread of people as before (as in the Russian revolution). Agonizing conflict and sundering of relationships on many levels occur, with an impact on attitudes and memories that echo far into the future. Even in the United States, and although the founding fathers of the new nation were farseeing in their time, the new whole was not all of one piece in the outlook of its citizens. They included, for example, a somewhat aristocratic landed and propertied class who inherited many of the values of the favoured classes in England and Europe. In the heyday of becoming an independent new nation, the differences did not prevent a convergence of will about the new nation. However, seeds evidently were there for the paroxysm of the civil war that followed barely three generations later. All of this impresses me with the relevance of looking back as well as to the present in any attempt to make a qualitative appraisal of relationships within or between whole nations.

However a nation comes into being its government will soon develop many arms, interests and expressions, reflecting and interwoven with the nature and diversity of relations among its subsystems and groups. Chapter 11 takes up the idea of an audit of the state of relationships within a nation, and the influence of this internal process state on relations with another nation. This chapter now returns primarily to interpersonal and small-scale relationships, with a focus on devising a framework to identify and compare them systematically.

The Realm of Human Relationships: An Ordering of Kinds

The nature and scope of human relationships has in varied ways been a primary concern from Chapter 1 on. It remains, however, to take a further step in identification that accords with a progressively expanded view of the full scope and systemic nature of relationship. A clear view of what the phenomenon is logically precedes the attempt to carefully distinguish its many varieties.

On Further Defining and Telling Relationships Apart

The identifying features of human relationship offered here are of a broad generic kind that complements the outline definitions advanced in Chapters 1 and 2. This aims to further underpin the formal analysis of relationship modalities that follows.

1. Relationships partake of life, a life emergent from the conjunction of few or many people, who in their engagement are components of this life.
2. As life systems relationships are dynamic, complex and in variously patterned equilibrium and movement.

3. A human relationship generally involves participant consciousness of connection or union as 'we', 'us', our family, group, community or other whole.
4. Relationships are highly diverse in their composition, and the scope, variety and *mix* of members helps to determine their kind and qualities.
5. The qualities of a relationship are not under the sole governance of individual members and their identifying qualities have meaning distinctive to relationships.
6. Groups, organizations and big human systems interact and relate in ways that both influence and derive in part from their inner member relationships.
7. The experience of an established relationship can exist beyond the lifespan or continued availability of the other. And, passed-on qualities and memories of a relationship may be a contributory influence in further generations.

Features 1 and 2 in this list point to the living, dynamic yet patterned nature of relationship processes. They imply that relationships are complex process entities that may develop a certain equilibrium, but are not cemented in an unvarying state. They also can be said to have a birth – and sometimes a pregnancy as, for example, when two young people are in a new but deepening relationship and *other members* of their respective families anticipate meeting each other and coming into direct relation for the first time. Feature 3 uses the wording 'generally involves' to allow for cases where one or even both parties may not be conscious of a relationship although it is distinctly apparent to observers. The widely varied make-up of relationships reflected in feature 4 is developed as one of the 'axes' in my classification (to follow). The big range of relationship qualities noted in feature 5 foreshadows a second axis of distinctions. Aspect 7 allows for the case of a felt relationship with a distinctly *remembered* other. Together, these defining features give room for a great range of kinds and qualities of relationship.

A systematic ordering in keeping with these generic features and previous discussion resists any very simple array, and aims here toward inclusiveness. The central challenge is to develop a versatile typology of classes and within-class categories of relationship. The use of more than one basic type or 'axis' of distinctions further empowers a classification system. Axis 'Q' is concerned with generic qualities of relationship; qualities, *for example*, of close bonding or nearness versus distance, whether or not the relationship is intense and charged with feeling, whether there is conflict or harmony, and whether the parties mostly compete or collaborate. A second axis (S) distinguishes classes of relationship by their compositional structure, across a spectrum from one-on-one personal relationships through a number of levels to relations involving whole nation states or other big systems of people. Any particular relationship would be classified in terms of its position jointly on Axis Q and Axis S.

AXIS Q: A Qualitative Typology of Relationships

The immediate focus is on *relationship* qualities, as distinct from separate individual characteristics or experience of members that is not within or about their relationship. The classes and within-class alternatives distinguished here have complex origins in the author's thought and career-long experience and study. They are presented not with an attitude of finality, but as a considered working distillation and path of development. They differ but do not all exclude any overlap, and there is no assumption that a single category will be sufficient in the qualitative typing of a particular relationship. Since relationships come into being and tend to evolve over time, if they are examined at different stages of development then variations in their identification may well result – as later illustrated. Altogether, 10 classes of relationship are distinguished, each with three or more subclass categories that are briefly identified. *Interested readers are invited to contact the author for additional detail, especially if research application is envisaged.*

Class Q1: *Relationships marked by high, low or variable intensity, or subdued flatness*

Relationships marked by intense mutual involvement are a main category within this class. Another category applies in the case of relationships that are notably uneven in intensity, often low to sometimes high. Relationships of an opposite kind might be either 'flat' and unexpressive *or* low-key and casual. A spread of relationships on the intensity continuum is thought to be favourable. A person whose relationships were all very intense could burn out or stress others. Low intensity relationships tend to be 'safer' and to be functional in many everyday associations. An emotional flatness of interaction, however, would leave a relationship seeming to be almost lifeless.

Class Q2: *Harmonious versus discordant and stressed relationships*

Whether relational interplay is generally harmonious, with mostly peaceful accord, whether there is distinct opposition and conflict *or* whether marked swings from concord to discord occur are principal alternatives within this relationship-specific region of difference.

Class Q3: *Buoyant active outreaching relationships as against kinds that are coasting passively or that are oppressed, shrunken, barely enduring*

Some relationships not only have an exceptional survival quality, for example in the face of external stressors, but they also remain very alive and vigorous – in a word, buoyant – in a wide range of contexts. They have a strongly initiating quality and might otherwise be described as agentic not just recipients of the agency of others (category Q3.1). Alternatively, relationships are internally quite active, but show little of this outwardly (Q3.2). In further cases, there is a distinctly non-initiating or non-venturing 'coasting' quality or a 'waiting' to be engaged and aroused to action by the energy and motion of others (Q3.3). In instances devoid of buoyancy the relationship could seem ground down, somehow enduring but almost without motion (Q3.4).

Class Q4: Relationships distinguished by their cohesion or bonding quality or a lack or obverse of this quality

The relationship may be cohesive, with close bonding and a strong sense of 'we'. Alternatively, the relation matters to participants but bonding is constrained and does not entail close *mutual* sharing of experience. Another possibility and category is that closeness or intimacy is being actively avoided and the relationship held (perhaps unsteadily) at arm's length by one or both parties. This differs from the further case of low-key relationships where participants 'know' each other, but with minor investment and no bonding impetus.

Class Q5: Relationships that are vibrant and full of energy (thus dynamic open systems) or that are lethargic and inward-looking relatively closed systems

Energy level and vibrancy is not the same as outreaching buoyancy (Q3), but high energy levels plausibly help to give rise to positive buoyancy. Thus some joint (Q3/Q5) ratings are expected. Within Q5, some relationships will be high energy (one category), others with wide swings in energy level and dynamism, and a third kind with little energy or 'glow'. The context of other relationships will play (or have played) a part in which alternative applies.

Class Q6: Relationships that feed on competition or thrive on cooperation and collaboration

Relationships born from competition or rivalry and desire to win and in some cases to dominate, subjugate or diminish the other are commonplace across many contexts in the culture. Engagements in which people join in generally collaborative mode for mutual support or nourishment, or effective team work, are also a frequent kind. In another variant the relationship thrives distinctively on competitive games or repartee as modes of valued encounter.

Class Q7: Relationships that are struggling or stuck, or flowing and evolving

The central distinction in this class is the presence, or the absence in diverse ways, of flow and evolving movement. In some cases the 'absence' is involuntary and there is an effortful struggle to improve things and move forward. Another way involves a static or repetitive, running down quality. A still further variant is a very tangled, erratic quality that can work like a cage enclosing the participants.

Class Q8: Relationships radiating warmth, coldness, affection or aversion

This class includes cases where participants light up together and where their engagement radiates warmth that tends to relax others and may invigorate other relationships. In a second mode, the participants are absorbed in one another, with evident strong attraction or love. More quietly bonded relationships comprise a third related category. Cases where the relational temperature is cool or even icy form a contrasting fourth kind. An aversive looking down on or disdain for the other (perhaps to bolster self-esteem) characterizes the remaining variant distinguished.

Class Q9: Relationships on the alert, with perceptive attentiveness or hair-trigger reactivity – or the obverse of these qualities

People in a relationship can be alert and ready to respond in very different ways. Where there is an ambience of trust and secure feeling the attentiveness may take the form of mutually perceptive listening and taking-in of the other's meaning, as well as expressing one's own (Q9.1). Lacking this ambience of trust and secure feeling the participants may be alert to any possible denigration and involuntarily poised to react in strong defence (Q9.3). Sometimes neither of these qualities apply – the parties are casually inattentive a lot of the time (Q9.2), *or* they each benignly feel that they are on the side of the angels, expressed or not (Q9.4).

Class Q10: Relationships between parties who are transparent about their own relational processes or guarded and unrevealing

This class focuses on the aspect of relationship transparency, especially the degree to which the members are expressively revealing of their own relational processes in company with third persons or groups. People (couples, families, even large groups) quite often do not wish to show the working and nature of their own relationship during engagement with a third party (Q10.1). In other instances, people evidently feel so easy and secure in their relationship that in most situations with others they are spontaneously and freely revealing of their own process together (Q10.3). Another possibility is that one party tends to be open and the other unrevealing about their relationship (Q10.2).

This completes essentials of the qualitative scheme. Some research potentials are mentioned at the end of this chapter. Interesting practice usage may occur to the reader especially after going through the illustrations that follow after my outline of Axis S, next.

AXIS S: Kinds and Categories of Relationship Based on Their Structure

In approaching a systematic schema of structural classes it is assumed that all relationships can be viewed as arising from two parties called here A and B. *Either or both of these parties can be one person or several or many people.* When B, say, is many (perhaps a whole family or larger connected group), besides forming one whole in relation to A it may well contain smaller relationships nested within it. The outline that follows distinguishes five main structural classes of relationship, beginning with a class in which one party is an individual and the other is singular *or* plural. Each class is further divided into two or more categories and in most of these there are finer subcategories. The distinctions are discrete and unfold logically and in these respects are more objective (though perhaps less interesting) than those in Axis Q. *A more detailed presentation for interested readers, including finer subcategories, is available from the author.*

Class S1: *Relationships of one person with a single or multiple other*

In this class, one-on-one relationships are the most familiar form (category S1.1). People also have associative connections with collectives of others, joined in small systems, such as a family or team (S1.2), and with communities (S1.3), organizations (S1.4) and nations (S1.5). As well as being experienced from within the relationship, these and most relationships also can be viewed from the outside position of an informed observer.

Class S2: *Small-system to small-system (or group-to-group) relationships*

This class centres on relations between similarly small relational systems. Some of these kinds of relationships are familiar to most people, for example between two couples or other dyads (S2.1), and between families (S2.2) and teams (S2.3). For members of either system this association is a 'we-with-(multiple)you' relation. Generally, there also would be relationship subsystems within each of the component systems/groups.

Class S3: *Group-with-larger system relationships*

This class involves relationships between structurally dissimilar parties in which the smaller system may be nested within the larger system (category S3.1) or lie outside it (S3.2). The relations may be interdependent or oppositional. Each system, while constituting a whole in their association, could have many relationships within it, which contribute to the working quality of the group-with-system association.

Class S4: *Relations between and among organizations and communities*

Interactive associations between large systems conscious of each other also are common. This class differs from Class S3 in that both parties are of broadly similar dimension and complexity. However, they may be similar (S4.1) or distinctly different in other ways. They may for example be different kinds of organizations (S4.2), for example manufacturing, mining, educational, human service or educational. Or, one may be a commercial organization and the other an affiliated community with its own qualities and interests (S4.3).

Class S5: *Relations between nation states and other big systems*

The origins and histories of nation states feed into their working and interrelation, as earlier noted. Some internal relational processes (such as the relation of government ministers or the head of state with their constituents) can have particular visibility in the nation's relation with another big system. One underlying factor is that of how alike (S5.1 relation) or different (S5.2) the systems are in their ethos, political arrangements, government and economies. Beyond their direct interchange, states often are affiliated members of larger groupings (S5.3) that affect inter-state relations (Greece's membership of the European Union is an example). There is also the case of relations between state and nonstate ethnic or other people-systems.

As between the two axes, appraisal on Axis Q is the more challenging, but taken in combination the axes multiply the variety of distinctions that are possible, yielding a highly discriminating potential taxonomy. The examples given next are just that, a small number of illustrations from an extremely large potential canvas. A (usually) simple first step is to identify the kind of structure on Axis S and then devote main attention to identifying the qualitative features.

Positioning Relationships on the Two Axes: Illustrations

Observer-judges who have witnessed or become closely informed about a particular relationship are expected to agree generally on where it fits in the *structure-based* classification scheme. In the area of qualitative distinctions unpractised judgements will be less consistent. I think it realistic and advantageous to locate most relationships in at least two and up to four qualitative classes from Axis Q. Four classes is a proposed maximum, to ensure identification by distinctly fitting categories and omission of any that are quite a 'loose' fit. *Within a class* the best-fit principle would apply by selecting *one* category only – except to note transitions from one applicable category to an adjacent one in cases of known active movement in a relationship. The following illustrations demonstrate application of the approach. They include category meanings from a presentation of the approach with added detail.

The Therapist–Client Context

In 'individual' therapy relationships are *complementary* dyads, for which there is a subcategory within category S1.1. A case in point is the well-known filmed interview between 'Gloria' and Carl Rogers (see Rosenzweig, 1996 and Zimring, 1996), which also has some clear qualitative features. Over the interview, the therapist–client relationship reached the category in Q8 of a 'quietly positively bonding favourably experienced relationship'. The quality within Q9 of 'empathic focus on the other's subjective experience' clearly applied too. Other *demonstration* sessions by Rogers in the same collection (Farber et al., 1996) can be similarly identified. Readers would see that the case of Mark (ibid., pp. 334–356) is distinctly different. In this (to Rogers) 'baffling' interview the process was quite unlike the relational qualities with Gloria.

In Rogers' extensive therapy with 'Jim Brown' (ibid., pp. 240–250), most interviews were marked by few words and long silences. In the intensity sphere an 'emotionally flat unexpressive relationship' was the applicable category, though the hospitalized client's occasional eruptions of strong feeling that broke through led to the later designation 'relationship intensity often low to sometimes high'. This was coupled with the Q7 quality of a 'strained relation with one or both parties trying to improve communication'. However, the relationship eventually developed into the Q8 'quietly bonding' quality and 'empathic contact' was reached. With another Rogers' client, seen for 11 extensively documented interviews (ibid., pp. 143–230), the last-mentioned qualities also emerged, though there was another (Q4) feature identifiable as a 'significant but carefully balanced and not intimate or *mutually* sharing relationship'. In this relatively early case, Rogers' listening and reflection components were very consistent and disciplined, leaving little room for direct disclosures or a distinct sense of 'we'.

Yalom's (2001) therapy relation with 'Betty' (the 'Fat Lady' – 250 pounds) developed little in the first year, judging from his close description. He could hardly look at her, felt repulsed by her body, and bored and frustrated by her jolly and entertaining observations and virtual absence of self-talk – though he wanted to help if she would/could let him. Category S1.1 applied, but was pulled by the client toward the 'casual encounter' option in this class. The qualitative categories include the Q1 'low key, low intensity' alternative, the Q7 category 'relationship static or slowly repetitive…' and a Q10 'avoids revealing' quality. Then, finally, the unspoken became spoken in the therapist's confronting response to the client's style and obesity and his perplexity about her motives in therapy. He also drew her into a challenging and dynamic therapy group. Movement occurred and she became ready and able, for the first time, to maintain a radical diet change (down to 160 pounds). She became much more self-disclosing (as was the therapist) and used the therapy relation in a different way. Eventually, the therapy partners were ready to conclude. Their mutually valued relationship as described had included periods of high intensity, the Q6 quality of 'collaboration in joint or team work', and the Q9 aspect 'participants attend, listen and take in the other's meanings' now applied. The mentioned Q7 and Q10 features had dropped out. The reader may be interested to study and type other examples involving relationships with therapists of differing orientation, possibly including Fritz Perls and Albert Ellis, who also interviewed Gloria. (Many such interviews are accessible in libraries and from online sources.)

Illustrations from Family and Group Therapy

In the family therapy context the qualitative categories would tend to be from classes Q2 (conflict/harmony), Q8 (warm/cool/aversive), possibly Q7 (stuck/flowing), and probably Q4 (close/apart) and/or Q9 (attentiveness/reactivity). Comparing categories that applied earlier in the life of family relationships with those that apply at the end of therapy can be illuminating – as in an example from a remarkable account of family process and relationship by Lang & McCallum (2000). Both parents and their two children, a boy and a girl, were involved. For illustration, I will focus on Donna's (the daughter, age $14^{1}/_{2}$ years) experienced relationship with her family. Shortly before therapy began, she had overdosed on strong medication found in her home, in an apparent suicide attempt. At the first therapy session, Donna was in the city with her mother and had announced that she could not and would not return home to the literally unbearable family situation. The qualitative categories in keeping with her experience are 'relationship stressed by severe conflict', 'entangled, erratic relation that could disintegrate or form a cage', 'participants are alert and on guard for any sign of negation or attack' and 'engagement where one party avoids revealing their relational processes'. Donna's parents did not communicate directly and she felt they used her as a go-between.

After four eventful whole-family sessions there was a phase of couple therapy with the parents only and then one more conjoint family session. In the meantime, Donna had left home with her parents' support and gone into a private boarding school she was happy with. This transformation of context, coupled with major changes in perspective and communication within the family, were transforming her life. Donna's relationships with her family and with each of its members now were strikingly different than when therapy began. For her the relation in the harmony/conflict area evidently had shifted to 'little conflict and generally harmonious and peaceful association', the relationship had changed in the warmth/coldness area, the 'entangled erratic' quality no longer applied, and there were distinct gains in the Q9 area to 'perceptive listening'.

Face-to-face small groups are in the same structural class as families (S1.2) since each engaged member would develop an idea or sense of the group whole. In the therapy group powerfully envisioned by Yalom (2005) in his book *The Schopenhauer Cure* – an experience-based (see Yalom & Lescz, 2005) but fictional work – 'Philip' is a philosopher who poses the greatest challenge to the therapist-leader and other members. He is firm in the view that his hard-won 'peace' comes from separateness, from eschewing emotion and avoiding any strong attachment to people. Discovering and locking on to Schopenhauer's thought had worked as his salvation – and he is seeking to pass this on to others. He enters the group not for personal development but as a means to the end of satisfying an accreditation requirement needed for his practice. His person-with-group relationship in the first months fits the 'emotionally "flat" or unexpressive relationship with little overt sharing' quality in Q1, and the Q4 feature of 'carefully distant or avoidant relationship emphasizing differences'. However, the interactive dynamism of the group, with its strong mix of confrontation, receptivity and experiential sharing, finally drew Philip into significant engagement, leading to change in relationships within himself and *with the group*. The former categories ceased to apply; there was more intensity, listening and collaboration, and a positive bonding quality.

Other Group and Larger System Relations

It can be expected that individual-group relationships will evolve and change in the course of an experiential learning or therapy group (Barrett-Lennard, 1998, pp. 148–162). In the different context of *a team or work group* individual-group relationships are more likely to stabilize so that subsequent change may only be noticeable when other members leave or are added. Ideally, a distinctly collaborative (Q6) quality would apply in one or other variant, and there would be a cohesive 'we' quality (Q4). In larger communities or organizations, unless they are exceptionally cohesive, relationships between individuals and the whole can be expected to differ widely from one person to another. In communities, individual–community relationship quality may rest heavily on the person's expressed attitude and engagement with those immediately around her/him. *If* s/he was in a leadership or initiating position, estimation could be based on his/her way of engaging and quality of communication with a wide circle of members.

Group-with-group relational processes (S2.3) occur all the time among sporting teams, within organizations and in many social contexts. The relations often are competitive or even combative. In other instances, of course, collaboration is a vital feature. Some groups may bond positively with each other in a joint 'we'. Or, their relationship process may be cautious or carefully avoidant (as in Q6), especially in the presence of third parties (perhaps an employing organization) from whom both groups desire preferential treatment. Relating groups may be guarded and unrevealing about their inner processes or open and transparent (Q10). Such groups may relate with their 'parent' organization (category S3.1) with a pattern of qualities that differ from their group-with-group relation.

Although it is not feasible here to extend this illustrative discussion of the application of the taxonomy advanced I would be pleased to receive examples from readers – as well as refinement suggestions or other critical feedback. There is another major region of relationships involving people, namely, between humans and members of the non-human world. Chapter 10 is devoted to a careful exploration of this world. Some of the categories distinguished above (especially structural ones) could be adapted to human–animal relationships. Significant dyadic relationships of person-with-animal abound, and one-to-many (c/f category S1.3) and small-group-with-large-group (c/f S3.2) combinations are common in farming and husbandry contexts. However, the distinctions I make in this further domain have their own original order (Chapter 10), and the reader will find that the topic raises many vital issues about kinds and qualities of relationship.

Conclusion: Glimpses of Reader Application and Potential Research

The charting order presented here is novel, carefully considered, not final. I regard it as a working foundation of an ordered way of distinguishing relationships, one that has some precedent in broad idea from the system of distinguishing living species. As with any classification of complex phenomena the approach presented reduces great naturally occurring variety into a comprehensible conceptual and descriptive order, an order whose value is ultimately tested by its usefulness in contexts of application and research. Besides the one-on-one therapy context, practitioners working with couples may wish to use the schema as one way of assessing relationship qualities at or near the start of therapy, and again at one or more later stages. Some *clients* might even be invited to go through a slightly simplified version of the Axis Q scheme, locate their relationship in that framework, compare estimations and follow up any triggered feeling-thoughts in their therapy exploration (not my own idea but that of a colleague I respect). With a whole family, the various relationships could be mapped, also at more than one point. Practitioners working as group relations facilitators may discern evocative applications in that context. The schema also would have potential sensitizing value in counselling training and other developmental contexts.

Research applications could well begin with a focus on the 'reliability' of qualitative judgement choices. This would be designed to formally check on the consistency of classifications by suitably prepared judges who are provided with appropriate relationship samples. More concise distinction of some categories and/or improvements in portraying particular classes might flow from such a check. Using the tested schema, there would be numerous possible applications in therapy and other research. One of these would focus on potential category shifts in client–therapist relationship qualities from early to late individual therapy interviews *and whether these shifts were related meaningfully to outcomes of therapy*. Another possible application would study *couple relationships* through therapy to determine whether/what kinds of (desired or predicted) relationship change occurred. Experiential learning or therapy groups would lend themselves to study of expected kinds of relational change. Participant judges also could be called on to estimate a configuration of desired/ideal qualities in a particular context. Is there, for example, substantial commonality in leader- or worker-desired qualities of relationship in different kinds of organizational settings? Research-minded readers would no doubt think of other research foci pertinent to their interests or setting. Some will have interest in community settings and qualities, which the next chapter searches into.

7

Community as Relationship and Vicissitudes of Belonging

What is 'a community'? The term can be applied to collectives of people that have something in common (perhaps nationality, ethnicity or location), but with little or no actual connection with each other. In more careful usage, a community is a body of people who are aware of their connection and feel some bond or quality of belonging. It evidently is in our nature to hunger for group affiliation beyond the immediate family. We want to be related in a larger 'we' that reflects and contributes to a sense of who we are and where we fit in the scheme of things. The communal whole can be a rather loose and permeable relational system, or a relatively tight and closed one. In size, its members may range from dozens to thousands. While there is a similarity in the needs for affiliation involved, it is evident that communities form in diverse ways, are of widely varied quality and composition and no longer need to depend on close physical proximity of members.

Origins and Variety in the Becoming of Communities

In early human history, multi-family tribal groups probably were the first form of community. Tribes would have a number of practical advantages over isolated families in terms of member protection, hunting, allowance for diverse roles and division of labour, a wider mix of relationships and, not least, a broader gene pool. Later, when villages and towns formed, the advantages of large, relatively stable membership increased, especially where these wholes developed organically and with strong communal bonds. The ways in which people come together and find communal attachment in modern environments, with technology-assisted linkage and living patterns, need not hinge on location and are more variable in form and in what members look for and how they bond.

Communities of association and belonging can have strikingly varied prominent features. In the case of many indigenous communities mutual attachment to a natural environment has profound meaning to community members (Abrams, 1997). A local culture with unique language usage and outlook, or strongly shared religious or other belief, may stand out. Other potential connecting factors include common ethnic affiliation and traditions (especially as a minority within a diverse larger society), or a 'calling' or special vocational interest that draws people together whose life meaning is partly built around that calling. As earlier noted, a community experience may emerge or grow stronger under the impact of a shared crisis or disaster – depending on the quality of pre-crisis relationships and resilience (Twigg, 2009). It can also spring from mutual discovery of an associative context that draws those involved to feel at home and supported in their outlooks or way of living. An affirming communal experience may be transient yet strong and salient in the memories of those who shared the experience (Rogers, 1977).

In communities that begin with a distinctive founding ideal the visions of the original participants may focus on strongly desired alternatives to experienced social constraints or discrimination against their religious beliefs. Such visions can be said to apply to the 'Pilgrim Fathers' settlement in Plymouth, New England, where freedom for the community members' beliefs and desired ethos and way of life evidently were primary motivations. However, as the enclosing colony of Massachusetts developed, fears of Calvinist believers in the locality of Salem turned into lethal intolerance of some deviant members thought to be aligned with forces of darkness and evil as witches. Closed visionary communities can be especially hazardous, as in the extreme case of Jonestown where over 900 members died together (Mancinelli et al., 2002).

Kibbutzim were founded in Israel as utopian self-sustaining socialist communities, and flourished there between the great wars and after World War II. Unsurprisingly, those that remain have evolved from their founding visions, are less centred on their whole-community experience and tend to be more engaged in commercial activity (Jewish Virtual Library, 2012, from *Encyclopaedia Judaica*). Spiro's searching earlier study (1970) of a particular kibbutz found that it was 'no longer bent on presenting itself as a blueprint for communities elsewhere but occupied with its own wellbeing' including concern for its long-range future (Barrett-Lennard, 1994; Teibel, 2010). Oliver's account in his 1976 book (pp. 201–214) reports mainly positive outcomes for children, of the participatory communal environment for learning, but notes also an increasing influence of the wider youth culture. The same author provides a carefully descriptive and critical account of a range of utopian and designed therapeutic communities.

Utopian communities that survive often become less distinct over time from other groups in the encompassing society. Even the 'old order' Mennonite community in Southern Ontario (as known to the author from having lived nearby), though retaining much of its very distinctive earlier lifestyle, interfaces peacefully with the surrounding population and institutions, conducts a large public produce and crafts market and has an easy relationship with non-traditional Mennonite groupings. In any significant community, and strikingly so in the group just mentioned, the participants are inclined to turn to each other not only as a natural expression of relationship, but for practical assistance in immediate need and to share and utilize knowledge of their community's larger world. Old Order Mennonites do not subscribe to mainstream insurance schemes but share risk as a matter of course and converge to materially assist each other in the face of crisis or disaster.

Community Experience and Health in Contemporary Mobile Societies

Whatever form a community takes, the development of an active network of relationships seems crucial to its vitality and a sense of communal belonging by members (McMurray, 2007, chapter 1). Ideally, everyone would be acknowledged or looked out for by other members and each person or family would be contributing, by their presence or active engagement, to the maintenance and ethos of their community. Typically, in current urban settings there is a significant movement of people leaving and entering or seeking to enter communal groups. People who do not experience a communal affinity, or who feel 'outside' any group, may be desperate to find a context where they do have the sense of being within and part of something with others, a 'something' that also supports and contributes to their sense of who they are.

In an established community some members would think about what makes for or diminishes the well-being of their communal whole. In a confident community the members look outward as well as inward, and are conscious of the relation between their community and 'outside' systems on which their collective partially depends and which it also contributes to. The qualities of those encompassing systems, and their relations with even bigger systems such as large nations, clearly can make or break constituent communities. In a supportive or sufficiently benign societal context, communities can develop their own kind of life and presence, a presence supportive of members and their personal relationships through the ups and downs of their lives. Well-functioning communities also take an active stance in relations with their environmental systems and toward the preservation and development of their distinctive and valued qualities.

Thus, 'healthy' human communities are living systems of association, support, affirmation and meaning. Specifically, they are self-organizing open systems that rely on and can be nourished by their connection with other healthy systems. They respond to external circumstance as well as to fresh information and initiatives from within. Members are not copies of one another and their diversity contributes to 'growth in the scope, subtlety and wisdom of communal consciousness' (Barrett-Lennard, 2005, p. 99). They tend to conserve tested values, but the ways these values are *expressed* evolve and vary widely between members. System change is not pursued for its own sake but, at best, to preserve and enhance the life of the community. This life exists in interdependent relation with the lives of its members, while also having its own properties and momentum as a communal culture (see, e.g., Etzioni, 1968, pp. 45–49 on 'emergent properties').

As noted in Chapter 6, communities are broadly distinct from organizations in that they are not primarily about production for profit or providing a service to outsiders. They form or exist for their own sake as 'centres of belonging' with vital bearing on the associative meaning of their members' lives. Thus member bonds tend to be stronger and structures looser than in organizations – as further considered in the next chapter. Since human life is developmental in its nature, and communities are a manifestation of this life, a well-functioning community will tend to refresh and renew itself. This happens partly as a natural consequence of the generational and other turnover of members and relationships, of people having experience outside the community, and changes in the environment of the whole community. A strong and lasting community would grow over time beyond the collective wisdom of a particular generation of members. Further generations then can benefit from this growth and extend it.

Community Life in Transition

Most people are no longer anchored in a single stable community, but are in motion in a moving-on world. Careers and job changes; new and changing relationships; relocations and alterations in lifestyle: all can lead people into and out of communities. The communities themselves may endure through considerable turnover of members. Communal systems that have evolved over time and been rich with shared relational experience and meaning adapt and hold on to life. They are 'homes' to which people return if or when they can and which, in any case, survive in the memories of former members and continue to influence what they look for. 'Sense of community' is hard to pin down conceptually, yet is a quality that may be reflectively felt by members or sensed by perceptive observers or visitors to a community.

Stable settlements of people and the form(s) of community that flow from such settlement are becoming the exception in contemporary urban society. Individuals who live in temporary association, even where this is valued and formative for them, can also feel adrift and without continuing attachment as they move from one 'harbour' anchorage to another. Some harbours offer refuge or sanctuary, others serve as landing places for the traveller to gather resources for the next phase of travel and still others may prove to be siren-like in attracting and exploiting visitors without receiving them as persons. Of course, it is not just the harbour but also those who anchor there and the confluence of circumstance that co-determine the outcome. Our societal world may help a person to learn skills of 'travelling' more than those of putting down roots and inhabiting a place together. The travelling skill may include ability to quickly form attachments-for-the-moment while also looking out for what comes next. It may even include resourcefulness in engaging communally with valued qualities of sharing and bonding that can however be broken off again, since there is always another potential setting.

Contemporary culture includes many organized and managed collectives established under the banner of 'communities', though not ones that have formed and evolved organically from relational needs and life circumstances. Retirement villages have become one prominent example. Oliver (1976) examined visions of collective life that evolved in tribal contexts with development of moral orders and practices growing from the experience of participants and their forebears. In contrast to these forms, there are utilitarian systems pre-structured and put in place by social architects and planners and the commercial interests of organizations that do the building work for these systems. 'Evolutionists' committed to supporting, preserving, and (if called for) enabling self-generated community processes tend to see human nature and community as woven into the larger fabric of life and natural environments. For utilitarian planners the envisioned practical needs of participants are central and environments and resources are fashioned to meet these perceived needs (ibid.). The latter emphasis tends to see people as consumers and it is a short step to emphasize shifting consumption 'needs' and opportunities. Then communal bonding as a priority never develops or falls easily out of sight.

A pragmatic moving-on world significantly affects contexts and qualities of community. Many settings have some properties of communal association though their raison-d'etre is to equip participants for their vocational and life journeys. Schools, universities and other training/educational associations are a case in point. Where the focus is largely on individual learning and development, the experience of community is secondary, a by-product that can nevertheless have significant bearing on whether or how members seek out and respond to opportunities for future communal association. Intensive residential workshops – to take another example familiar to the author – may develop a strongly communal quality that is valued and vividly remembered by participants. Some participants may stay in touch with each other but, overall, the importance lies in what members take to other professional and relationship life contexts. The discovered communal features enrich their experience-based awareness of the process and potential of life communities.

Arguably, a vibrant community embodies a subtle blend of change and constancy. As a living entity it is always in motion in some respects. At the same time, a certain regularity of process and endurance of values seems vital for the community to have an identity experienced and perhaps treasured by its members. A life-tested matrix of connection underpins a sense of belonging, of being associated in a kind of partnership that grounds members in their worlds. I say 'worlds' since a single community is no longer the whole world of most people. Not only is there the high mobility factor but also, in rapidly increasing degree, there are 'virtual' communities of engagement of people via the internet and other media. These networks of connection and exchange, often without any face-to-face contact, are fostering new kinds of association based on commonality and choice and thus with significant meaning to participants. Although they may not last or engage people deeply yet, in some cases at least, these associative networks have valued qualities resembling those of more physically tangible communities. Member experience within them is likely to affect first-hand relationships that are a part of physical communities. In other words, the 'virtual community experience' flows into other communal associations. It can, of course, also substitute for and reduce engagement in more substantial physical communities.

Radical change in local environments from mining, logging, land clearance, introduced diseases, pollutants from manufacturing and many other causes can jeopardize or overwhelm existing communities. And there is also a vulnerability to natural disasters such as tsunamis and major earthquakes, floods or landslides. The effects of warfare or selective, violent state suppressions can fragment or effectively wipe out whole communities (see Chapter 9). However, bonded 'organic' communities do not die easily and survivors may work hard to maintain connection and rebuild their communal world. In other cases, population movements and other societal changes gradually 'dissolve' a community. The impact of these changes varies with the resources and resilience of a community's membership and bonds, these in turn being partly a function of how deep-rooted the communal sense and quality is. Some communities seem able to re-create themselves and recover from assaults that would disburse and effectively end other collectives. Resourceful subgroups may emerge that have a crucial role in a community's coping response to the crisis (Quarantelli & Dynes, 1977, p. 31).

Recovery and Transformation of Threatened Communities

A community can be eroded or disabled by internal division as well as from external factors impinging on it, or (more likely) from these two sources in interaction. If threats from the outside are severe, a community might erect barriers and seek to isolate itself or, alternatively, mobilize to attack other collectives who are the perceived sources of threat. Insulation from the larger society can make the community more vulnerable to highly controlling leadership and to personally disempowering belief systems. In these circumstances, 'concern for self-preservation may become the driving force, warping the community into a defense camp' (Barrett-Lennard, 2005, p. 100). The price of aggressive defence stresses internal relations, however, especially if members assume more machine-like alignment to combat the danger. At the extreme, the community may become a highly controlled organization and a violent antagonist to its neighbours. In an alternative transformation, participants bend their efforts to see into the reality they face, understand whether their own community is contributing to the threat, and discern how they might collectively change their way of relating to other bodies to reduce or remove the threat.

It is difficult for a community that is suffering from serious internal stressors, especially if there are factions that are very distrustful of each other, to take problem-solving steps or seek outside assistance with their own processes. If there were no convulsive inner tension yet a process of struggling to survive for any of a multiplicity of possible reasons, a community would in principle be able to use enabling consultants to further discover and effectively utilize its resources, and potentially to regain health. Communities that are 'tired' and largely repeating themselves in a depressed level of functioning may also find opportunity to reach outside themselves for assistance with their own working, security and health as collectives.

Community development programmes, especially when initiated or encouraged from the outside, tend to focus more on material developments, legal and justice issues, housing, educational or medical facilities and the like and somewhat less on the development of relationships within the community as a strengthening end in itself. In principle, both kinds of goal can be pursued in a way that each contributes to the other. In the case of external initiatives for change, extensive consultation within the community is intrinsically desirable and much more likely than externally planned change to lead to a valued enrichment of community resources and process. It is also in keeping with the democratic and social justice principles emphasized in community work. In a leading text in this field, Kenny (2006) has systematically delineated the roles and principles of community development (CD) work. The roles she lists include a variety of tasks, abilities, knowledge and skills. Facilitation, networking and communication skills are emphasized, in the first instance 'to help a community identify, develop and fulfil its needs' (ibid., p. 19).

However, the enumerated tasks begin with 'researching and analysing community issues, needs and problems' and include 'developing, interpreting and implementing community policy' and 'educating the community about their rights and responsibilities' (ibid., pp. 17–18). The information as a whole implies that the CD worker is seen as having the expertise to take substantial initiatives to steer the process on a pathway seen to be in the community's interests. Broad goals such as empowerment, gaining awareness of rights and learning how to negotiate assertively are assumed in advance and there appears to be some inconsistency with the principle of discovery-oriented and enabling facilitation of community values and goals.

Hawe et al. (2009) affirm that communities need to be understood as 'complex ecological systems'. In this light any significant intervention can be 'seen as a critical event in the history of a system, leading to the evolution of new structures of interaction and new shared meanings' (ibid., p. 267). Block (2008) speaks of the human need for a 'structure of belonging'. He finely describes different facets of what goes into such a structure and illustrates process and ways to aid community transformation. However a CD worker proceeds s/he is providing a model, and her/his modus operandi needs to transcend any simple cause and effect understanding and appreciate the dynamic self-propelling interaction of triggering and feedback processes that occur in complex systems.

Qualities of Community Strength and Wellness

There is a growing literature on community strength, though with varied implications as to the meaning and criteria of 'strength'. Some of this work is broadly concordant with the perspective advanced here although the language differs. Pertinent sources include reports by Black & Hughes (2001) and Pope (2006). I prefer the more specific term 'wellness', which does imply effectiveness and strength in the working of communication and relationship in a community. These features are highlighted here because of their relative neglect as a direct source of priority goals as well as their fit with the overall thrust of this book.

In a working community of people the members are in reach of each other, directly or through other members. They have a common language, often with an idiom that is more or less distinctive to the community. Members' lifestyles are not all the same but there is a mutually understood and largely shared morality, value system or code underlying their relations. There is also a certain quality of interdependence in practical affairs having to do with the working of the community. Most fundamentally in present perspective, the community is a system of association and relationships. I already have offered a normative view of qualities of well-functioning people (p. 53) and relationships (p. 20) and will similarly focus in summary on the proposed features of community process health. These overlap the desired qualities of personal relationships, but in their combination and scope are specific to the context in focus here. In outline, a *well community* is conceived as having the following interrelated characteristics:

1. A quality of felt belonging experienced by the members.
2. An organic, cohesive quality that also makes for a 'we' sense – not a 'we' against the rest of the world but a home place within it.
3. A broadly shared tolerance for diversity and a disposition and capacity to transcend differences for the common good.
4. An ethos that fosters growth process among the members and in their families and groupings; growth that acts back to enhance the communal whole.
5. An ethic and atmosphere of encouragement and respect for the varied qualities and resources of members.
6. Engagement processes that encourage broad-based initiatives and make for distributed and community-centred leadership.
7. An openness to the experience and recognition of actual processes and events within the community *and* an interested attentiveness to the

surrounding world; these aspects together making for a dynamic open system quality.

8. A tendency *both* to conserve experience-tested qualities such as those listed (1 to 7) *and* to an evolving refinement and refreshment of goals in application.

Item 1 in this list has been discussed as applying to any associated grouping of people justifiably identified as 'a community'. In a well-functioning community this strongly present feature is a magnet to its members, and naturally makes for the cohesive 'we' sense encapsulated in item 2. The bonding of a healthy community does not, however, rely on everyone having very similar styles and qualities since diversity is also advantageous. Developmental growth of members and relationships is likely to increase this variety, a variety that includes complementary interests and resources (aspect 3). These things contribute to fruitful initiatives and a spreading of potentially facilitative leadership in the interests of the community. Such growth also will contribute to members' constructive engagement beyond the (permeable) borders of their community (aspects 4, 5 and 6). People in a healthy community are not just occupied with maintaining what is communally desirable but are keenly aware of actual happenings, attitudes and other processes – in their community and beyond it (implied in aspect 7). In some new-formed communities members may fasten on its special qualities and their development and only later mature into open awareness of external relations. This feature and aspect 8 imply a protective stance toward what the members consider special and valuable about their community, though with an openness to its continuing evolution.

Conclusion

Communities that are embracing and vital to their members' sense of belonging and meaning are precious systems that often are casualties or under threat in a fast-moving world, a world in which people tend to be encouraged to overcome personal obstacles, find their own paths and pursue their *individual* development and destiny. There may always be some tension between the goals of *self*-realization and a strong communal engagement that reduces self-preoccupation, enhances belonging and nourishes shared group life and community. Self-realization need not be ego-centred and can develop within communal engagement (Blatt, 2008). Fresh study would be required to determine whether or how often *all* of the qualities of well-functioning community mentioned above are to be found in existing communities. I would expect that some aspects are far more often potentials and possible goals in life communities than they are fully achieved qualities.

The reader may be rethinking the question of what exactly is the phenomenon of community both generally and in his or her own life. Certainly, people cluster and associate voluntarily in collectives that can be of huge importance to them. But are these generally living communities in the sense that I have advanced here? The complexity and variety of the settings in which people live and the bombardment of media and professional information on what we 'should' value and seek to implement in our life settings make me wary of confident generalization. The ideas presented toward the end of this chapter, though carefully distilled, come partly from a values stance and stand as propositions. Other parts of this book lend further meaning to the perspective and issues examined in this one. The next chapter in particular, which is concerned with the nature and working of organizations as collective work-places and theatres of relational experience and influence, complements this one.

8

Large Organizations as Systemic Worlds of Relationship

Big organizations of widely varying nature and function have a major property in common: they are containers of a diverse multitude of relationships. One prominent group markets goods, these organizations existing in interdependent relation with the systems that produce those 'goods' and the people and systems that purchase them. Varied organized institutions provide human services to the wider community and others promote and serve the recreational and social needs of their members. Further main categories include professional and trade associations, government departments and civil service and military organizations. Most of these systems have a long and indefinite lifespan. Some others are project-centred and dissolve on completion of the project. Still others fail to thrive or are taken over and absorbed into larger organizations. Their inner working varies with the kind of system, its management, external realities, experience over time and shifts in practice influenced by worker members. However, regardless of the tightness of structure and control, the organization is not a mechanism because its human members and their relationships are not mechanisms. Organizations develop a supra-personal identity and ethos that partakes of the consciousness of people leading, within and surrounding them.

The needs and priorities of an organization at the time naturally and in large measure determine who is recruited or accepted into the membership. Recruitment into senior positions often results also from people in and outside the system knowing each other or knowing people in common. Most members are part of a smallish team, and these teams or sections are connected with each other in larger groupings. Some individuals may have responsibility within more than one group and, because of the specialized nature of many tasks in large organizations, specialist members often are vital informants to the person who is formally their supervisor. Organizations that extract raw materials or that trade, manufacture or sell goods, and even those that provide human services, usually do not devote high priority to the inherent well-being of their own members. Their leaders need to be, but often are not, facilitating 'helpers' in Schein's (2009) sense. However, the system's long-term viability and a positive social contribution arguably depend on a healthy internal human relational

environment. When many members feel good about their work and their relations on the job a positive radiation into the wider community is likely to
follow.

Organizations necessarily are open systems, interacting as a whole and
through their members with many features of the larger world that surrounds,
engages and interpenetrates them (see Thompson & McHugh, 1995, chapter 3;
and Webb, 2006, e.g. pp. 31–33). The opportunities, needs and style of an organization, how it is led or managed at various levels, and its relation with outside
systems, all feed in various ways into human relationships within the system.
Communication is basic to joining and partnering in activities or attitude.
When working members are deprived of relational contact although engaged
in coordinated activity, as in some assembly line or other repetitive physical
production, the work itself may have little intrinsic meaning and mainly serve
as a relevant symbol and means to an end for the workers. The relation of
observable working conditions to work satisfaction *and* productivity is
complex, but the climate of relationships within an organization is seen as a
major factor on both levels.[3]

Organizations as Generators and Custodians of Relationship

Entry into an organization means entry to a fresh world of relationship,
including associations that come with the job and personal affiliations that
are not task related. The whole large organization, of whatever kind or
mission, is a complex system of interwoven human activity and association.
Attitudinal relations between groups or divisions as well as relationships
between individuals have vital bearing on the system's overall functioning.
Generally, two basic aspects can be distinguished in relations between
members. One of these is instrumental and typically involves the passing on
of information and/or materials from one person or group to another. Farace
et al. (1977) highlight the variety and complexity of task-related message
exchange and other instrumental communication in organizational settings.
The other basic aspect is concerned with feelings, personal communication
and connective experience in relationship. Ease and fluency in relationship
contributes to member influence beyond their task expertise or formal position. Both relational feeling and instrumental elements apply jointly in
nearly all working relationship contexts. Formally, many interrelations have
a vertical dimension, as in worker–supervisor and manager–group relations.
Listening and process consultation (Schein, 2009, pp. 132ff.) are relationally

---

[3]   Research evidence through the mid-1900s (Barrett-Lennard, 1972, pp. 48–68) already supported
       this conclusion. In 1939, Eton Mayo critiqued inquiry that 'ignores completely the mutual
       dependence and complexity of the facts of human association' (in Roethlisberger & Dickson,
       1967, p. xi; see further Mayo quote in Dickson & Roethlisberger, 1966, p. 117).

oriented and compatible with differing responsibilities and mutual concern with instrumental activity.

In subjective expression, 'you–me', 'they–me', 'we' and 'we–them' relational processes are ubiquitous in the felt experience of participant organizational members. For a given person, some of these relations are likely to matter greatly, while others are casual or perfunctory. Meaningful human attachments in an organization can be few, sporadic and unpredictable. In more favourable settings and satisfying roles participants welcome and come to depend on their affiliations with other members and their shared productive work. Where people are interacting with other people in a system, varied first-hand relationships naturally form. The quality of these lived relations is a partial consequence (as well as a contributing cause) of levels of psychosocial health in contemporary cultures.

Schluter & Lee (2009), in their practical manual on 'relational management', view organizations as pivoting on relationship processes (whether recognized or not) *in all of their activities.* Effective managers, in their view, necessarily are skilled in the arts of communicating and fostering rewarding connection between people. In an earlier manual, Campbell et al. (1991) present a hands-on account of 'development consultation'. This is concerned with facilitating developmental change in relational awareness within organizations and their systemic working more broadly. The writers believe that the communication and feedback processes set in train in their consultation 'ensure that it is impossible *not* to change' (ibid., p. 15).

Relationships in a large organization develop through a spread-out management 'team', specialist professional members, line workers in different areas and supporting administrative or clerical staff. Through job-related and informal contacts the support staff get to know people with similar roles in other areas. As noted, these associations can shortcut formal exchanges in ways that are crucial for the working efficiency of the organization. Generally, the more casual associations, task-related or otherwise, form a significant, largely predictable and unthreatening part of the relational environment. Familiarity is an important variable in managing the diversity of relational contexts that, in their uneven qualities, can confuse new members.

An organization, especially through its internal leadership and those with owning or regulating interest, is deemed to have a large share of responsibility for the human relationships that it brings into being. While its existence does not directly *govern* the kind and quality of these relationships the fact that these emerge and develop within the organization, with its own mission and character, implies consequential systemic influence. The causation is not simple (see Chapter 5) since the emergent relationships are not only a result of the larger whole (and the members' outside worlds or relation) but also come to be influences in their own right, on each other and on the larger system. In seeking to grasp the overall relational character and climate of an organization, several variable features can be highlighted. An important one is the aspect of competition or rivalry within the system, especially when this is harnessed to a strong focus on outcomes.

Relationships in Systems Centred on Outcomes

Any organization has reason to appraise the outcomes of its activity. According to its kind, profit may be a pivotal concern, growth, wealth accumulation and/or success in competition can be central drivers, perceived standing among related systems or in the wider community may be a top priority, recognized high achievement by members (as in universities or research institutions) can be a paramount concern, the reach and size of its membership may be a major issue (e.g., as in many professional and volunteer organizations), and enhancing personal, social and/or spiritual life quality may be an inspirational force. Political and other organizations often have more than one agenda, including submerged or unofficial drivers of leader initiatives, such as desire for power and/or other personal or faction gain.

An overriding focus on outcomes that are financially profitable, prestigious or otherwise organization-enhancing draws constant attention to extrinsic success, usually at the expense of attention to process and relationships. As well, outcome results tend to be assessed by comparing performances within the system. These comparisons readily place individuals and/or groups in competition with one another and engender a culture of rivalry. Rewards for performance can accentuate this rivalry. Though an element of competition may increase task-focused energy, a strong and constant outcomes focus would tend to diminish intrinsic motivation, to increase stress and to reduce trust and warmth of association. Creative innovation is another potential casualty. Where ambitious groups with a distinct or special mission see themselves as pitted against other forces in their system, the natural internal diversity of style and viewpoint within such a group diminishes. At the extreme, a 'groupthink' mentality can emerge.

In big organizations, strong competitive rivalry between groups or main divisions may have some energizing effect, but it restricts open cross-communication and can narrow or stress relationships within these subsystems. Where success in competition with other organizations is an overriding concern, this works as pressure on the system to increase efficiency, with risk to internal relationship quality. Relations within an organization necessarily have 'external' effects as will be further discussed. Bringing change in the culture of big organizations such that human relational well-being issues have similar priority to other organizational objectives is a huge challenge. Distinction has been made between transactional and transformational leadership (Bono & Judge, 2003; Kovjanic et al., 2012). The former is largely task-centred, exchange-based and reliant on extrinsic motivation. The transformational leader values and (at best) inspires self-engagement, communicative rewarding relationships and cooperative work activity as a source of meaning. In such settings members may identify strongly with *their* organization, want it to thrive and assume they can help this to happen.

Take-Home Effects of Organizational Life

Contemporary organizations tend to be moderately concerned with the well-being of employees on the job. In my observation, however, they mostly do not confront implications of being a context in which members are living a big part of their lives (perhaps half their waking hours) and from which they take home significant effects to their families and communities. In the too frequent case of vulnerable members leaving their daily work situations stressed over what they have experienced, especially from troubling interaction or lonely cut-off feelings on the job, this has to affect how they re-enter engagements outside work. It may be true that 'workers want to be understood and validated as conscious, creative, thoughtful and passionate human beings' (Diamond & Allcorn, 2009, p. 2), but also the case that experience in employment often extinguishes any expectation of being received and treated this way. Any setbacks in a person's private world of close relationships have no immunity from the influence of relational attitudes developed through experience in organizations, from school settings onward.

From their experience as organizational consultants with a psychoanalytic thought base, Diamond & Allcorn (ibid.) see organizations as frequently defective containers of experiential and relational systems, heavily influenced in their identity and working by unconscious processes. Shorn of their specialist language, these authors imply that positive potentialities of the human self generally are unnourished in organizational life, potentially with damage to the self and relationships. Further, if organizational leaders are driven by forces outside their consciousness then the whole system can in crucial ways be 'flying blind'. This 'unseeing' must affect the working of human relations throughout the system, with carry-over into members' outside lives. A lack of recognition of the systemic interplay of influences in the organization is a likely accompanying feature. In contrasting positive potential, insightful awareness of relational processes in organizations is a developmental process likely to be beneficial in outside personal life as well. Even where self and other are fairly clearly distinguished, the intersubjective 'third' – the phenomenon and process of the emergent relationship itself – may not be recognized or effectively taken into account (ibid., chapter 4).

Work in organizations is of course a main source of livelihood, especially in industrialized economies. Income earning is extrinsic to engaging in work for its intrinsic meaning but obviously serves an enormously important function for most workers, often on a symbolic as well as practical level. Having a job in a visible major institution, in a chosen career and affirming level of appointment, or in any relationship-sensitive context that helps to validate the employed person, supports self-esteem and assurance in non-work relationships. Aspiring to such a job, and not being 'successful' in attaining it, has the likely reverse effect of diminishing the self-in-relationship – if not moderated by other circumstance. High job status and income, of course, is not reliably advantageous in personal relations. If these features do contribute to self-respect and enrich the person's friendship circle then life relationships can be expected to benefit.

If systems and tasks within an organization contribute to significant stress or discontent and a poor quality of life on the job, and these effects are carried outside the work environment, this is 'bad for' the organization itself in various possible ways. Possibilities include undue staff turnover, reduced productive energy on the job, a falling reputation in the wider community and an inability to grow or evolve. In a recent study of a diverse sample of employed adults 41 per cent reported that they typically felt stressed out during their work day, and under half were satisfied with growth and developmental opportunities through their work (American Psychological Association, 2012). 'Take-home effects' apply not only to employees and their families but can cumulate to affect the vibrancy and health of the local or even national community. Large organizations not uncommonly make grants or target funding to selected community projects, with positive effect. However, if the internal relational health of the system is not itself a priority the resulting deficiencies can be expected to leak into the wider community that employees inhabit.

Organizations as Human Habitats: Qualities and Health

Organizations are created human habitats, which in many cases impact heavily on the environments of other life forms. In what senses are these human habitat systems responsible for their own internal quality and external impact? In whom is this responsibility vested: the owning authority, shareholders, directors and/or top leadership of the organization or its working members? Since organizations vary so much in respect to authority and decision-making, the only general answer may be that responsibility is shared in varied balance across all of these levels. Ambiguity from lack of focus on this issue can make it easy for those involved at any level to feel that influence, initiative and responsibility lie elsewhere in the system. Less often, it seems, a broadly shared feeling of assumed responsibility prevails. In the more developed or well-to-do economies large organizations can be held legally responsible for their effect on the natural environment, and most new mining, manufacturing and housing development projects need to be assessed in this respect before they can go ahead. The crucial further sphere of social and human relations impact is less often considered in any depth.

The volume of reports edited by Starik & Sharma (2005), on 'sustainable organisations', brings together original investigative studies by Gallagher and others that focus not only on immediate impact but also on sustaining resources and qualities of the environment over the lifetime of any major project or development. It is argued that in order to be well functioning an organization's membership needs to be perceptively aware of its environment in a way that is conducive to both human and environmental well-being for the foreseeable future. A fully ecological awareness, necessary for organizational well-being in the long term, would embrace these emphases within the broader understanding that human society and the natural world are interdependently conjoined (see Chapter 10). A volume edited by Gozdz (1995), with a complementary mission, brings together numerous contributions concerned with the internal, broadly relational process of organizations, especially toward the creation of a communal quality of association and its fruits.

Aspirations for organizational health also depend for their realization on continued advance in knowledge of ways that large organizations work, how they tend to evolve and how their qualitative health as human systems can improve without reduction in output performance – as assessed by criteria that also are evolving. Organizations not uncommonly call on outside specialist consultants to assist in their development. If the consultants are highly qualified for and have the mandate to assist in genuine soul-searching within the system, fruitful outcomes are possible. One broad result could be the development of a new quality of experienced partnership and responsibility among members at all levels. However, freeing up fresh creative thinking not only about the products or services of the organization but about its basic working as a human system can yield unpredictable outcomes. Besides those who are energized and innovative in their response to the process other members may find it disturbing and prefer to manage their piece of the territory in the way things presently run. Searching dialogue about what is seen as desirable and possible can lead to substantial consensus in some groups but not in others. Lack of consensus may even be the norm in a large many-sided system. It does not imply a static state if parts of an organization change and other parts 'slog on' much as before.

Neville & Dalmau (2008) point out that contemporary organizations tend to contain more than one culture and that such variety can be natural and fruitful. They believe 'that those who now attempt to impose a unitary culture on an organization often unwittingly damage both the organization and the individuals who comprise it' (p. 6). It can also be fruitful to look at the system through a variety of lenses or try out its fit with various images, for example, as Morgan does in his classic work *Images of organization* (1986). Neville & Dalmau (2008) further see organizational behaviour as having unconscious components living beneath 'a self-image that is strongly tied to images of rationality and objectivity' (p. 15). A well-publicized 'brand' – a catchy phrase and/or visual symbol – derives from a self-image, actual or desired. The same authors draw on Jungian archetype theory and classical mythology, coupled with an infusion of systems thinking, in a vigorous and evocative exploration of non-conscious patterns and determinants of organizational behaviour.

In exploring organizational cultures, Neville & Dalmau (chapter 2) also review various ways that have been advanced to classify system styles. These range from distinctions that borrow freely from a language of personality types (or psychopathologies) or that create categories distinctive to the level of culture or large systems. Gibb's (1978) approach to assessing qualitative modes draws on both of these levels. The modalities he distinguishes are labelled *punitive, autocratic, benevolent, consultative, participative, emergent, organic, holistic* and *'cosmic'*. Underlying these, in Gibb's perspective, are different levels of trust within the system, higher trust being a generally growthful direction of change.

Where morale is strong and members of an employing organization have an attitude of ownership of 'my company', 'my service', union, church, school or university, political party or other organization, their work in that setting expresses a vocation and sense of belonging. Energetic engagement is intrinsically motivated, and there tends to be natural concern for the well-being of their system and a readiness to collaborate as partners rather than compete with colleagues (Herriot, 2001, chapter 7). Various factors help to foster this sense of ownership: work that is interesting or rich with meaning, felt security in 'their' system, a sense of being valued and supported by fellow workers/colleagues and those with leadership and managerial responsibility, and a personal readiness to step in and assume agency in their vocational world. Rewarding personal-working relationships with colleagues is an implicit feature of this described context.

The sheer scope and size of many organizations would tend, however, to work against a substantial sense of identification with the whole system, especially for members in rank and file positions. Departments and even work groups can be encapsulated 'silos' (Diamond & Allcorn, 2009) that restrict awareness of the larger system and, thus, provide little opportunity for a sense of partnership in the whole organization. Even without such blockage a true sense of shared ownership cannot be produced by policy (unless members literally are co-owners). Many organizations have policies and approaches oriented toward influencing the self-identity and loyalty of members. They may, in effect, be seeking to 'colonise the selves' of employees, as carefully discussed by Webb within her critical sociological examination of *Organisations, identities and the self* (2006, pp. 154–161). Given that the complex human self has varied potential configurations that come into play selectively (Chapter 3), a self-configuration may often be bound up with career organizational membership. Moreover, the interaction of complex selves can be expected to produce some uneasy or even conflictual relationships. Any well-functioning contemporary organization would be prepared for this and have resources available for constructive response to relationship difficulties and collisions (see, e.g., Copeland, 2005).

Organizational Transformation and Change

There is an extensive literature on organizational development and change. This work explores various change strategies, objectives and processes (see, e.g., Bennis et al., 1985; Palmer, 2006), although it tends to have in common the idea of systematic interventions and related assumptions that privilege particular directions of change. The broader term is 'transformation' (c/f transformational leadership) and this can at best be facilitated or helped along, though not produced, by measures dedicated to enabling it to happen. Some authors are very firm in a view contrary to most ideas of planned change and how to produce it. Neville & Dalmau (2008) are particularly eloquent in their expression of this contrary view, as follows:

> Transformation … is most certainly not something that a change agent does to an organization. Rather, it is something that happens to an organization, as a seed transforms into a plant, or an egg transforms into an insect or animal when the time and conditions are right. The change agent working in the ways outlined … is not trying to change the organization, but to put it in touch with its own transformational energy while helping it to become aware of what, at some level, it already 'knows' about itself and its context. (Ibid., p. 77)

This view is very much in accord with the present author's attitude in working with a client in therapy, as expressed in a piece titled 'On *not* seeking to change my client' (Barrett-Lennard, 2003, pp. 51–57). A consultant in the present context naturally would want to have some helpful effect, but may believe that significant change is an organic growth process that has its own energy and basic direction; a process that s/he may at best help to release or enable. I do not mean to suggest that this is a passive engagement in which a 'midwife-consultant' simply follows. It requires highly concentrated, focused listening, an awareness of context and structure inside and outside the organization and the capacity to imagine and share meanings that help to transform information exchange into dialogue and problem-solving. It is quite unlikely that the organization is like a finally tuned and integrated organism. There will be different and probably opposing voices, each needing to be heard and clearly acknowledged so that truths of perception and judgement and felt responsibility are exchanged and *the energies behind these voices no longer cancel each other out*. As a result, an approximately common direction of transformation that the closely listening consultant helps to articulate may be found.

As in the case of individuals and personal relationships, events that disturb an existing equilibrium sometimes trigger awareness of need and energy for change. Even incidental or unexpected happenings in themselves of no great consequence may be a suggestive stimulus for another look at associative patterns of activity that in turn leads on to fresh discriminations and small steps of transformation. A large organization has many parts and is of its nature an unwieldy whole. Some of its parts may interface with 'outside' systems almost as closely as with adjacent parts of the same organization. Certain semi-autonomous parts (a research and development division, for example) may have more immediate potential for change or self-transformation than other parts. It can be in the interests of the organization as a whole to allow and encourage this unfolding development to take place – with some finesse from the central leadership to help ensure effective interchange and flow between the contribution of this part and other branches of the system whole. Organizations that appear to be static, or stuck in a fixed pattern, or to have no apparent interest in change, are thought to have latent energies for refreshment and some kind of unfolding. If this potential energy is never released it seems likely that the organization will wither, be absorbed and reconfigured in another system, or disintegrate. Organizations in which many people are invested as a source of livelihood and meaning have their own life force and do not terminate easily, within the larger societal systems of which they are part.

Conclusion: Impact and Responsibility

Organizations are ubiquitous; they are shot through contemporary cultures and we swim in them. We live big and consequential parts of our lives engaged in educational and then in work organizations, and we constantly associate with organizational systems that provide necessities of life, and goods, services and experiences beyond necessity. Our cultures are infused with professional, government, religious, recreational and other kinds of organized associations to which we variously belong and which we encounter in everyday life. Many of these are ramifying systems that, besides their internal membership, depend on engaging a great many non-member clients and supporters. Indeed the boundaries of such systems may be fuzzy. For example, are the active shareholders outside or inside a large commercial organization? Such systems include varied voices and even subcultures, and may effectively liberate groups of their members or confine and diminish them.

Arguably, human well-being requires that big organizations need to further confront the implications (1) of being a context in which participants live a great part of their lives and from which they take home significant effects to their families and other life relationships, and (2) of their impact in other ways on the surrounding or societal community on which the organization itself ultimately depends. When this confrontation occurs some change in identity can be expected to flow. Ideally a main axis of change would be for the organization to attain a vision of itself not merely as a means of production, wealth creation or significant service but, beyond and above this, as a people-resource and partner in sustaining and creating the human relationship world of which it is part. This ambient world tends to be sorely in need of wide-ranging human relations recovery and development. Any far-seeing organization can choose to recognize itself as a custodian of human relational life with vital relevance for societal well-being in an interconnected world.

9

Relationships in War
and Genocide

Acute mistrust and conflict between peoples continues to be a tragically destructive feature of our world. There is great need not only to end threatening and warring tensions in many contexts, but to go beyond this in finding ways to heal the system-wide wounds and drivers of such conflict. Sources of this conflict include differences in worldview, ethnicity and tribal loyalties or deeply held religious conviction. These differences may be compounded by poverty or great inequality in living standards, by life-threatening insecurity and/or by memories of past oppression and 'underclass' experience that perpetuate deep distrust. Extreme leadership ambitions and short-sighted economic self-interest are other potential factors. But beyond all of these predisposing conditions there is something more. This has to do with relations and tensions *within* either of the systems in conflict, due perhaps to an oppressive authoritarian regime, strong divisions by class, economic power or ethnicity, or a situation in which a relatively powerless majority of people gain some sense of potency in identifying with the powerful presence of a revered or dominant leader – as has been the case in North Korea, for instance. And, a highly competitive culture can itself breed inner-onto-outer tensions.

This chapter examines ways that wars start and end and the phenomenon of peace, and considers an approach to the healing of relations between peoples. The exploration is in keeping both with a generally searching interest in relationship and the author's fresh immersion in process and thought specific to this field. A way of thinking about big-systems tensions and warring conflict is one broad result, and provision of many examples of how such conflict begins and ends is another. Consideration of relational recovery processes within and between national and ethnic systems is also a feature. The study invites further unfolding and testing of principles in a future of connected contribution by others with related deep concern.

Peaceful rather than combative ways of solving problems mostly are given short shrift in television and other media, and even in sporting and other live contests. Does this imply that humans by nature are highly competitive and ready to fight for supremacy? Or, is our nature marked by a tendency to join and bond in receptive relationships? These and other issues come into the search that follows (1) to understand the drivers of hostility, distrust and resorts to armed attack on 'enemy' systems *and* (2) to explore ways to recover from destructive or lethal conflict between people and the systems of which they are part. The journey of this chapter briefly revisits elements in our make-up and then looks reflectively on the phenomenon itself of big-system functioning and some of the ingredient features that have produced inter-system tensions and conflict. Many particular instances of warring relations within and between nations, and issues involved in the course of these conflicts, are examined as the chapter goes on.

Deciphering Big-System Inner–Outer Tensions Leading on to War

Our nature as humans is readily seen as a factor in the ways we relate to each other. In light of the ancestral origins of the human species and the strong tendency of higher animals to establish a hierarchy of dominance, a potential to engage aggressively is an expected inheritance. However, alongside this tendency is an unlike, equally self-evident twin: a powerful inclination to bond and, along with this, a frequent capacity for altruism and empathy. Perhaps both of these 'opposing' tendencies were vital to the survival of early human families and tribes. As societal systems developed, groups of belonging – self-perceived as 'we', 'us' or 'our' community or nation – became larger and more complex. These organized groups had more to defend and aggressive competition tended to be focused outward onto other groups of *they* and *them*. Human capacity for symbolic representation advanced and became almost a world within the world of primary experience. Verbal images of Us and Other came to evoke the contrasting potentialities within our human nature. A detailed study by Cashman (1993, chapter 2), however, found little research support for, and much argument against, the notion of a general built-in instinctual or genetically based aggressive nature being a principal driver of war.

As human societal worlds expanded to include large nation states, uneasy relations between these states could still seem to reflect a duality in our nature. Big nation states brought new levels of complexity, however, such that inherent personal tendencies, though of continuing importance, were insufficient to account for the working of big societal 'organisms'. The different ways these social mega-systems begin influence their later structure and working. For example, one origin is an essentially peaceful and organic growth from a smaller social organism; another national system begins with the joining together of smaller communities either by choice or conquest. The revolutionary overthrow of a previous system of government in a major region is among further origins – all as more fully discussed in Chapter 6 (see subsection 'Relationship Origins and Configurations in Nation States').

When a nation, itself born out of struggle and conflict, was later embroiled in a tense standoff with another nation, the threshold for resort to armed conflict might well be lower than in a similar case facing a nation whose evolution had been peaceful and included successful negotiation with other powers. In another example, if a nation's origin or development resulted in powerful centralized leadership and control, then dealing with a state of tension with another nation might be approached with a focus on top leaders on the other side on the assumption that their leadership, too, had unified responsibility and control in their country. It might then be supposed that forceful negotiation with the opposing top leader(s) would be sufficient to resolve the impasse. In the different case of a nation whose leadership resulted from a track record of popular election, the government's stance toward dealing with dangerous international tensions would be influenced by their own need for broad voter support. These possibilities, albeit simplified, help to ground the view that national origins and organization are vital to any full understanding of belligerent dealings between nations.

Another mentioned variable in a very complex equation is the relation among major groups inside the nation in view. A nation facing outward lacks a unity of resolve if there is strong internal mistrust and tension. One common manoeuvre in this case is for the leadership to cultivate a perception of external danger to promote a common purpose. Where no credible external threat can be advanced, but internal dissent is strong, internal turbulence may be handled in a sharply repressive way. In a nation under despotic rule or with a very sectarian and authoritarian government, violent suppression of an opposition movement is one resort, which may degenerate into civil war (as in Syria and formerly in Libya while this was being written). Where the relation between the government and the citizenry flows basically from a democratic tradition, internal division may lead to a change in the head of state by their party or parliamentary action, new laws may be introduced and/or a fresh election held. In the further extreme case of part of a nation wanting to secede and become independent, this may occur quite peacefully, as in the former Czechoslovakia, or it may result in a fight for independence (usually with some outside assistance, such as preceded the formation of Bangladesh) or in the broader civil war as developed between North and South in the United States (discussed in Chapter 6).

Where protagonist nations are markedly different in their origins and systems of belief and government, vulnerability to uneasy relations or conflict is likely. Taking one nation by itself, it is common for one faction to be more steeped in their inherited systems of belief and social outlook than another constituency is – the latter perhaps a well-educated and more prosperous middle class. Whether such polarity produces conflict depends on the wider context. In a contemporary pluralist nation and society there will be many groups of diverse interest and outlook, and any broad polarity might cause heated debate, but a convulsive effect of such difference is very unlikely. In a context of major and rigid control by one or other group (as has seemed to be the case in Iran, for example) assertion by a more liberal but politically weaker faction can lead to that group's forced suppression. The narrowly conceived interests of individuals and groups within almost any nation can have a great bearing on demands for internal policy shifts or government-to-other-government competition for resources (such as oil). The interwoven dynamics of tense internal and external relations may fuel suppression as just discussed or contribute to great power conflict.

Nations, or regions within nations, are *homelands* to the people who have long inhabited them. The occupation by another nation's foreign forces is a threat to 'my home' and its ethos. The affected peoples' deep relationship with their home reflects its pivotal role in their life meaning and sense of who they are. Understandably, they would wish to defend this, and the strongly felt identity that goes with it – one of the dynamics evidently at work in Afghanistan as this is written. 'Suicide terrorism' may be resorted to in the absence of conventional military organization, where particular members deliberately sacrifice their lives and the lives of others for the greater good as they would see it. A plausible broad *aim* is to shock the occupying/governing powers into abandoning their grip so that the homeland and culture can be restored to the people indigenous to it. Of course, different motives by those behind such desperate measures come into play as well. A major study by Pape (2005) has shed strong light on the likely nature of the underlying processes.

Pape studied all documented incidents of suicide terrorism from 1980 to 2003, 462 incidents in all, which occurred in a wide diversity of contexts. He found no evidence of emotional disorder or pathology among the attackers, who were mostly from working or educated classes and not Islamic fundamentalists. In nearly all cases the attacks were against people in or from democratic nations, although native citizenry in the occupied territories also were in the line of fire. Pape's inference was that the attacks were used as an instrument of coercive power by the resistance organizations to compel democratic governments – especially through the impact on public opinion of large numbers of people being killed, including civilians and often children – to withdraw from the homeland territories they occupied (ibid.). However, the truth in this interpretation is probably over-generalized. 'Suicide missions' have been resorted to historically and in some recent instances, as a mode of warfare in which trained and willing individuals are in effect the ultimate 'intelligent guidance system' for lethal attacks (see, e.g., review by Leray-Meyer, 2005). To the attacker, or 'sacrificial warrior', the action is far from suicide: it is one in which their earthly death is integral to the price and means of having a significant impact on behalf of the people and cause they believe in. Moreover, this cruel warfare adaptation is no more destructive of human life than other warfare actions within and between nation states.

Secessionist struggles, rebellions and civil wars may last a long time or sometimes be over fairly quickly. Both sides, with no clear-cut winner in sight, may desire to end the conflict and suffering, but the massive breach of trust is such that even *if* a settlement could be negotiated the perceived risk of the other side reneging is too great to stop hostilities and disarm. In a lasting conflict the protagonists only know each other as adversaries or enemies, and thus have no experiential basis for committing to a quite different relationship (see Kirschner's [2010] examination of this issue). As implied above, 'civil wars' often are regional combustions, not ones that engulf entire pluralist states: examples include Chechnya in Russia and Kashmir in India (see Cederman & Gleditch, 2009). The historical and contemporary conditions motivating such agonizing regional-state conflicts often have features in common (such as an ethnic or religious minority 'drowning' in a sea of Other) as well as needing to be understood in their individuality.

Sometimes a powerful force for change occurs without any armed uprising, emanating perhaps from widespread unhappiness with a long-standing and rigid regime. This force may suddenly coalesce in the form of a mass peaceful protest, which by its scale and insistence produces a collapse not of every influential structure but of the previously governing authority. This was the case not long ago in Egypt. In a state with a more powerful internal security system together with a different military culture or supporting militias, a similar process may begin but be met with violent suppressive force, which either crushes the movement (as in Iraq under Saddam Hussein) or triggers armed resistance that leads on to civil war. The events in Libya appear to have been an instance of the latter kind. That conflict was also an example of a community of nations intervening against violent internal suppression of mobilizing dissent. The major liberating shifts in Egypt and Tunisia no doubt contributed encouragement to groups in Libya desiring to 'liberate' their nation from its autocratic rule – and also brought to the surface big tensions in other states in the region.

Cashman's unusually wide-ranging study (1993) of the causes of war examines possible influences on many levels and considers available research that bears on several hypotheses. The 'human nature' level he considers has been mentioned. Beyond this, *the impact of stress* on leader attitudes and even personality is given detailed attention (ibid., chapter 3). The impacts of either side's images of the Other, often laced with misperceptions that can lead into war, are generously illustrated from actual and possible cases. The author notes also that a 'perception that war is inevitable, combined with the perception that the present time will be more advantageous militarily than a future time, creates an especially dangerous set of circumstances' (ibid., p. 67). Cashman provides grounds to argue that these perceptions were a factor in the onset of World War I. Wars usually appear, as in this case, to have been seriously miscalculated in their duration, the resolve of the enemy and the draining distortion of economies, not to mention the human suffering and massive decimation of relationships that shadow the future.

Small hunter-gather societies or tribes seem to be more aware of the damaging costs of lethal conflict than more 'developed' societies have been. Cashman cites Dyer (1985) as noting 'that of the hundreds of hunter-gatherer societies which modern man has encountered, almost all have had the same attitude toward war: it is an important ritual, an exciting and dangerous game, and perhaps even an opportunity for self-expression, but it is not about power in any recognizable modern sense of the word' (Dyer, 1985 as quoted by Cashman). Dyer also is cited as judging that this 'pre-civilized warfare' was mostly a 'rough male sport for under employed hunters, with the kinds of damage-limiting rules that all competitive sports have' (Cashman, 1993, p. 31). Although most nation states somewhere in their history have resorted to war, or warring defence, there is great variation in their conflict activity (ibid., p. 124). Put another way, it appears that nations as a species are not conflict prone. There is a correlation between the size and power of nations and their involvement in war, and totalitarian and other states that are pressure cookers internally clearly are more prone to war than established democracies.

Cashman's book is a mine of information regarding theories of international war. Each worthwhile theory helps to focus and illuminate particular issues, some other theories seem simplistic and none fits all cases. This outcome does not surprise me, or Cashman in the end, since individual nations are complex systems, even under authoritarian rule, and relations between nations add another layer of complexity. Consideration here of some of the ingredients of this complexity, and of the monstrously inhuman processes of war, leads to the issue of how wars end in an opening to peace. Later, my exploration will focus on issues in the preservation of peace through healing recovery from the searing relational injuries of war.

Difficult Paths to Peace: Terminating Wars and Genocide

Wars in the modern era generally end before there is literal annihilation of the loser's forces and infrastructure. Combatant states, especially the one nearest to collapse, can be so exhausted and hurting so badly that a crucial shift in balance occurs between pro-war and anti-war considerations, that is, between everything that weighs toward continuing the war and everything weighing against doing so. The 'everythings' can be a varied mix: the escalating suffering and hardship of people, shifts in public consciousness and/or internal coalitions, collapsing military capacity and leadership changes. Third parties in the UN era often urge negotiation and endeavour to broker peace, partly from economic self-interest and in response to the pain and criticism of their own vicariously involved populace.

In relations of protracted conflict, the systems include people whose life meanings have become embedded in the conditions or process of conflict and the quest this entails. Popular media mostly have a common interest in arousing and attracting their customer audiences by brief and simplified encapsulation of dramatic events with little search into their context and tapestry. Not surprisingly, also, an emphasis on competition and adversarial processes in the culture tend to carry over into large-system relations. All of these things challenge efforts to make the transformative shift from conflict to peace – whether within nations, between states or between a state and a covert enemy or terrorist organization.

Ending Warring Conflict and Genocide Within Nations

National governments that turn against groups of their own citizens do so in different ways and the violence ends differently. Genocide is an extreme but tragically not uncommon case. Instances within memory include Nazi Germany's systematic extermination of some six million Jewish people before and during World War II, an atrocity that continued right up to the point of Germany's wartime defeat. As in this case, one way that such genocide ends is by the forced collapse of the central government under whose connivance or authority the genocide is conducted. Another large-scale example was the starvation, killing and incarceration in the early 1930s, under Stalin's rule, of millions of Ukrainians (called the holodomor and comparable with the holocaust in its scale), with the evident intention of subjugating a people of distinctive culture and independent outlook. The holodomor ended probably because it worked as intended in the short run and other concerns took over, including the industrial development of Ukraine and the looming prospect of another international war.

The genocide in Cambodia occurred in the wake of profoundly destabilizing conditions associated with the US-led war with North Vietnam, with effects that spilled over into Cambodia. A rebel movement there became able (in 1975) to overthrow the weak and embattled Cambodian government and establish a reign of terror to enforce a completely different social and economic order. In the process, those in control killed more than one-fifth of the whole population in the breakdown of any humane sense of relationship. This 'Khmer Rouge' regime finally was forced out of power by a unified Vietnam, became a shrinking guerrilla movement and eventually disintegrated. Thus the shift to a peaceful order was initiated by the intervention of a neighbouring nation (Vietnam) – partly to protect its own interests and diaspora. Then a new coalition government could be formed under UN guidance and this appears to be restoring Cambodia to healthy internal relationships.

In Rwanda, the shocking genocidal violence erupted in an extremely volatile post-colonial context containing the two ethnic groups of Tutsis and Hutus. This did not happen 'out of the blue', but followed an extensive background of ethnic tensions, and periodic murderous conflict between these groups, with ineffective colonial and peacekeeping operations. Some earlier interventions (not UN sponsored) that sided with one or other faction helped to feed the ethnic tensions. The fuse for explosion of full-scale violence was lit by the Hutu President's assassination, triggering the government-based (and media-supported) promulgation of licence and instructions for extermination killing of Tutsis and 'traitorous' peace-advocates from any faction. After some 800,000 deaths and the escape of most remaining Tutsi civilians to neighbouring countries, the Rwandan Patriotic Front of mainly Tutsi fighters finally overthrew the government, eliminated some of its members and supporters, and consolidated a position of dominance that has held ever since. A great number of people were arrested and selective healing efforts – later mentioned – were instituted in the profoundly traumatized nation.

In the internecine conflict and genocide in recent time in Sudan, the government centred in the North engaged in violent suppression of resistance and discontent in the South, in a conflict best described as a one-sided civil war. Extreme suffering and great numbers of deaths from combat and associated famine and disease occurred. Yet there was no outright defeat of the South and with UN assistance and limited political backing down in the North a negotiated peace finally was brokered, including an agreement that paved the way for a successful vote on independence for the South. In overlapping time there has been genocidal persecution in the Darfur region of Sudan. Extreme racial attitudes by powerful Arab groups in Sudan against the largely defenceless black African peoples of Darfur, abetted rather than restrained by the national government, have been a pivotal factor. Those killed or who have died of starvation or disease number in the hundreds of thousands (Martin, 2007). Possibly two million fled over the border where the majority remain in refugee camps that amount to big tent cities, and their displacement remains unresolved as this is written, notwithstanding the best efforts of UN agencies and other organizations.

Sometimes, a major natural disaster interrupts and has such great impact on the participants in a warring conflict that it produces a common cause that contributes to the outbreak of peace. The deadly Indian Ocean tsunami in 2004 was a crucial factor in breaking the deadlock between the Free Aceh movement and Indonesian government, now with a common cause (the rebuilding of traumatized and shattered regional communities) that contributed to a mediated formal peace accord eight months later (Beardsley & McQuinn, 2009). The involvement of *external* powers to end an internally oppressive regime is fraught with the risk that this will just inject another adversary with its own perspective and interests, and work to widen or prolong the tragic tensions and human damage – as can be seen in Afghanistan. Even the UN-backed multi-state intervention in Libya in support of the (finally successful) internal revolution against a virtual dictatorship under Gaddafi leaves uncertainty around the healing of relationships and building of a unified democratic state.

From War to Peace Between Nation States

The two world wars of the 20th century destroyed human lives and relationships on a scale without precedent. No major nations were left outside and independent of those cataclysms, nations that might otherwise have been in a position to mediate overtures of peace. The first Great War finally ended in an agreed armistice and treaties, more imposed than negotiated, and secured under conditions of profound exhaustion and antagonism – with required reparations by the loser and no healing between victors and vanquished. The seeds were there for what became World War II (see, e.g., Chapter 5 and Reves, 1947). In that latter case, the Allied requirement of unconditional surrender (particularly demanded by the Soviet Union) no doubt prolonged the war and, on the other hand, opened the way to political restructuring of the defeated Axis powers. The outbreak of peace after World War II resulted in the compromise arrangement to divide Germany into zones of occupation by forces of the principal victors, reflecting a wary mistrust between the Soviet Union and Western powers.

Thus the very different political and economic systems installed in East and West Germany were hosted by unlike powers that had been drawn together by war partnership against a common enemy. The victors wanted the Germany within their sphere of influence to be a redeveloped communist ally (for the Soviets) or a more democratic amenable partner (for the other allies). The erstwhile wartime allies confronted each other with deepening distrust. Within a decade, nuclear-armed nations stood poised for a potentially annihilating war if attacked, and a dreadful tension hung over their peoples and most of the world. Divided Germany stood as a symbol and possible igniting spark in this enormously perilous standoff. Nuclear war would have been unwinnable and civilization-destroying, an outcome that gradually became evident to the leadership on all sides. Peace with Japan had been forced by overwhelming American military superiority, the terrifying prospect of more atomic destruction of Japanese cities, and the vital compromise of agreeing to leave their revered Emperor still on his throne as figurehead of the nation.

Stanley & Sawyer (2009) propose – unconvincingly for the world wars – that 'interstate war termination is the result of a bargaining process between two interacting sides', this requiring development of 'an overlapping bargaining space'. The relative openness of belligerent leaders to 'realistically' monitor the progress of the war, estimate its outcomes and make informed decisions is necessary for effective use of this space. Leaders, however, can be entrapped in inflexible positions, with internal changes needing to occur in order to get 'unstuck' and into an effective bargaining space (ibid.). These authors work to test their rationalist model against real-world cases and do make some adjustments in this light. My own sense is that the 'messy' complexity of process in nations actually at war, each with their own view(s) of reality, poses difficulty for such an approach. Surprisingly, the promising idea of 'bargaining space' was not linked to any consideration of third-party involvement in contributing to this space and its effective utilization.

A decade after World War II ended another international war involving major nations was launched. Egypt under President Nasser unilaterally proclaimed nationalization of the Suez Canal under Egyptian control, in a context that included notably poor communication from and to other interested powers. Britain, France and Israel then attacked Egypt and rapidly advanced their military objectives in the vicinity of the Canal. Successful militarily, the operation was a disaster politically and in human terms, with many nations condemning the attack on Egyptian sovereignty and threatening varied retaliation. The United Nations, quietly supported by the United States, passed resolutions formally ordering cessation of hostilities by the invaders and the relinquishing of captured locations. This UN action ended the state of war (after at first refusing, Israel reluctantly withdrew, with conditions). No healing of relations between Israel and its Arab neighbours occurred and, a decade later, those neighbours and Israel attacked one another in the 'Six Day War', that ended with Israel's occupation of the Sinai, West Bank and Gaza, and annihilation of its opponents' attack forces. Under a later Egyptian president, formal peace was finally declared between Israel and Egypt, has held since and appears to be sufficiently in the interests of both states (and other interested powers) to continue into the future.

Since World War II, there has been on average an international war every five or six years, beginning with the war on the Korean peninsula – in large part a struggle between communist China and the United States, although formally multi-national and involving the UN. The fighting finally stopped after drawn-out and complex negotiations through what amounted to an armistice not a peace settlement (see Rose, 2010). In a word, the conflict never wholly ended – as seen in the continuing face-off between North and South Korea and the former's nuclear ambitions. The less confronting for the West but great human tragedy of the Iran–Iraq war was another in the series, as was the bloody drawn-out war in Vietnam that finally ended with withdrawal of the United States. The earlier warring conflicts involving India, Pakistan and Bangladesh, which did have as one outcome the birth of a new nation (Bangladesh), was a further instance. In addition, there have been the two US-led wars with Iraq, ending with the realization of immediate military objectives but scarcely adequate societal peace, the conquest of Tibet by China, and the wars between external powers and oppressive regimes in Afghanistan.

The United Nations has had a role, sometimes crucial, in most of the wars since that body was formed in 1946. It has occasionally authorized warring campaigns intended to prevent greater human injustice and suffering, has helped to constrain the spread and longevity of other wars, contributed vital mediating and peacekeeping operations in a number of cases and has been instrumental in numerous refugee settlements, the provision of famine relief and in other ways. Nations generally have wanted a 'legal' international basis for their wars – with the notable exception of bloody internal conflicts. There is of course interdependency between the UN and member nations and thus the greater the power of the nations choosing or embroiled in war the less is the practical influence of the UN once a war has started. Mediation before a war begins, either under UN auspices or on the initiative of mutually trusted nations or groups – such as the European Union – is greatly needed and seemingly possible. Besides its more obvious applications, mediated communication has a potentially vital role in the further mode of warfare to mention.

Making the Impossible Possible: Engaging 'Terrorist' Systems Toward Peace

Terrorist organizations can have a long and influential lifespan, with commonalities in process and very different endings – as in two cases to mention. The Liberation Tigers of Tamil Eelam (LTTE), to give their full name, operated for over three decades, reportedly conducted some 200 suicide attacks and numerous assassinations (including Prime Minister Rajiv Gandhi of India), participated in several ceasefires and engaged in what in the end were abortive peace negotiations with the Sri Lankan government (Bhattacharji, 2009). The government finally abandoned negotiations and crushed the LTTE forces and its leadership in an all-out military campaign resulting in extensive civilian casualties – though somewhat constrained at the end by potential edicts of the UN Security Council. There had been a phase of military intervention by India, assisted negotiations that failed to bear decisive fruit, and the conflict ended in outright defeat of the Tigers and a great many deaths and relationship casualties among Tamil civilians. Close study of process in earlier negotiations that had promise but collapsed might yield valuable insights for negotiation in future internecine conflicts.

If organized terrorism is seen as a form of warfare, rather than just criminal activity without credible political aim, eventual negotiation or possible agreement to end hostilities is an option. In this respect, the case of the (Provisional) Irish Republican Army (IRA) in Northern Ireland is instructive. The IRA's initial strategy, to free their homeland and unite Ireland, was to use sufficient damaging force to produce collapse of the Northern Ireland administration and inflict enough casualties that public opinion would compel the British government to withdraw from the region. This aim was not achieved through the diverse features and vicissitudes of a long campaign. Ultimately, following contacts with the non-violent Social Democratic Labour Party and secret talks with British civil service administrators, the IRA called a ceasefire in the mid-1990s, conditional on its political wing Sinn Féin being included in the political talks to follow. Conditions on both sides then produced a temporary collapse of non-violent negotiation, but finally a new ceasefire agreement by the main parties to terminate violent conflict and proceed on a peaceful course was established (see searching study of the drawn-out process by Cox et al., 2006). Terrorism in this case was not an impediment to an apparently conclusive peace agreement, and some on the IRA side would argue that it helped to force a space where this could happen.

The terrorist organization and activity associated with Al Qaeda, notwithstanding the death of Osama bin Laden, evidently is still dangerous to an unknown range of potential targets. It would seem that there has been enough experience by now that some substantial understanding of what drives and sustains terrorist combat activity by this movement and others is achievable. Covert message communication through intermediaries should be possible, though difficult to undertake against the history of viewing earlier lethal attacks (notably on the 'twin towers' in New York) over-simply as criminal acts – as the IRA attacks were originally deemed to be. I have no knowledge of *how* suitable intermediaries might be utilized, but believe that there are others who have such information (Afghan government-known contacts with the Taliban evidently occur). Communication, of course, does not only take place verbally. Policy development and actions, including shifts in attitude that are clearly conveyed in action, may help to establish a climate for other initiatives that finally make healing steps possible.

Toward a Relational Approach to Healing from Wars and Genocide

Big human systems at war or the lethal conquest of one people by another is seen as both reflecting and inducing *profound* disorders of relationship. Any real healing from such grievous wounds must be a complex and formidable challenge. As with any healing it is to some extent reliant on built-in recuperative tendencies that apply on personal and systemic levels. For these tendencies to work requires not only an outbreak of peace but also a shifting ethos and working of relational systems within the former belligerents. A corpus of people with the commitment and gathering knowledge to facilitate the healing is also necessary. An integral aspect of their orientation would be to gain a searching understanding of the climate of attitude, ambition or fear, and the experienced motivation and viewpoints, that had helped to drive the conflict. This understanding could broaden to a tuned awareness of the respective lived frames of reference of the protagonists – starting with their governing and 'moral' leadership.

Long ago, Reves (1947) offered a striking articulation of the sharply differing viewpoints of the main national actors in the quarter-century period between the two world wars. Taken one at a time, each nation's view of the surrounding world and their interests and place in it fuelled profound distrust, antagonism, fear in some cases, and readiness for warring attack and defence. Reves' valuable characterization is highly suggestive though not sufficient for a contemporary understanding of the many attitudinal and relational currents feeding into one nation's interaction with another nation state. This present discussion offers a potential window of entry to such understanding that pivots on systems of relationship.

One approach would take into account what we know generally about human motivation, or, about the working of small relational systems in tension and conflict where it is easier to see what is happening. Or, we might gather evidence of population attitudes in the two (or more) major systems. If war is threatening we might place our confidence in a particular conflict resolution strategy or another way of tackling difficult disputes for which there is some formula. The chances, however, are that in practice none of these or similar approaches (notwithstanding any useful features) will work effectively because they oversimplify the diverse multi-level interacting relational structures and dynamics within each system. This complex internal dynamic would have many relevant levels, including face-to-face relationships (which, for example, may often be authoritarian or mostly egalitarian in nature), the working and linkages of larger groups in which people work or share interests, community religious beliefs and traditions, the structures and dynamics of major organs of government leadership, politics, commerce and human services, and the emergent mega-systems of whole nations. A promising approach to healing would need to address or take account of all of these contexts of relation and further levels of association and attitude that they would lead into. Simple solutions would not be expected to come from facing the complexity of relational process within and between whole societies.

Warring *internal* conflict must usually arise in conditions that *include* profound dissatisfaction and grievance with features of the existing governance. Often, the perceived discrimination and treatment of an affected minority who lack political/social rights or suffer other grievous circumstance within the national setting is a crucial factor. The serious grievances may involve (among other possibilities) land rights, legal systems and policing, educational or employment opportunities, persecution of people of particular belief or culture, judicial or non-legal control systems, and/or deeply felt issues of identity and desire for self-determination. All such grievance issues need to be listened to, negotiated and addressed in some way by national government leaders and relevant administrative authorities, in any course of a peace-affirming and healing process. Strong external prompting and assistance may be necessary for this to happen. The ensuing process needs to have tangible outcomes such as altered arrangements and revised institutions in important areas, new qualities of association between concerned groups, modifications in the exercise of government, and protected opportunity to conserve, practise and/or develop cultures of belonging.

In a nation torn by bitter dissension and conflict, the power centres may have a tight nucleus, especially on the side of the official government facing desperate voices of groups in opposition to the prevailing forces of control. However the acute strains or internal conflict ends, there will be a legacy of profound rupture of the relationship systems that link and divide the protagonist people-systems. There will, as well, almost certainly be serious losses, breakdowns and distortions of relationship within systems on each side of the conflict. In the recovery process, however undertaken, it is thought essential that many people from the formerly combatant groups come into each other's presence and begin to dialogue and see or glimpse each other as drawn from the same human and national family. Some of this may occur spontaneously as people go about their connected lives, but this is unlikely to suffice in the wake of organized, *psychologically and physically armed* conflict and destruction. In their search to illuminate processes of peace and reconciliation in the Sri Lanka context, Ramiah & Fonseka (2006) emphasize 'conflict transformation' as a process with multiple paths to 'restore and renew broken relationships' (ibid., p. 11). One such path or step would be to draw people with similar roles but on opposite sides of the conflict into first-hand communication. The very fact of this occurring (difficult itself to achieve) would help to turn the direction toward healing.

In Rwanda true reconciliation and healing after the mass slaughter of Tutsi people by Hutu militia and, often, by the victims' Hutu neighbours, poses almost insuperable difficulty and challenge. Various organizations and projects, government, judicial, religious and independent, have had the mission of producing or furthering reconciliation, but the results nationally are in question (see Clark & Kaufman's valuable compilation [2009], *After Genocide*). The government-sponsored National Unity and Reconciliation Commission (NURC) is concerned specifically with recovery from the 1994 genocide horror (Nantulya et al., 2005), but excludes consideration of the full sequence of events that led up to extensive fighting and murders by *Tutsi* forces (Rwanda profile, 2013; Zorbas, 2004).[4] It excludes casting the genocide as ethnic conflict, and these taboo areas of 'silence' limit open confrontation.

Nonetheless, the several thousand *Gacaca* ('grass roots') courts established have permitted a great many people to be brought to account in varied degree and much more community participation, sharing of stories and ventilation of feeling than the judge-led formal courts. According to Zorbas (ibid.): 'Gacaca's overarching goal is to promote reconciliation and healing by providing a platform for victims to express themselves, encouraging acknowledgments and apologies from the perpetrators, and facilitating the coming together of both victims and perpetrators every week, on the grass.' A close in-principle appraisal of the process appears within the searching philosophical exploration of genocide by May (2010, pp. 264–267). In all, the Gacaca programme appears to be valuable in idea and practice, although the large-scale application makes for variability and uneven effectiveness.

The conscience of the Western world was affected by the horror that exploded in Rwanda, while the West, and even the UN, stood by. This reaction helped to motivate many and varied offers and programmes of assistance when the fighting stopped. Many of these have had practically supportive or even healing effect locally. They have included and aided projects in the educational sphere, in sports and expressive arts and in opportunities for therapeutic

---

4   The interested reader would be able to track down later articles and a book by Zorbas who, in 2002–03, worked for the United Nations High Commissioner for Refugees in Rwanda.

dialogue (Barefoot Artists, undated; King, 2010; Kreitzer & Jou, 2008; Staub et al., 2005). Much of the effort has been focused on recovery from personal trauma and on development projects toward the normalizing of educational and other opportunities for children. Yet the degree of literal reconciliation and recovery of shattered relations between surviving victims and perpetrators of the slaughter is seriously in question. Gasana (2009) drew on findings of an extensive NURC survey study, and concluded that '[the fact] that Rwandans from all ethnic groups can cooperate to produce development objectives does not necessarily mean that they have rebuilt their relationships'. Further, without this rebuilding, 'there can be no long-term development' (ibid., p. 149). Developmental reconstruction needs to happen in a context where openness can become the norm through actual relational recovery and the building of *trusted* associations at all levels in the societal organism. This it seems could take generations in Rwanda.

Genocide, as in Rwanda, is a special case of intra-national mass violence (even the holocaust was conducted out of the sight or direct participation of the general non-Jewish public). Lesser but serious ethnic crises have been relatively commonplace. Öberg et al. (2009) conducted an elaborate analysis of 67 cases that occurred over the period 1990–1998. Their focus was on interventions that sought to prevent escalation to armed conflict, or to minimize such conflict. These included verbally expressed *statements about the crisis* by third parties, relief efforts, mediated communication between disputants and resolution proposals. More coercive measures included warnings of sanctions, offers of rewards for non-escalation, severance of economic or diplomatic relations and UN authorization for military enforcement measures. Verbally expressed attention and concern were the most common categories. 'Third-party coordination', facilitation and relief efforts happened with some frequency, followed by warnings and other measures in minor proportion. Most coercive responses only occurred after hostilities had broken out. Major powers and neighbouring states accounted for the greatest *number* of interventions and the UN and other international and regional organizations were involved in sometimes-crucial ways. *The report is silent in regard to any concerted community-to-community problem-solving and healing dialogue in these cases.*

The healing of relations *between nations* who have been at war has to undo extreme attitudes fostered on both sides to drive the will to sacrifice and endure the many dangers and privations of war. In a word, this includes undoing the image of the Other as an evil and extremely dangerous enemy bent on conquest and destruction of the world and values We cherish. Our defeat (as seen by survivors) would have meant destruction of the social order and ethos down to the life of each person. The needed change is a huge shift and, if it does not occur, peace may be an interlude rather than a closure – as it was between major powers after World War I, or between some of the states welded into the former Yugoslavia during the Tito regime. All-out war infects people and societal systems at all levels and restoration of health within and between the former enemies is a complex integrative process; a process that involves alterations in direction, shifts in public consciousness and movements in relationship on multiple levels. Awareness of these levels could be furthered by development of a *stressed-system model*, one that encompasses patterns in small-scale (face-to-face) relations, patterns in larger groups and their interrelations, and community and organizational processes up to those of major systems of government. This would be a demanding research endeavour to do well (see also last part of Chapter 11).

Sometimes, the recovery of relations between states who have been at war does seem to happen without special or focused programmes with a direct healing aim. An example of this is the transformation of relationship between Germany (and also Italy) and the main Western powers that those nations were at war with. Perhaps this resulted in large part from effective removal of the obstacles to peaceful association. For example, in contrast to the sequel from World War I, Germany was encouraged and directly assisted in significant rebuilding of its shattered infrastructure, institutions and economy, and cooperative relations were established in academic, cultural and political-government contexts that were less a matter of restoration and more about building anew. The gradual evolution of what became virtually a European super-state, in which Germany is a pivotal player, is an entirely different context for the working of self-interest, one that would seem to rule out the danger of regression to the model of the 1930s. It could be very instructive to search into all the other possible and interacting factors in the shift from profound mistrust and bitter hostility to a predominantly cooperative and even friendly association. The more personal wounds of relationship loss have not all disappeared, however, and deeper and more widely distributed dialogue about what drove the forebears of present generations of people into such extremities of conflict and suffering is called for still. And, serious economic stresses in some of the nations involved work to threaten the hard-won peaceful relations between them.

It is almost a truism to say that we live in an increasingly globalized world that makes for massive interdependency of nations not only in Europe, but in the Americas, Africa, Asia, the whole Pacific region and between continents. Trade relations, exchange of knowledge and cultural interchange are crucial to the well-being of nearly all of us. War between nations has less imagined 'benefit' than ever and visibly greater cost to both or all belligerents. Yet conflict can and does still arise, especially as a spinoff from tensions and armed conflict within nations. The United Nations has representatives in all major or sizable nations and offices that can reach every member state. It has been involved in a great many peace-keeping operations, using peacekeepers under UN auspices from willing member states, and contributes a critically important moral and practical presence and resource on many levels, especially to smaller nations. There is no comprehensive system, however, *both* to monitor the build-up of tensions before they escalate into fighting *and* to immediately organize preventive action and remediation or, still less, full-fledged reconciliation and relational healing programmes. The UN effectively is a super-cooperative of nations. It has a moral authority and a reach that few if any of the constituent sovereign nations have. Arguably, those nations would do well to cede carefully selected present powers to the UN – as states within federated national republics do to nations of which they are part.

Conclusion

Each decade since World War II has included one or more breakouts of war between nation states, and warring conflict or genocide within states has been beginning every year or two. The terrible cost of such conflicts includes not only the loss and crippling of individual lives but the even more extensive loss and damage to relationships among the survivors. While human competitiveness and the caprice of leaders can be factors in the outbreak of war or genocide, many current and historical influences in complex interaction typically are involved – as the numerous and varied examples reviewed in this chapter imply. Tensions and other dynamics within states are major sources of influence in wars between states as well as being pivotal in intra-state warring conflict. War represents a breakdown of relationship, but is not like a quarrel between individuals. It is tempting to oversimplify the causes of large-system conflict, and processes of peace-making and subsequent healing. Factors such as very different political, belief and knowledge systems contribute a certain vulnerability in the presence of historical oppression, great inequality in living standards, population pressures, internal discriminatory practices and tensions, leadership ambitions, and the like. Arguably, the search to understand and prevent war can be informed by humane values and a systemic approach that works hard to decipher the complex processes entailed.

In the aftermath of war between major nations, recovery in the form of developmental healing confronts a region of process beyond the present reach of full, definitive understanding. It also seems clear that big systems and the relations within and between them have a multi-layered and self-reinforcing momentum that would make broad healing change difficult to enable. However, establishing healing as a vital goal is a big first step, and applying less-than-perfect knowledge is a practical constraint but not a reason for inaction. The challenge I see is to recognize knowledge limitations, search laterally and in depth, and constantly seek to extend this knowledge. This extension includes gathering case information and fresh observation and formulations that lead on to a coherent and usable body of thought. This chapter, to me, embodies an approach and first step in such 'gathering', which readers may wish to extend and refine in respect to aspects they find of greatest interest or salience. Efforts at the levels of inquiry and conceptual understanding and of practical action need to develop into a truly powerful combination, both to reduce the large-scale violence we humans do to each other and to expand consciousness of our complex but fathomable interrelatedness.

10

The Shared World of Human–Animal Relations

We humans are one species in a vast web of interconnected life forms that share our planet's biosphere and range from invisible microbes to the great blue whale. Mammals alone number some 5,500 known species, and birds count for another 10,000 (Osborn, 2010). All of these closer relatives, and most of our more distant ones, share a reliance on oxygen, internal temperatures in the liquid water range and organic foods. Human–animal relationships and interdependence also go much further than these commonalities imply. The question of where we humans sit in the spectrum of life and of our disproportionate impact is a brief initial focus in what follows. The chapter goes on in its main part to examine the particular *kinds and range* of our relationships with other species in the sentient world, including the vital friendships and partnerships so many humans have with animal relatives. I will argue for the importance of being aware of our close and interdependent relation with other inhabitants in the shared lifeboat of the ecosystem of nature we all journey in.

Humans in the Larger Scheme of Things

Homo sapiens are latecomers in the history of more advanced life forms. An encyclopedic record of all the living organisms we know of that evolved over the last three and a half billion years would barely have room to mention us. Moreover, unless human evolution was stopped in its tracks, our species in its present form will be superseded by *more complex* distant descendants – thinking forward a million or so years in time. Even within a much shorter time frame, given that microbial and other species with very short lifespans can and do evolve so quickly, it is possible for the tables to be turned on more advanced and apparently dominant species like ourselves. The environment for life, especially the oxygen-rich atmosphere, was essentially created by ancestral life (Pidwirny & Jones, 2010). Human evolutionary development adapted to the late environments in which it occurred makes us creatures of the natural world in common with other life forms.

Humans might well be considered an invasive species – even a plague as Hugh Mackay (2010) bluntly describes us. By punching so greatly above our weight in terms of contemporary environmental impact, we put at risk the life system that gave us birth. Our very brief history in the timescale of evolution also implies that we are much less tested than most of our present relatives among the complex (mammalian and avian) life forms, let alone those of the many earlier species that have endured. Yet we tend to see ourselves as being the most advanced kind of life, even 'above nature' in the eyes of some humans. It is within our power to protect *and* to destroy, but either way our knowledge is spotty in regard to the vast web of interconnection among living species. All this should make humans much more modest than most of us are about our place and standing, and even our longevity, in the scheme of things.

Looking back from the future and assuming no freezing of history and evolution, our present cultures will appear at an early stage of understanding the intricate relations among the hugely diverse community of species and common enveloping habitat. As is true of humans with each other, relations based on self-interested exploitation of fellow life forms risk quite destructive outcomes. One possibility is the creation of microbial species that are a direct threat to human or other life. And, in working to eradicate a 'pest' species a more destructive alternative may take its place – as in the case of the poisonous imported 'cane toad' in Australia. Healthy survival depends on scientific and public mindsets that expect complex interdependence and are drawn toward seeing into the working of interactive processes in the nature of which humans are part and partners. Enlightened and generally considerate relations with our fellow species, and a caring stance toward our shared precious habitat, seem critically relevant to the common good.

The Different Modes of Human Relationship with Non-Human Beings

Interspecies relations are ubiquitous, ranging from bacteria that inhabit, nourish or infect their hosts, and on through the whole domain of life. Relationships between humans and other advanced species are my main focus. Mammals generally have affiliative needs, and are keenly aware of 'Others' both within and beyond their own kind. Interspecies bonds are not unusual. Domesticated dogs and cats, growing up together, can be in friendly relation, and there are many other different species that learn to get on perfectly well. Horses in my observation try to avoid being alone and will keep company with a familiar sheep, goat or other animal if no other horses are in reach, and they can similarly be drawn to the company of friendly humans. A strong social tendency, holding across a great variety of species and contexts, is generally accepted by biologists as originating in the survival advantages of sociality in the process of evolution (Alexander, 1974; see also Darwin, 1872, 1874).

Human–animal associations and attitudes are a fascinating domain, both in contemporary life and in antiquity. As instance of the latter, in Egypt many animal and human–animal hybrid effigies, thousands of mummified cats and numerous other animal mummies bear witness to the vital human–animal connection in their early but 'high' culture. In Minoa, pre-1500 BC, dancing and leaping with bulls was practised –evidently with greater danger to humans and less to bulls than in the more one-sided bullfighting of much later time. The Bushmen of the Kalahari have had a certain reverence and regretful sorrow for the large animals they killed for food for their families and groups, using poison-tipped spears or arrows. Indigenous peoples in North America often felt an extremely close kinship, involving significant communication, with the animals and birds in their world (see, e.g., Abrams, 1997). The people of many tribal cultures, including Australian aboriginal groups, have felt deep spiritual and intimate connection with special landscape features and both mythical and certain live creatures in their natural environments.

Significant human–animal relations, so diverse in kind and quality, are arranged here in six broad groupings in terms of their function from a human point of view. Most of these groupings contain subvarieties in turn, and the distinctions are convenient ways of keeping track of the great variety of relational activity and quality in this domain. Some relationships, of course, have more than one function or meaning and the groupings reflect principal intentions.

1. The Relational Contexts of Companionship and Play

Friendships

Human–animal relationships include caring friendships, ones in which the animal partner is cherished and the human is not in any fear of judgement. They include those collaborative contexts (as in the partnership of shepherd and sheep dog – see next context) in which a human partner warmly values and rewards the animal's efforts. The training involved works in both directions, since the human is also learning the animal's ways. Dogs are perhaps the most familiar species that tends to engage in highly responsive ways with humans, but pigs, horses and sheep reared by hand and other domesticated animals, including some birds, can connect strongly. In relationships with pets and other house animals companionship often is the main function. Although cats do not (to most people) have the expressive repertoire of dogs, strong companionable ties can develop with them as well. There can be clear indications of affection or joy in many such associations, and both everyday observation and considerable research with varied species imply that responsive empathy is not confined to humans or even to primates (de Waal, 2007, 2009).

Exposure to dolphins (especially) and some other marine mammals can evoke a strong sense of affinity and relationship, with a returning resonance from the animal partner. Jane Goodall, Dian Fossey, Frans de Waal and other investigators have shown that significant trusting relationships can develop with many members of our closest relatives, especially including chimpanzees and gorillas. Mutual unthreatening familiarity (or directly 'knowing each other') is presumably a major contextual factor for bonds to develop. Other more transitory associations can be quite positive, at least on the human side, as in the case of those human visitors to zoos who experience a special interest in particular animals. Although the animals are captive, particular bonds may become strong with zookeepers who have a continuity of relationship with their charges through the ups and downs of the animals' lives.

The companion animal helpers of blind or otherwise handicapped people can involve particularly intense relationships and serve as a valuable context for understanding human–animal bonding. Sanders (2003) specifically disavows the view that symbolic consciousness and language are necessary for perceptive interaction and a functional awareness of the perspective of the other. He further proposes (ibid., p. 407) that key issues such as identity, personhood, empathy, mindedness and culture 'may be fruitfully explored if we turn serious and appreciative attention to the human–animal bond and the social exchanges that both define and result from this unique form of "socia-tion"'. If personhood and mindedness arise centrally from social interaction, including the context of human–animal relationships, they have significant counterparts in the animal as well as human *partners*. Not only in the case of companion helpers but also in the broader case of household animals there is a literature that views them as potentially significant member-participants in the family system with a role in also shaping relationships among family members (ibid.).

Play

Most children relate very readily to young animals, whose play tends to be very free after initially 'clumsy' exploration. Playing with dogs and other animals provides enjoyable recreation and a sense of partnership and bonding with a more-than-human world. Interspecies play when it occurs among animals presumably also enlarges *their* experience of the living world. Such evidently new experience includes the striking case, photo-recorded by Norbert Rosing, of a grown polar bear and husky sled dog in animated but gentle play (see Stuart Brown's account, 2011). Humans and animals often relate to each other with lively self-expression. Children and young animals alike, exercise, learn and develop through spontaneous play activity (Sanders, 2003). The play is not a win–lose contest, though it may include 'allowed' non-serious victories (e.g., by the smaller/weaker participant) and is arguably a context for the display and development of altruism (see Chick, 2008). Children and the young of higher animals energetically respond to an imagined or self-produced world in much of their play, play that contributes to building their adaptive skills and awareness for the more serious world to follow (Brown, 2011; Wenner, 2009).

This preparation through play probably was a selective advantage in biological evolution.

Communication has of course a crucial role in any relationship process and some of the language of play, like running, leaping, and responsively approaching and retreating, is common to a wide range of advanced species. More specific non-verbal elements are mutually learned or co-created in play as in other relationship modes (e.g., Kennedy, 2005). My own observation suggests that play *with* animals tends to be a freer more spontaneously expressive world of engaged interaction than play-sport between humans – with exceptions of course. (Play between parents and their young child can be expressively liberating for the parent.) With animals, play also tends to be physically active, emotionally satisfying and mentally undemanding. Human adults tend to live in a world of targeted 'functional' activity in many spheres, with some time out for passive or onlooker entertainment, while the nourishment of play is neglected. If play is completely neglected in interactive contexts with young children, the adverse developmental consequences can be very serious (Chick, 2008). Engagement with an animal evidently provides, for many humans, the truest times of relaxed companionship and play.

Sometimes, relationships of children with fellow humans are wholly baffling to a child who has different mental-emotional proclivities (and possibly somewhat different neural 'wiring') than most people and never gains confident ability to navigate in his or her world. A not uncommon extreme is to withdraw into a mode of coping deemed autistic. Such a child may (given opportunity and not in every case) relate more readily and comfortably within the world of relationships with animals. In this easier 'home of relationship', the person may become knowing, self-expressive and even empathic as, for example, in the striking case of the autistic animal scientist Temple Grandin (1995). Grandin's bent to think and process experience non-verbally and in distinct images underlies and links to a rare ability to tune into the sensory and associative/learning world of animals. Fruits of this special ability led on to her vocation. The livelihood of many humans also brings them into close relation with animals as next discussed.

2. *Workers Together: An Important Sphere of Relationship with Animals*

Partnerships

Associating as fellow workers has been an important context of human–animal relationship for millennia. Farming and early agriculture has been one of the main settings in which animals and people work in varied partnership. Quite often the animal's engagement is highly responsive, as a significant expression of their capacities and affiliative needs. A mentioned example is that of a sheep dog with a herder who is sensitive and valuing of his/her animal partner and skilled in communication relevant to their work together. This work involves control of other more subservient animals valued by the herder in a somewhat looser relation. Altogether there can be quite a mix of relationships: between the human and animal workers, between the animal partner and herded animals, and within that herd, where some may take the lead and others follow. Occasionally, an unexpected relationship intrudes, as witnessed by the author. A former baby lamb that had lost its mother and been bottle-fed at a farm household, in company with people and dogs, finally was returned to the flock. In the incident to mention the flock was being rounded up by a sheep dog totally accustomed to his dominance with sheep. Running on 'automatic pilot', the busy dog went to control the full-grown former baby lamb lagging behind, who was now much larger than the kelpie dog and with horns. The indignant sheep turned on the dog, gave chase head down and the latter ran for its life.

Working partners often are physically powerful animals: horses, oxen, camels, yak or elephants. An effective (interdependent) working relationship is not abusive of the animal partner. Clearly abuse does occur and the animal (e.g., an elephant) sometimes returns violence in amplified measure. Animal partners can be highly responsive to the particular human with whom a relationship is well developed, but unresponsive to a different partner or stranger. Human and animal partners need to get acquainted for significant bonding to occur, although this need not take long with 'domesticated' and other highly social species and may happen very slowly (or in practice not at all) with some other species. Although training and rewards are involved in working partnerships, it would in my view be a superficial and mistaken understanding to regard the process simply as a function of operant conditioning of an animal who is responding to an image of concrete rewards to follow shortly – which in fact frequently does not happen. Affiliative needs clearly are not confined to humans (de Waal, 2009) as already noted. Arguably, the affiliation in many human–animal encounters has become its own reward, while also growing out of an evolutionary journey in which such bonding was life-supporting to the species.

Dolphins who are skilled at herding agile fish into tight clusters near the surface have adapted this skill in close cooperation with local fishermen in Laguna, Brazil. The dolphins see the fish via echolocation in reflective cloudy water and use their own way of signalling to the waiting men exactly when to cast their round, hand-thrown nets. This long-established practice is mutually advantageous: many fish are caught by the men and the distracted fish that escape the nets are easy prey for the dolphins. This linked learning appears to have been a mutual discovery and refinement process (Pryor & Lindbergh, 1990; also see Wikipedia: 'Dolphin').

Before the end of World War II, it was judged (growing out of B. F. Skinner's work) that dolphins could be trained for wartime combat duty, for example to deliver depth charges to the hulls of enemy ships (perhaps in involuntary suicide missions for the trusting dolphins). Whether from ethical concern or fear of 'mistaken deliveries' this idea was not taken up by military authorities. Trained dolphins were helpful, however, in detecting sea mines in the port of Umm Qasr in the 2003 Gulf War (Kreger, 2003) and were and are prepared, along with other marine mammals, for varied defence and intelligence-gathering purposes. The training ground activity in San Diego Bay, where dolphins and sea lions are trained for crucial naval assistance roles, is described in a report by Rajewski (2011). Horses, of course, were often used in the past in cavalry attacks, potentially lethal to either or both of the warrior partners. In World War I, the Australian Light Horse soldiers brought their trained cavalry horses all the way from home to some Northern theatres of war.

In ancient stories and modern experience (for example in Monkey Mia in Western Australia) instances of the human–animal connection with dolphins are legion. In some Australian and other settings, people wade out to dolphin depth and may touch or swim with them, in engagements that the animals are highly responsive to (Connor & Smolker, 1985). Seals, sea lions and other intelligent and social marine mammals also can learn to engage with humans in mutually beneficial activities, including the entertainment of onlookers and, on the animals' side, their protection and rewarded associative exercise of skills beyond human capacity.

Master–Slave Relations, Harsh and Benign

There are other working contexts, of course, in which the relation is one of exploitation by a human partner who 'uses' the animal only as a means to an end; virtually a tool to achieve an outcome consistent with the person's goals or needs and relationships with other people. The animal tends to respond grudgingly to the threat or actuality of punishment. The human partner in this case may have little awareness of the animal's felt experience or even that s/he is a highly observant and feeling being. There is a relationship of sorts, marked by tension, absence of trust and the immediate potential of conflict and pain. Relations with draft animals or treatment by riders under stress can be abusive or even violent to the animal partners. Under conditions of threatened starvation individually known animal workers, including horses or sled dogs, may become food for their handlers, as in some polar expeditions.

In more benign master–slave associations, animals are sometimes recruited to capture other species: other birds, by birds of prey, and fish in the case of cormorants rendered briefly unable to swallow (see Baldwin et al., 1996). Humans can be wholly dependent on working animals, in instances mentioned and, notably, in the case of seeing-eye dogs with their blind masters. As observed by the author, in large teams of work horses familiar simple commands and perceptive encouragement seems vital to maintaining unity among the team. Sensitivity to relations among the animals is sometimes important in their placement in a team (with counterpart in some human work teams). In closer and trusting human–animal working relationships, a certain responsive empathy develops in the animal partner as well as in the human.

Relationships with animals are not under the total control of either partner, since they too are emergent phenomena that to a degree develop their own life and influence. It is too much to expect a long-familiar pattern to change readily by decision of the human partner alone, who cannot simply step outside the established pattern for a new beginning. If, however, s/he is now in a different mental-emotional and awareness 'place' than when the relationship formed gradual change could naturally occur. Similarly, if the life circumstance of the animal changes then their approach and input to the relationship would tend to differ. Such is my view, at least, in the case of familiar human–animal partners.

3. Human–Animal Relations in the Context of Research and Discovery

Field Studies in the Animals' Natural or Home Environment

Research on and making use of animals is of course another major region of connection. Along with systematic observation and concern to extend organized knowledge the natural scientist's motivation may include significant personal interest and appreciation of the subjects they study so closely. The relation in this case is not one of mutual engagement since the human observer tends to be as unobtrusive as possible, but absorption in the Other, even if one-sided, is a significant form of association. (In practice, some awareness of a hidden or distant human presence by sense-intensive intelligent animals is often possible.) Migration studies of birds and of land and marine species comprise one extensive subsphere of engagement by research observers. Where the human observer focuses on mass movement of the animals, and even more where automatic detection or counting equipment is used, the very arm's-length way of associating implies a limited although consequential kind of 'relationship'. Such study may pave the way for interactive association in a conservation programme or in close experimental work.

A more hands-on association, at the borderline between experiment and field observation, involves tagging or mounting equipment on animals for detailed study of their natural behaviour or particular abilities. One focus is 'simply' to track the animal's movements – perhaps as they migrate to follow food supplies or reproduction opportunities as the seasons revolve. Another focus is to understand the animal other's range of perception that might, for example, include sensitivity to magnetic fields in the case of some migrating bird species. In this case and others, a temporary 'capture relationship' (and associated trauma) is likely, as the animal is fitted with a tracking device or an instrument that would interact with their suspected additional sense. Then, after their briefly bruising first-hand contact with the human investigators, the animals are released back into their home environment Some devices (e.g., microchips) are permanently attached and others eventually separate; in both cases without *appearing to* complicate the animals' life within their own communities.

Naturalistic study of animal lives and relations in their own habitats, conducted with caring concern for their preservation and well-being, includes two examples to mention. One is the protection and study of mountain gorillas in Rwanda and adjacent regions, especially study that includes and follows in the tradition of pioneering work by Jane Goodall and Dian Fossey (1983/2000). The first stage is development of trusting relationships, both one-to-one and group-to-group, between particular humans and gorilla individuals and groups. Some close, almost intimate, observer contact has been recorded in excellent documentary film aired by the BBC and possibly familiar to the reader. Reciprocal recognition of individuals and some depth of mutual affiliation were clearly established in this work. Substantial learning about ways gorillas relate to each other and how they can relate to humans and vice versa has been a significant feature. Among Western Lowland gorilla groups, kinship systems apparently can make for peaceful and inclusive association even among related males (Bradley et al., 2004). Among mountain gorillas close relatives are likely to become aggressive competitors, especially among mature males.

A further example includes long-term observation of killer whales in British Columbia waters, work that also includes the recognition and monitoring of individuals and family groupings of whales and DNA-based study of relationships across generations (summarized by Francis & Hewlett, 2007). The orcas associate among themselves in two main cultures with quite distinct social lifestyles and food sources (mammal flesh versus fish), and with little or no interbreeding. The resident group is less avoidant/more relaxed with humans than the more individualist and silent hunters of the mammal-eating group. This region of relational investigation includes case studies of young orcas in difficulty, one of whom (Springer) had become separated from his mother and pod of relatives, the other (Luna) also isolated and whose mother had died. Rescue operations and/or close monitoring by concerned humans applied in both cases. In the absence of inclusion among their own kind, the young orcas tried it seemed to maintain the human connection, sometimes causing consternation to people in small boats (ibid.). Their story includes episodes of strong public and scientific interest and implied felt relationship. Many people were drawn into concerned and sometimes conflicting efforts on behalf of the animals. Springer survived and eventually was able to join and bond with a relative group. Sadly, boat-following Luna finally was sucked into the propellers of a tugboat and killed.

The Human–Animal Relation in Experimental Work

There is widespread study of animals held captive under varied conditions not considered by investigators to be harmful, but away from the animals' native habitats and communities. The association with humans may be intensive, with

rewarded forms of animal cooperative response and development of a significant partnering relationship. It typically ends in eventual release of the animal
participant, with or without sufficient preparation for return to their home
familial group or community of animals. It includes research on echolocation
imagery by dolphins in which fine obstacles and nets are used to study the
limits of their detection in visual darkness. Their detection using sonar from
below, of objects above the water line, is studied in animals who obligingly
accept being briefly fitted with 'eye cups' (as observed at the Vancouver
Aquarium by the author) so that their optical vision is not operative. Although
investigators in dolphin studies are sensitive to issues of animal perception, *the
influence of their relationship* on what the animal can or is willing to do invites
new lines of study that include a focus on the relationship itself.

In the different case of animals used experimentally in controlled laboratory
studies, to advance knowledge for human benefit, large numbers have been
'sacrificed' in the course of gaining this knowledge. Although cruelty is not
intentional, ethical constraints have tended until recently to be minimal in the
research use of small rodent species such as rats, mice or guinea pigs. This situation is changing: in Canada, for example, significant ethical safeguards apply
in research contexts to members of 'all vertebrate species'. Some medical
research, however, looks to the potential of animals to provide or grow tissue
or other 'spare parts' for therapeutic transplantation into humans (see listed
Nuffield Council on Bioethics report). Generally the 'rights' of laboratory
animals remain on a quite different plane than in the cases of primate or human
life, and even where simpler species are protected the 'relationship' with them
clearly is one-sided in terms of governance. This is not to argue that exploitation of simpler animal lives is *never* justified. Very much harder to defend is the
use of highly aware and intelligent animals such as rhesus monkeys in invasive
research involving drugs, implanted electrodes and other treatments that
finally kill the animal or leave them permanently damaged – as occurred in a
biopsychology laboratory in a large university department I once served in.
(Nowadays, regulating ethical codes would rule out any such work or very
tightly constrain it.)

Harlow and colleagues (1965) raised a number of rhesus monkeys in total
social isolation from a few hours after birth for periods of 3 to 12 months. On
first exposure afterwards to other monkeys or humans the animals displayed
terror and went into extreme shock. One three-month-old died from 'emotional
anorexia' and another had to be force fed to survive. The filmed reactions were
disturbing to this viewer and other onlookers, and the research now would be
deemed ethically unacceptable notwithstanding the goal of throwing further
light on human development. (The researchers *claimed* that most of the animals
gradually recovered from the deprivation and trauma [ibid.].) No doubt there
are other studies of isolation rearing, and there is extensive work on cross-
species 'imprinting' of attachment as vividly demonstrated by Konrad Lorenz
(e.g., as noted in his popular books; Wikipedia: 'Konrad Lorenz'). Advancing

knowledge by means that are respectful and considerate of fellow species and that also are deemed efficient in the face of human need and investigator scientific and career priorities makes for complex paths and balancing of priorities. However, whether the study of animal response to disease and contaminants and their treatment is advantageous to humans *over all other options* is unresolved (see, e.g., Anderegg et al., 2006).

4. Relationships in Animal Conservation, Eradication and Health Care

'Conservation' of animal species has become an important value for many people. Stated less positively, since most species would look after themselves given the chance, this mostly equates to limiting human exploitation or environmental impact that could decimate or extinguish the species. The main relations under this heading are between groups or populations of animals and humans who care for or about them. The popularity of 'wildlife' documentaries presented by David Attenborough and others is testimony to widespread fascination with other life forms in their natural settings (and at a safe distance). It seems that the best documentaries promote a sense of commonality and relational feeling in the human observers, and a stronger concern for the interesting relatives that share our patch on planet Earth.

National laws or international agreements now protect many animal species that were formerly hunted down to small population or near extinction levels. They include elephants, rhinoceros, North American wolves, polar bears, fellow primates, and most whales and other cetacean species. Alas, many others, including the Tasmanian tiger, the early megafauna of Australia and New Zealand, and passenger pigeons – formerly the most prolific bird species in North America – were brought to extinction by human action, and a great many others are under threat of extinction (see International Union for Conservation of Nature 'red lists'). In some regions native species are protected, more or less effectively, by local legislation such as the Threatened Species Conservation Act 1995 of New South Wales. The colourless *word* 'extinction' refers to the complete obliteration of a whole species of life form. Its frequency is at a historically high level and evidently increasing, even among mammals and birds, mainly as a result of loss and degradation of their life habitats (Butler, 2011; Wikipedia: 'Habitat destruction').

The identification of a species as destructive pests or 'vermin' invites an eradicating response that, if directed to a class of fellow humans, would be genocide. Not uncommonly the animals that are now 'pests' in a particular region were introduced by humans, for example in the case of rabbits, cane toads and foxes in Australia, or rats and cats in New Zealand. Native species also can fall on a human hit list as in the mentioned extinction case of the Tasmanian (marsupial) tiger and species elsewhere in the wake of human settlement. There is also a great deal of unintentional decimation of animal species in the development of farmlands, open cut mines, oil and gas extraction and other industrial and 'resource' developments – and the ever-present growth of cities and highways. Without human intervention animal and plant communities tend to evolve a self-regulating balance. Generally, humans are a huge threat to self-balancing systems.

'Culling' an animal species that breeds strongly and is well adapted to its environment, in order to keep 'stocks' down (e.g., to preserve crop yield), mostly is done without selectivity, for example to take account of the presence of dependent young still alive but unable to survive. The issues of full impact over time or of how animal suffering can be minimized during the culling are neglected or insufficiently considered. Preventive methods of population control may also be possible as well as more humane. Distinctly stressed or abusive relations *between people* also affect relations with animals. These effects can spill over into mistreatment of family pets and domestic animals more broadly (Ascione & Shapiro, 2009). Human–animal relationships always occur in larger contexts, settings that sometimes include violent conflict between people. In human wars animal casualties and suffering result from habitat destruction as well as being in the line of fire. The bombing of population centres probably kills more domestic animals and pets (seldom taken to air raid shelters) than it does people.

In contrasting vein, major resources are invested in the health care of animals, both preventive and devoted to treatment and healing from injury and illness. While concern over animal suffering is a factor, other (self) interests also are involved in the specialized remedial care, for example of companion and worker animals. For veterinary doctors generally, their field is a calling and caring profession as much as in the case of physicians who serve human patients. Veterinary clinics and hospitals are widely accessible in 'first world' societies. Animal refuges may be available as well, to take care of lost, injured or abandoned animals without access to veterinary clinics. Compassionate volunteers devoted to the well-being of their charges and to finding homes or releasing them where possible (or to reluctant euthanasia where no alternative is found) largely staff these refuges. Protection and health care are added testimony to the huge variety of human–animal relations, as are the 'proxy uses' of animals next considered.

5. Relations in Human-Organized Contests and Entertainment

The first 'taming' and riding of horses began in antiquity and it is plausible that competition to see who could ride the fastest began soon afterwards. Horseback riding enabled a speed of movement in hunting and fighting. The relations involved in contemporary racing include those between the horse and trainer, horse and jockey and horse with stable hands, the competitive relations among the horse-and-rider dyads and the strong vicarious engagement of onlookers with the racing participants. The valuable horses may be warmly and well-treated in most contexts, though with ulterior motives openly expressed in wagering and pushing horses to their limits on the race track. At best (and with best results from a human standpoint), the human–animal relation is a partnership, even though of a master and servant kind and mostly to satisfy human competitive and social needs. In such partnerships, horse and rider communicate largely through a developed body language, as described in Brandt's (2004) searching interview- and observation-based study. Positive human–animal relations may continue after a horse's racing career ends in 'retirement' and/or breeding contexts. The treatment of racing greyhounds has been much more uneven.

Greyhound racing for organized human entertainment was a 20th-century development, substantial in a few Western countries, lightly present elsewhere and with no presence in some regions. It is not comparable with horse racing in scale or width of social appeal. Betting on race outcomes is not always involved, but is a feature in the more highly organized settings in the UK, US (though illegal in some states), Australia and South Africa. 'Successful' racing greyhounds have fairly short careers (to about age 4) and their fate afterwards has been highly variable, with many dogs destroyed when their human purpose no longer applied (see Lynn, 2007; Humane Society of the United States October 2009 report on greyhound racing; Wikipedia: 'Greyhound racing'). At best, ex-racers are re-acculturated and kept or adopted into families as pets. Camel racing is practised in some Middle Eastern and North African countries, in Mongolia, parts of India and even Northern Australia, not uncommonly with child jockeys. Camels appear to be less relational with humans than horses are, in racing contexts, but their cooperative and interdependent association in desert regions clearly has been of great importance to people historically.

Bullfighting for human entertainment and usually ending in the death of the bull is still practised on the Iberian Peninsula extending into adjacent France and in some Latin American locations. This ritualized sport does involve a high level of skill and some danger to the human contestant, as well as pain and associated suffering to the bull. For the bull it's a fight to the death making for a one-sided relation of lethal conflict for the animal. For the involved onlookers it could be seen as an outlet for emotions that cannot be safely or legally expressed in other contexts. The reader could readily extrapolate in regard to the human–animal relations involved in cockfighting, where the birds may be armed with blades or spikes attached to their feet and human skill is little involved, or in other human-engineered animal contests in which the animals are in danger of life or limb.

Old-time circuses that kept, displayed and used animals in a variety of acts have declined in prominence, due partly to development in standards of animal welfare and strong questioning of practices by animal rights groups. Circuses of their nature are prone to exploit animals, though not necessarily to the point of abuse and, at best, the animals arguably are in a safer, more supportive environment than their 'wild' counterparts. Individual animals do get known in close relation and the total picture of human–animal relations in these settings is complex. The European Circus Association (undated) has advanced spirited argument supporting the value and health of circuses in that region. They are held to contribute to human awareness of and positive relationships with animals, and there is an ethical code of conduct for the treatment and care of the circus animal participants.

6. Animals in Human Food Supply and Hunting Contexts

Animal lives end in this further major region of human–animal association, since they are bred and used for human consumption, and often also for production of leather and fur garments and for the value placed on horns and/or other bodily components. The animals may be raised in the open and 'range fed', perhaps to maturity and with some human contact and handling. The human controllers in this case are mostly responsive to the 'foodstock' animals' health and growth needs. The animal may of course live with some sense of danger derived from elements in its treatment (e.g., branding, forced movements and other handling) and its ancestral origins as potential prey of carnivores. Where the animals are reared or fattened in the artificial worlds of feedlots or chicken batteries they become literal commodities to the governing humans, and any conscious relationship is almost non-existent. Pacelle's documented account (2011) of the treatment of animals mass-produced for food in artificial environments, both in their lives and in their manner of death, is disturbing to read. From his roles as CEO of the Humane Society of the United States he reported from experience on the difficult, step-by-step process of producing system change against vested commercial interests and denials to awareness of the time.

In first-world settings it is considered most humane to conceal from animals that they are in mortal danger until the moment of stunning or death. In North America the design of the most modern abattoirs – largely based on Grandin's work – provides for the animals approaching slaughter to move through sweeping curved ramps without any distracting obstruction or frightening treatment. A short article (Grandin, 1993) distils the practical principles discriminated for animal handling and treatment, which rest largely on her understanding of the way the animals in question perceive the world. The human–animal relations entailed are rather different in the case where animals are killed in the wild for food by indigenous peoples whose prey usually are aware of the danger and often have a chance to escape. Killings often are quite matter-of-fact and can appear to be unfeeling, although in other contexts conducted with a certain reverence as earlier mentioned. In 'the wild', the communities of animals include grazing species that live in danger of their predatory neighbours, but are well prepared to make best uses of their resources to escape. Humans uniquely have tended to memorialize with trophies their (one-sided) hunting prowess and dominion over the world of big 'game' animals.

Fish, as a major source of human food, are hunted and caught in a great variety of ways. Baldwin et al. (1996) provide a comprehensive and detailed list. The people engaged in commercial fishing necessarily work to catch fish en masse, not one by one. Although there are benefits from knowing a good deal about the world and behaviour of fish, the hunter–prey relation in this case usually would not involve relational connection with the experience of the fish netted and drowned in air – and tacitly assumed to have a primitive consciousness. More awareness of the resourcefulness of fish, and of engagement with them, is within the purview of rod and line anglers. Fish stocks, including sharks and reef fish, are being depleted in most parts of the world. Water temperature increases that bleach coral beds also diminish their sanctuaries. The human–marine animal association largely centres on fish as a food source and, aside from ethical issues, is not viable in the long run even in the 'commodity relation' as practised.

This exploration, organized by kinds and class of human–animal relationship, has been an investigative overview. The explicit relationship emphasis is original, but the reader would find in the sources I have cited much additional information regarding human to animal treatment practices. Study of these sources also could suggest finer discrimination of relationship categories than those I have used. As in other chapters, I hope that some readers will take up the challenge to further this inquiry or integrate it with action plans. Broad underlying implications of what has been so far presented form my next focus.

Relations Between Humans and Other Species as a Pivotal Axis of Life

As discussed, there is such a great range of contexts in which animals are crucial to human life that any idea that we are an autonomous species above and apart from the rest of life would be a fancy, far removed from the real world. Expressed another way, humans are a huge presence that has a multi-sided relation to and impact on animal life. But the connection is more than an exchange; our essentially interdependent relationships with (other) animals develop their own momentum and qualities, and do so within a biospheric system of life as an extraordinary and intricately complex whole. As an alpha species with a high level of consciousness, humans clearly have great responsibility along with exceptional power within the living systems of nature. We put our own future at serious risk if we 'harvest' the finite abundance of life only for our purposes and nourishment as a single species. Also our potential for altruism and an ethical path is violated if we look just to a narrow conception of our own species interests.

In practice, humans tend to be very protective toward individual animals with whom a significant relationship has formed – not unlike the case where the other is a fellow human. Animals that are *not* individually known, even if from the same species as those that are, may be treated quite differently – even 'culled' in a conservation context, sacrificed in research, killed in a contest, or slaughtered and eaten. Experienced relationship seems to be the key factor in making the difference. Sometimes, the sense of relationship *does* extend from known animals – as companions or fellow workers – to unknown members of the same species. And, it seems that we *see ourselves* increasingly in our most human-like primate relatives. A broader sense of animals (especially mammals and birds) as fellow-experiencing ancestrally related creatures – with their own kinds of acute awareness, feeling and potentials for attachment – appears to be developing. If felt attachment with other life forms is indeed growing it could be the saving of the experiment of complex life on our planet. A heartening find late in this writing is titled *Assessing the human–animal bond* (Anderson, 2007). This includes 20 research questionnaires and references to some 50 other devices and procedures! A highly informative history of observation, thought and feeling toward animals, assembled by Preece (2002), may also spark the reader's interest as it did mine. Readable works on the emotional lives of animals include those by Bekoff (e.g., 2007) and *When elephants weep* by Masson & McCarthy (1995).

Animal welfare and the 'wellness' of human–animal relations pivot on an apprehension of the living world, simultaneously from the inside as an involved participant engaged with other kinds of known participant *and* also from a zoomed-out position in which we see things together in their dynamic interactive working. Fraser's remarkable book (2008), concerned with *understanding* animal welfare (and abuse), searches into animal experience and life informed by scientific observation and ecological and philosophical-moral perspectives. Fundamentally, much of his work has to do, in my terms, with the human–animal relationship viewed both close-up with much illustration and also through a wide-angle lens beamed jointly on social-cultural, scientific and ethical issues. A fascinating historical study of how animal consciousness, rights and welfare have been viewed over time since ancient Greece and Rome is included. As one instance, it seems that the mathematician Pythagoras was a passionate believer in the close kinship of animals and humans, and held that the slaughter of animals was a species of murder.

The fact that carnivorous animals kill and eat herbivore animals and some-times other meat-eaters, and in most cases would not survive without doing so, is scarcely an example to humans who could survive and physically prosper (as many do) without animal flesh. Relying on animals to concentrate needed protein also is a highly *inefficient* use of the plant resources those animals consume. I believe that many humans feel some degree of guilt about eating fellow creatures, especially of the same species as animals they have experienced in responsive relation, and could well become vegetarian if they had to do the killing themselves. There is one aspect of a much wider dividedness in the human perception of animals. On the one hand we see ourselves as a different order of life than (other) members of the animal world. On the other hand, the similarities are so evident and far-reaching that the continuity of life becomes compelling – as it already was to some individuals and groups in antiquity (ibid.). Great sameness and distinct differences go hand in hand across the spectrum of more complex life. The sameness underlies our closer relations and feeling for animal partners. Differences play a big part in how humans 'use' animals and, in other cases, leave us in awe of them. Differences of another order apply to a further whole realm of life to simply acknowledge.

Each person contains and depends on a vast community (billions) of tiny lives. The majority of these lives are bacteria that live in our gut and have a crucial role in effective digestion, nutrition, intestinal health and other useful functions (see, e.g., Sears, 2005; Wikipedia: 'Gut flora' [extensive references]). The human organism is host to this multitude that lives within us in symbiotic relation. There are of course other robust but pathogenic microbial life forms able to get past the body's defences in the human bloodstream and/or that may invade other organs. Internal 'wars' between microscopic combatants are commonplace and pass unnoticed if they are readily 'won' by protagonists defending their host. (Antibiotics may help to destroy a virulent micro-enemy, though at risk of built-in defenders being killed in the crossfire.) A systems-sensitive stance is a necessary aspect of advances in understanding this whole sphere of relation. It is also vital to effective understanding of our very consequential relation with the world of plant life.

In broader ecological view, Rowe (2000) sees the whole earth as a self-organizing system whose surface envelope, or ecosphere, had the capacity, like a vast living womb, to breed and produce organisms. Thus 'life' in Rowe's view is not synonymous with living organisms but more generally also applies to the larger environment of nature that gave birth to them. Capra (1996), from his searching review study of the nature of living systems, identifies self-organization and the working of complex (non-linear) dynamic exchanges of influence and relationship as central principles (see Chapter 5, this book). The metaphor of 'web' applies from the level of living cells to the whole ecosphere of interdependent life.

Conclusion

Other animals are our fellows in the intricately connected spectrum of a single overall journey of life. They are a marvellously varied band of relatives, with whom we relate in a great diversity of ways: broadly as companions, as fellow workers, as subjects of our research, and in our roles as conservers, master regulators and health workers; and whom in other contexts we exploit for entertainment or raise to eat as a primary food. How we relate, qualitatively, varies greatly between these categories and within them. At one extreme we interact in the weakest sense of relationship, virtually without awareness of the animal other's living sentience. In scope, our relation may reflect fear, indifference, a wondering interest and respect or companionate warmth and empathy. It is argued and implied here that the general tendency and balance of these kinds and qualities of relationship is of great consequence for the fruition and sustainability of a life-supporting world; an inclusive interwoven world that the human species is putting at grave risk. This danger is presently confined to our home planet and could be transcended. Assuming the continued life of our species, more likely than not it will in time become involved in relations within and with other worlds.

Part IV
Research and the New Paradigm

11

Researching Relationships: From the Plural Self to Big Systems

This chapter explores issues and research methods to call on (or to avoid) in studies of relationship broadly relevant to the interests of this book. It is carefully about research process, not an overall review of content. The kinds of investigation considered are those meant to strengthen and advance theory and to aid practical understanding. A starting focus is on the *methods* that can or might serve useful purposes in this complex region. The chapter then explores present and potential new lines of study over the range from intra-personal and small-system relationships through to the working of big-system relations. Much of this work, both done and possible, is not confined in approach to a single context (e.g., psychotherapy) or even to one level (interpersonal relations, for example) since the principles and important aspects of method are applicable across a spectrum of relationship systems. While research sometimes seems plodding and dull it is also, in this realm, a region of opportunity and excitement.

What Kinds of Research are Useful or Problematic in this Complex Region?

There is of course no one criterion of usefulness, and the potential value of studies of varied method and focus depends a great deal on the way the work is implemented. The following outline of different complementary types of investigation is offered as an orientation and as a stepping stone to the next part of this chapter.

1. Naturalistic Observation-Based Studies

To survey and establish main contours of a class of relationship, open 'wide-angle' observation and description is particularly relevant, especially to start with. Careful study of data gathered directly from participants, or from

145

observers, can yield a picture of the phenomenon in view, of its architecture one might say, including component features and where they sit in relation to each other. Altogether it is a broad region that can be considered under two headings, according to the way the data is gathered and the kind of analysis that would follow.

1A. *Systematic Qualitative Research*

Careful planning goes into this kind of study, though specifically not of a kind that pre-judges the shape of what might be discovered. Information is guided in its broad direction via invitational inquiry non-leading as to content that gives participants room for expression of their own experience, observations and meanings, which then constitute the main data. Some information naturally is added about who the informants are. A frequent step is then to generate a classification system that reduces and organizes the data from each person and for the sample group. The result is a distillation of the informant view of the phenomenon under study. A current methodology of this kind is closely described and illustrated by Hill (2012) who makes allowance for more and less elaborate qualitative analysis. Investigators would bear in mind that the informants, the data analysts and the investigator-interpreter all share in creating the pictures and understandings that emerge.

Research is a human endeavour always influenced by investigator perspectives. The challenge is to be aware of this influence and to avoid self-confirming methodology or inferential steps that are not thought through. In the present context, two or more judges may be employed to study the data in the form it is gathered and jointly work out a detailed approach to and framing of these data. A third person or 'auditor', who examines and helps to define the process of their work together, could also be involved (ibid.). The researcher may work as participant-observer, in open and sensitive mode, to the complex and many-sided process investigated. Or, s/he may stay carefully separate, near but on the outside, in the interests of 'objectivity'. In either case observer and observed are not only connected in a mode of relationship within the research process but mostly share membership in a wider culture or system of association that values inquiry and evidence. Questions of the kind 'Why am I, or why are we, doing this?', 'What *do* I/we hope to find out?', 'How might this be a stepping stone to further studies and knowledge advance?', and 'Is it likely to yield results or insights of practical value?' desirably would be part of an investigator-observer's preparation in the very human domain of relationship study.

Discovering the shape of the phenomenon studied by carefully discriminating component events or features and how often or consistently they occur is often a valuable first step. A further step in the same or a subsequent study might be to arrive at a picture of how these things unfolded and moved in a describable sequence. A kind of dialogue with the ingredients of observation that carefully looks back and forth and around what is seen is a vital factor in the emerging picture. This step, in a data-rich and subtle tracking of process, appears to be the least practised and most difficult to portray. In a relevant exception, Reid (2013) finely encapsulates a very similar idea in her discussion of reflective research practice. Arguably, such reflection has great potential for deriving the full value and meaning from the investigation. Relationships are involved at all stages in a qualitative research enterprise: generally with colleagues in planning a study; in gathering the data from participants and at times mentally re-engaging with them while examining the information they provided; observed within the content of the data itself; in any collaboration by more than one investigator; and in the reporting aspect viewed as communication with envisioned colleagues and readers. Finlay & Evans (2009) have written a book on 'relational-centred research' in which the participants are regularly involved and treated as active contributors to the research enterprise – effectively, as co-researchers.

1B. Action Study of Interactive-Relational Phenomena 'On the Fly'

In this related kind of research, a sudden dramatic social phenomenon or crisis event is tracked and studied in its human relations processes when or shortly after it happens, with whatever means the investigator can bring to bear. The phenomenon could be an industrial strike or an outbreak of violence, a natural or human-made catastrophe, the response of a community or organization to a crisis, or even the outbreak or process of a war in its human relations aspects (see Chapter 9). Hurricane Katrina in New Orleans in 2005 is one example of a devastating natural catastrophe that generated extensive research and related documentation (see Erikson & Peek, 2009). It would be a study in itself to determine, however, just what research data was gathered from residents *on site and at the time*. Report topics suggest minimal direct inquiry into relationship experience (Erikson & Peek, 2009; National Hazards Center, 2006).

A given study of this kind can resemble the first-mentioned systematic qualitative research, but of its nature is short on advance planning and includes improvisation as the situation unfolds. Participant-observers could well have helping/rescue agendas in the midst of the crisis and only be available to respond to the research inquiry after the event itself recedes. In the Katrina case, suddenly the greater part of the city was under water and most people desperately sought safety or waited for help amid the chaos. Interviewing for research and documentation, if conducted sensitively, also can have spin-off positive value as a debriefing experience for the participant witnesses. In any case, the purpose of this kind of research tends to be largely practical, that is, undertaken with concern to prevent or reduce the human damage from eruptive phenomena of a similar nature.

2. Study of Naturally Occurring Phenomena Where Much is Already Known

Astronomy is a field where a vast amount of observation already has taken place and a great deal is already known and theorized about that helps to inform further observation. By comparison, systematic study in the domain of human relationships, especially work that relates to this author's perspective, is at a very early stage – except in a few subareas. Work that is in the much-is-already-known category draws on prior study in its framing and focus. It has a theoretical base and typically involves extension or refinement of what already has been done, and thus is more targeted from the start than the kinds of research exploration first mentioned.

A genuine search for further knowing, and careful planning that takes account of what could realistically be concluded from the study as planned, are both vitally relevant. Sophisticated statistical treatment of the resulting data is not automatically required, but may be justified *if* in keeping with clear aims of the study and conducted with significant understanding of the assumptions and limitations of the particular quantitative analysis. Elaborate statistical analysis, for example, to find the chance probability of getting a particular result, is best avoided if investigators don't have a critical understanding of what such 'chance' means and are totally reliant on a pre-packaged system to do the analysis and provide results. Whatever the method in detail, the research desirably would make a contribution to theoretical understanding, suggest further inquiry and/or throw additional light on practice.

Carl Rogers' (1954) multi-level study of the therapy case of 'Mrs Oak', outlined in its content in Chapter 3, is pertinent here. It followed the less struc-tured early phase of client-centred research, the subsequent focus on the self as a pivotal construct and was linked to the then emerging emphasis on testing therapy outcome. The study contains four discernible stages: *First* is a careful observational description by the therapist of the emphases and unfolding of the client's therapy journey, amounting to a version of type 1, above. The *second phase* is a detailed account and discussion of extensive empirical data gathered over the course of therapy. This moves on to a close exploration of specific features of process and change that situates the study as an early example in its field of this more targeted second type of research. The *third stage* in Rogers' account returns to map the unfolding process of therapy via richly illustrative excerpts from the therapy discourse that amounts to a complementary version of type 1. Rogers' *last (fourth) phase*, his integrative summary conclusions, also has properties of my type 3 below, with some control features, but with a focus on individual personality and behaviour change rather than directly on rela-tionship. (The 90-page report is a tour de force as a single case research study conducted long before contemporary qualitative methods evolved.)

3. Study of Effects of an Action or Treatment with Use of Untreated Controls

Investigation of an existing practice in ways that make the interactive and rela-tional processes more distinctly visible may contribute positively to the quality and effectiveness of this practice. Sometimes this can be done by methods already mentioned, informed by a perspective that assumes that the process being examined is complex. If more exploratory methods have already yielded a harvest of descriptive information, interest can move from what happens to how it happens (Barrett-Lennard, 1998, pp. 233–234). A study that targets theoretically crucial features of a helping relationship and their association with outcomes of this 'helping' is an established example type (ibid., pp. 264ff.). Research data might be gathered in regard to a person's (or couple's or group's) relationship qualities or behaviour before the 'treatment' and again afterwards. A traditional form of control would be to make use of a matched untreated group (the matching may be a considerable challenge and is never perfect), tested and retested over the same time interval, thus to increase confidence that the studied practice process had something to do with observed change.

Sometimes the 'untreated control' aspect can be handled by observation or testing before a period of delay and waiting for treatment, then followed by a retesting before and then after the treatment itself (Butler & Haigh, 1954). This method does not require separate control participants, avoids their recruitment and matching, but may bias the treatment sample toward those who are both seeking help and willing to delay. If enough is known already about the phenomenon under study, and either method is implemented so that a clear result underpins a considered interpretation, this kind of research can help to further knowledge or suggest refinements to practice. Where these conditions do not apply, the results of such a study may at best have value as a learning exercise for the investigator and, at worst, mislead other investigators and practitioners.

4. Laboratory and 'Analogue' Study of Expected 'Cause–Effect' Linkages

Studies in which the data-focus is custom-designed to suit the logic and needs of the research introduce limitations and inference that make generalization to more naturally occurring situations hazardous. Work of this kind typically is guided by hypotheses that particular variables will move in step and with some kind of causal linkage. Even if everything else besides the influence of a treatment variable on an outcome (say) is, for practical purposes, held to be constant, this artificial situation does not take account of all the kinds of possible interactions that could spring into operation when the system is functioning outside the constraints imposed by the research. A naturally complex process of its nature also is likely to include subtle elements that may be picked up or intuited subjectively and that are vital components of the phenomenon being examined. Controlled experiment could throw useful suggestive light on particular interactions, but not reveal the unconstrained 'real life' working of the relational phenomenon under study. Investigator interpretation would be necessary for a plausible broader explanation, one likely to co-exist with other ways of understanding the results taken in context. Inapplicable 'double-blind' studies are mentioned below.

5. *Study of the Dynamic Working of Large Relationship Systems*

Research of this kind is even more difficult to do well, but is thought to be less fraught than the last mentioned kind with its potential for exact though mistaken conclusions. This type might profitably grow out of studies of one or both of the first two kinds distinguished above. It would assume that the phenomenon under study is complex, not subject to simple or singular determinants but systemic in its working – within which a variety (perhaps a web) of interacting components could be distinguished, as discussed in Chapter 5. The first phase of the research, aided by prior naturalistic study, would be to identify these component features and their positions in the system. Ideally, these would then be plotted over a succession of observations to see how one state of play in the system leads on to the next.

The methodology in this case would be dynamic. It could not, at the present state of understanding in the human relations sphere, be fully laid out in advance, but would unfold further in the course of more than one application to the phenomenon under study. This phenomenon might range, for example, from a stressed family system to a community's process in the aftermath of a natural disaster (see, e.g., Hodgkinson & Stewart, 1998; King & Cottrell, 2007). It might involve an international conflict. Since relational systems are emergent and 'open', a decision on a system's boundary (what is inside and outside the system) can hinge on investigator consultation and informed best judgement. Knowing how a relationship system works enables prediction, and could provide an evidential base for input that facilitates change in the system's course and minimizes harm or enhances positive effects internally and in interaction with other systems.

As implied, any of these broad kinds of research study depend for their usefulness on the particular ways they are implemented, that is, on the investigator's prior understanding and *the way the methodology is applied in a worthwhile context of inquiry*. Relationship research centres on the study of life processes occurring within and between dynamic systems. Controlled 'double-blind' studies designed to test the effect of a specific circumscribed variable (a certain drug, say) and rule out the 'placebo effect' of anything else (such as doctor or patient expectation) are seen as not applicable in the study of complex relationship systems. The principle of this methodology is also questionable. The fact that administration of 'placebos', even in drug research, is often accompanied by a degree of recovery or change implies that the human organism is working as a complex whole, not just by the piece-by-piece impact of particular agents on targeted elements within this whole.

Reid's (2013) conception of a 'person-centric research' framework and approach is very pertinent in the present context. Her model highlights relationship process in the research context itself as well, potentially, as in the data. She notes emergence as a principle and advocates methods that assume and capture the complexity of the human phenomena studied. I earlier mentioned her emphasis on highly *reflective* immersion in all aspects of the inquiry process and data. This includes data elements or 'strange' results that might otherwise be set aside as idiosyncratic or irrelevant.

Controlled hypothesis testing could not, as implied, be the gold standard in relationship research, although there is worthwhile experimental work done and possible. The study of complex interactive and systemic processes needs generally to begin with exploration research devoted to finding out the overall structure and process of the phenomenon under investigation – as in categories 1 and 2 distinguished above. In my present view quantitative measurement and hypothesis-testing study can best be undertaken only after the whole phenomenon has been descriptively mapped so that the context of targeted features is fairly well known. How a system maintains itself and evolves or changes in its dynamic configuration are likely to be vital issues both for conceptual understanding and for practice.

Research Paths: Intra-Personal to International

Previous chapters have advanced theory and touched on research that flows into what follows, which takes account of the classes of research offered above, but is organized on another dimension of variety. This variety reflects the scope of this book's study of relationship, from micro to macro contexts and systems. Self-diversity and associated intra-personal relations lie at the micro end of this continuum. International and other big-system relations represent the macro end. Big-system functioning cannot be manipulated for research purposes and so does not lend itself to the more experimental kinds of investigation in categories 3 and 4 above. Thus not all categories are represented within the dimensionally different spheres next considered.

Investigating Self-Diversity and Inner Relations

There is a considerable body of literature on the diverse or plural self (e.g., Dimaggio et al., 2010; Hermans & Hermans-Konopka, 2010; Koch & Shepperd, 2004; McReynolds & Altrocchi, 2000; Rowan & Cooper, 1999) but a dearth of systematic research. Dimaggio et al. (2010, p. 393) point to a lack of measuring or coding systems to explain the near-absence of research. The 'lack' is not complete since a couple of studies were earlier mentioned (Chapter 3) and there are at least two questionnaire methods stemming from different ideas and interests regarding the plurality of self. Altrocchi and colleagues linked marked plurality of self with lack of stable identity and possible 'dissociative disorder', and their Self-Pluralism Scale effectively asked respondents (using true/false items) how variable and diverse they consider themselves to be (McReynolds & Altrocchi, 2000). This approach does not link variability to different contexts of relationship. However, in another paper Altrocchi (1999) refers to earlier work by Donahue who viewed 'self-concept differentiation (SCD) as *the degree to which one sees oneself as having different personality characteristics in different social roles*' (ibid., p. 173). In the complex SCD method several social role contexts were tapped, including those with a friend, romantic partner, son or daughter, and fellow worker. In general concept (though not in internal theory or implementing method) this work appears to be the closest precursor of the research approach developed by this author, using his Contextual Selves Inventory (CSI) – already introduced in Chapter 3.

The CSI taps the way participants *experience themselves* in significant life relationships, as with a parent, partner, sibling, own child, teacher, workmate, and distrusted person or group. For each relationship participants rate themselves 1 to 7 (not at all like me to very or always like me, in that context) on 24 self-descriptive items. Since the self is conceived as primarily formed in relationships of differing kind and quality, somewhat diverse configurations of self are both expected and being found empirically (e.g., Barrett-Lennard, 2008). (Some of the CSI items are modelled after those in a 100-item self-concept instrument [Butler & Haigh, 1954; Ends & Page, 1959] that was ground-breaking in its time.) Fresh low-structure qualitative research that inquired into the ways participants see or *feel about themselves* in diverse relationships would have provided another source of input to the initial item selection. As it is, the item sample has been twice amended, and other adjustments were made for the most recent thesis studies (e.g., Fenton, 2011; Zec, 2011). Further research with the CSI could address such questions as: How self-diverse are different populations and cultures of people? How is their self-diversity linked to other characteristics of interest (e.g., gender, age, social or emotional well-being)? What is a healthy degree and quality of diversity? Just how do different self-voices get triggered in different relationships?

The CSI represents one promising methodology in the study of the complex relational self and its varied manifestations. Any theoretical platform that assumes or hypothesizes that the self is naturally diverse *and that this diversity arises from or is evoked by distinctly varied relationships* could give rise to pertinent research. Polster's thought in *A population of selves* (1995/2005 – also mentioned in Chapter 3) could provide another foundation for empirical research. Contemporary psychoanalytic theory that has a distinctly relational emphasis in formulating the process of self-development and conflict within the self could be another starting point (Wachtel, 2008). A learning theory or cognitive behavioural approach (pivoting on reinforcement processes) might be adapted to highlight learned development of distinctive self-configurations and open another way of studying these. I also expect that the ways that self is perceived in diverse relationships would flow partly from the perceiver-experienced levels of empathy and related qualities in those relationships, but this surmise awaits direct study.

Exploring Interpersonal Relationship Process and Systems

Couple and Other Dyadic Relationships

The members of a two-person relationship each have their larger connected lives of engagement. Thus, although each twosome can be studied and has importance in its own right it is not autonomous. There have been many studies in therapy, family and other contexts of the way one or both members of a dyad experience the other member's response to them (Barrett-Lennard, 1998, chapters 13 and 14). This sometimes is coupled with the aspect of how members *self-describe* their own response *to* the other. Thus these studies tend to fall within a transactional way of thinking about relationship. Most therapy studies within this grouping have been concerned with the posited enabling influence of the therapist's conveyed empathic understanding and/or their warmth, unconditional receptivity and the congruence or genuineness of their response.

The thrust of the many process studies measuring these qualities (or 'conditions of therapy' – Rogers, 1959) has supported their relevance to therapy outcome (Barrett-Lennard, 1986; 1998, pp. 264–291; Bozarth et al., 2002; Cooper et al., 2010). Although the correlational associations with outcome are in the positive range and often are statistically significant they are not consistently strong, due either to limitations in the methodologies or the underlying theory, or both. My inference is that the research shows that there is truth to the theory, but that it is not the whole truth. Besides the fact that this approach does not focus on the *emergent dyadic relationship system*, the theory does not take into account client expectancy, the relational life of clients outside therapy or the therapy relation seen in its practice context. This inference is broadly in keeping with Asay & Lambert's (1999) research-informed view that about 30 per cent of client change can be attributed to the therapy relationship, 15 per cent to expectancy (hard to separate out from relationship), a modest percentage to 'techniques' and the large remainder to client resources and (in my language) outside life happenings and relationships. The figures offered are not direct averages and will of course vary across different therapeutic contexts.

One main line of the many studies growing out of Rogers' theory have used the writer's Relationship Inventory (BLRI) answered by clients (sometimes by therapists as well) to assess perception of the therapist's empathic understanding and other 'conditions' variables (Barrett-Lennard, 1986). This work goes back quite a long way (Barrett-Lennard, 1962) and is where my study of relationships began. No sooner had these features of therapist response been successfully measured and shown to be related to therapy outcome than interest extended to also examining their role in parent–child, teacher–student and other pivotal helping and life relationships (individual and group), via slightly adapted forms of the BLRI (Barrett-Lennard, 1998, pp. 307–319). In a different second approach, external judges rate the therapist's empathy and other qualities. An observer-judge is a third person looking on and his/her judgements are based on behaviours (usually recorded) rather than participant *experience*, say, of being understood. Thus in this second approach Rogers' adapted conditions become responding skills applied by the helper. Trainees can learn the practised *ways of responding*, but this by itself has little bearing on Rogers' (1959) theory of relationship (see Pinsof, 1986, pp. 202–203, for further reasons for discontinuance of this approach). Even the theoretically close BLRI-based work in most of its applications has treated relationship as an interaction between essentially freestanding individuals rather than as an emergent life process with its own nature. Significant ingredients in the formation of a helping relationship are tapped but mostly not the resulting relationship system itself (but see below).

The concept of therapeutic alliance in the research literature tends to be broader than that of the therapist to client relationship although there is substantial overlap and sometimes the terms are used interchangeably (Asay & Lambert, 1999; Bachelor & Horvath, 1999). In most usage, 'alliance' accommodates the aspect of therapist–client concordance in goals as well as their relational bond itself. By itself the term 'relationship' does not point to a function, but is generic in human association, while 'alliance' suggests a goal-oriented collaboration. In practice, alliance measures (of which there are several) are mostly based on multiple-choice questionnaires answered by clients and/or their therapists (Bachelor & Horvath, 1999). The terminology has a less transactional ring than relationship viewed as pivoting on one person's response to the other. However, 'alliance' preserves the idea of two parties with distinctive roles within a collaborative activity.

With increasing awareness of relationships as dynamic *systems* not merely interactive exchanges, it became a natural further step to arrange a 'we' form of the BLRI to tap into couple, family or close-group 'we' systems. In this version the items read, for example, 'We respect one another', 'We usually sense or realize what the other is feeling', 'There is a friendly warmth in our relationship', 'We get uneasy when the other brings up certain sensitive things', and 'We each look at what the other does, from our individual point of view'. This form was initially used (in Portuguese translation) in a study of family process by Gomes (see Barrett-Lennard, 1998, p. 308) and was completed without apparent difficulty and with meaningful results. The instrument can be answered by either or both (or all) participants, and is targeted in a way that hones in on the emergent relationship itself. (If answered by a close observer of the relationship, 'they' would be substituted for 'we'.) The continuing momentum of more familiar uses of the BLRI, plus shifts in my own professional circumstance at the time, contributed to a dearth of follow-up research, using this 'we' form. This surely is an inviting domain for a fresh focus of original work – using the available RI adaptation or other instrumentation.[5]

---

[5] A complete guide in book form to the development, diverse applications, various forms and further potentials of the Relationship Inventory is in preparation by the author (publisher: Wiley).

Generally, however, the empirical study of twosomes (or trios, etc.) *in terms of their whole-system properties*, however pertinent in contexts such as family therapy, is a largely undeveloped area of empirical research. The mindsets of investigators in an individualist culture make it difficult to think about relationships on a level distinct from the behaviours and feelings of each one toward the other. Each person and their response is vital to the 'mix' but the resulting whole, in chemical analogy, is not a mixture (bits of this one and of the other one stirred together) but, as noted, is an emergent new compound with its own properties. Until theory-based research truly comes to grips with this transitional shift in level, and adopts a distinctive language for it, knowledge development will be restricted. Study of whether particular *inputs to* a relationship are relevant to individual outcomes, while still of interest, does not directly illuminate the new 'compound' of relationship itself or how these relationship compounds interact with each other. This is both challenging and exciting in its potential as a new focus of (literally) 'relationship-centred' research that is waiting to be actively taken up.

Family Relational Systems (Besides Dyads)

There is an extensive body of literature, including several journals, concerned with family process and therapy, that includes innovative and valuable work on relationship systems. Notwithstanding encouraging connections in general direction I have not encountered a closely similar stance to the thought presented here. The range and interaction of subsystems of relationship in family and other contexts has been the main focus of my work in this context, which traces the varied structures and likely dynamics of relational process in families of differing size, composition and outlook (Barrett-Lennard, 1984; 2003, chapter 7). New research might, for example, usefully test for the clear occurrence, working process and significance for family members of triadic and double-pair relational patterns in families. In smaller families these patterns may include all members and thus characterize the family whole. How these distinctive wholes are born from the more embracing kinship, community and cultural systems they are part of is another important potential focus of research.

There are many clinical publications, especially on the working of triads (see, e.g., Bregman & White, 2011; Titelman, 2008), but apart from Gomes' modest but innovative 1981 study, empirical research with direct bearing on the thought I have been presenting is difficult to find. Fresh investigation of family process that distinguishes the whole range of interior relationships and the context of outside systems can make a powerful contribution to knowledge and help to inform policy-makers and service agencies and also interested individuals confronting the complex working of their own families.

The Face-to-Face Group Context

Small-group engagement is ubiquitous in work, play and learning contexts. The subcategory of intensive groups for personal-interpersonal development has spawned considerable research. Most of the studies, however, have either looked at outcomes person-by-person – perhaps cumulated for the group – or at each member's relationship experience within the group. Data from partici-pants can and sometimes does also involve structured ratings or qualitative accounts of the group whole, as mentioned below. Data on the qualitative response or styles of leaders are most often in the form of member ratings and may be pooled for a 'group' result. There are few examples concerned with whole relational units.

My own work with a Group Atmosphere rating form answered at follow-up or after each group session is a modest example. (The form, listing 20 pairs of separated polar opposite words pertaining to a group, is published in Barrett-Lennard, 2003, p. 76.) The profile of ratings by members was found to vary session-by-session and it distinguished different groups in its overall pattern (Barrett-Lennard, 1998, pp. 296–297). It was evident from this work that a quite simple methodology could yield distinctive and interesting results. Another small-group study, conducted by Clark & Culbert (1965), focused on a twosome property. Each member provided data on the experi-enced empathy and relational response of each other member (via a form of the BLRI) that allowed a ranking of everyone else in the group from each person's data. These data were used to identify 'mutually therapeutic rela-tionships' – defined as those relationships where *both parties* perceived the other as responding to them with a level of empathy and related qualities in the upper half of their rankings. This 'favourable *reciprocity* of relationship' appeared in this study at least to be a factor in mediating process change over the course of the group.

A focus on group-wide qualities can be found in present research literature on therapy and personal development groups, although the prevailing individ-ualist and non-systemic mindset makes for unclear and uneven application even by investigators interested in how groups work. In contrast to this trend, Beck & Lewis (2000) offer an exceptionally comprehensive and system-sensi-tive view of the overall process in groups:

> Process research on the group psychotherapy is the study of the group-as-a-whole system and changes in its development, the interactions within the patient and therapist subsystems, the patient and patient (dyadic or subgroup) subsystems, the therapist and therapist subsystem if there are co-leaders, and the way each of the subsystems interacts with and is influenced by the group as a whole. (Beck & Lewis, 2000, p. 8)

Beck and her collaborators delineated phases in the development of therapy groups, based on close naturalistic study of a series of groups (Beck et al., 1986).

Each of the nine phases Beck et al. distinguished was characterized by one or more overall properties. Phase 2, for example, pivots on the development of group identity. Thus, in this phase the group becomes more than the sum of its members as some main properties of this 'we' are forged. Group members searched for and often struggled together over the key issue of the purpose of their group, its style of communication and 'code of conduct', and issues of leadership and roles. Scapegoating occurred but was largely resolved since Phase 3 was found to emphasize the quality of *cooperation* (Barrett-Lennard, 1998, p. 150, after Beck et al., 1986). In a previous paper, Beck (1981) had searched more broadly still into 'developmental characteristics of the system-forming process', arguing that there is a discernible order through which the living structure of a small group evolves when (and if) the process is becoming functional for its members. Altogether Beck's work has evolved through the first type of (qualitative) methodology earlier distinguished to include a theoretical base that is a feature of type 2.

My own account of process in experiential groups emphasizes the kinds and formation of relational subsystems, the possible emergence of factions (which Beck refers to) and some key overall properties of a group, especially its level of cohesion, intensity and tempo (motion and energy) (Barrett-Lennard, 1998, pp. 159–165; 2003, pp. 68–74). The relational subsystem aspects and properties could also be examined in *work teams*, although this appears not to have been a focus in research to date. Studies of group process within organizations need to consider other contextual systems that members also are engaged in, for the results to be illuminating and valuable (see further discussion below and in Chapter 8).

Teams in professional sport are another context with potentially distinctive group dynamics. The teams typically meet in training contexts strongly emphasizing skills development in coordinated activity, and in the enhancement of motivation to excel. Competing successfully against other teams is the overriding concern of coaches and players. Research on relationship experience within such teams and in the wider context of team members' lives could be evolved with a direct focus on relationship systems – with advantage both for the quality of life of members and for deeper understanding of the human relations working of competitive sport in the culture. There are, of course, also relationships with team owners and hosting systems and a potentially massive following of vicariously involved observers. Studies in this area could be of a qualitative kind and could also use or adapt instruments and methods employed in other relationship-centred group process research. There also is the differing sphere of low-key recreational play that is important to participants and that could be useful to study in its contribution to relationship development.

There appears to have been little empirical research *involving direct attention to relationship experience and systems* in big face-to-face groups. The extensive programme of large-group workshops (100+ members) conducted along

Rogerian or person-centred lines did not include systematic research, although there are some richly descriptive and integrative published accounts, especially by Wood (1984) and also by Rogers (1977). In reading Wood's account, published after further experience in large-group events, I felt it would be unlikely for a concluding synthesis from more formal research to be as freely searching, creative and finely nuanced. A formal study could complement but not substitute for such a distillation. A report by MacMillan & Lago (1996) illustrates the difficulty of obtaining good feedback data for research, while also speaking of its potential value. Their exploratory research was based on a 10 per cent return rate from a large-group European workshop, using questions that mainly invited feedback on personal gains through the workshop and how these benefits came about.

This author was involved in a limited exception to the general dearth of empirical study, based on a large-group residential workshop concerned with the development and experience of community and personal empowerment. Reports on this study appear in more than one place (Barrett-Lennard, 1994; 1998, pp. 319–320; 2003, pp. 89–97) and I will give only a broad outline here. An End-of-Workshop Process Questionnaire was conceived and formulated on the spot by a small subgroup within the workshop crucible itself. It thus reflected the live sense and idea of those members (Barrett-Lennard, 2003, p. 92) and involved the workshop community indirectly in some felt sense of ownership. There were open-ended questions, but only the more structured items provided usable data (all provided anonymously) in the conditions that prevailed. The return rate was 70 per cent of the 135 participants.

The first multi-part item listed a series of potential qualities of the workshop community. Respondents were asked to rate the importance of each aspect for a sense of community *and* whether this quality developed over the course of the workshop. The aspects ranked of highest importance were 'Climate of respect/caring/trust', 'Attentive listening to others', 'Tolerance for ambiguity and conflict', and 'Sharing and surviving crises'. Positive change was seen as a little higher for the aspects seen as most important. Although the listed elements are about qualities of interaction and relationship across the workshop none of them point to an emergent communal whole or dynamic, which evidently was not within the mindset of participants to address. For further use, items could be framed to include explicit attention to the overall system and/or subsystems of relationship.

Another questionnaire item asked the members to rank several contexts within the workshop as to their relative importance in development of a sense of community. Interestingly, encounter groups that ran in parallel with meetings of the whole were ranked first, meetings of the whole community came second, and one-to-one meetings came a close third. Even 'alone times' were important. The results accord with an impression that although the big meetings were by far the most 'magnetic' context and stretched people the most, there were difficulties for less forthcoming members and some members found them quite problematic. The data-gathering for this study was a last-minute development in the workshop, and rather hastily responded to, but it suggests process features and an approach that invites more fully thought-out and relationship system-sensitive empirical study of large, intensive face-to-face groups.

Investigating Relational Dynamics in Organizations and Communities

Organizations come in many forms, with diverse missions, and can be viewed in a variety of ways (see Chapter 8, and Morgan, 1986). Notwithstanding the variety in kind and approach, the research study of organizations *as systems of experienced and interacting relationships* seems to be little developed. One strategy in pursuing this focus is to build on from small-system study while also taking into account the very different dimension and structural features; these features playing a crucial part in the scope of (interacting) relationships to be expected.

This discussion aims to discern a path that will reveal and picture the relationship processes and qualities that characterize an organization, or some major part of it. One method would employ low-structure interviews with selected members, chosen with knowledge of participant roles, and selected to represent all levels in the system. Although relationships are such a basic phenomenon in organizations (Chapter 8), obtaining data on them is a sensitive region for research. At the least, careful prior consultation and ethical safeguards would be called for, especially in face-to-face settings where the data is not given anonymously. Assuming a given member has been briefed and has agreed to be called on, a natural first inquiry in the interview meeting might be to signpost the issue of how the person is actually feeling in and about their relationships in the organization and whether there are questions *they* first wish to ask. Further inquiry would have an invitational and conversational quality and not include closed questions unless for the interviewer to check his/her understanding of the other's expressed meaning. In the case of a carefully non-leading approach, this work could be conducted in keeping with the type 1 methodology earlier distinguished.

Inquiry questions that define the subject matter but are otherwise open-ended and invitational in quality can be, of course, variously framed. A draft of one possible framing is, 'I hope we might talk a bit about your experience of qualities of communication and relationships here. This would include the people you work and connect with, and your sense of relations and feeling between groups in the system. Are you happy to do this, in confidence and giving your own point of view?' Questions from the interviewee would be answered to help the other to stay on subject though still speaking from their own frame of meaning. Such conversations could be highly informative about participant expectations, personal experience *and observations* around relationships, including relations between their own and other groups, and felt attitudes from senior people in parts of the larger system they engage with.

A picture from the resulting data, when classified by content and linked to the informants' roles, could be drawn in ways that were highly suggestive of the qualitative working of the organization (or parts of it) as a system of human association and relationship. Varied inventive ways of assembling the information might reflect specific interests and/or the creativity of the investigator. Additional methodology could borrow from small-group research, especially as an organization tends to be made up from many face-to-face groups with particular function and responsibility within the larger system. How these groups interconnect and the qualities that emerge from their combination have vital bearing on the working qualities of the organization as a whole. Webb (2006, pp. 154–156) speaks of corporate cultures as partly being about constructing a 'we' of their whole system – besides the 'we' experiences in smaller component systems. The members of representative groups throughout such a system might be called on to describe their group's relationship with other selected groups and with the whole system. The members within some groups may give very similar pictures. Marked diversity of perception, or 'we' pictures aligned in two or more clusters that suggest factions, might be found in other groups.

Each of the main divisions of a large organization would include multiple groups, of which the official leaders would constitute a group that formed another relational whole that each of them could describe – these descriptions able to be compared or merged. The relations among the leader-members might be quite competitive (each concerned with the interests of their particular group) or varied in other qualities, and the relations in turn between divisions or branches of the organization would need to be studied for their bearing on the ambience and performance of the whole system.

The members generally of an organization vary in how much and in what ways they feel related to the whole system, and they could be asked about the linkages of most personal importance to them. The whole, with its somewhat distinctive culture (or subcultures), would tend to be an open system functioning interdependently with other large systems and with 'outside' individuals and groups in varied relation (see Chapter 8). The internal structure of many contemporary organizations is not heavily hierarchical and may emphasize cross connections and distinctive functions assigned to specialist officers and committees. Thus, any comprehensive audit of the working qualities of relationship would need to take account of the full complexity of the avenues for relationship.

Although organizations and communities can overlap qualitatively, in principle they are two different breeds as human relationship systems, in light of major differences in why members belong to them (see Chapters 7 and 8) and what their goals are. Communities tend to form as vehicles for association, relationship and the more personal enrichment of members. Community affiliations reflect and contribute to the sense of identity of members, and felt commonality is fundamental. Thus community membership tends to be an end in itself while organizational affiliation has a more means-to-an-end quality (see Chapter 7). These and other distinctions underlie meaningful study and comparisons among and between such systems. In terms of broad methodology the options for research are similar to those described for organizations. Meaningful relational features to study seem to be rather different.

Members may come into a community one by one, but more typically the building blocks are couples, families, friendship groups and people who bring some relational linkage(s) with them. Although communities come in many shapes and sizes, when a community is forming networks of association develop and link up so that members come to feel affiliation and belonging with the larger whole as it evolves. The vitality of a community depends on these relationships, which would be a natural focus of study in research. Chapter 7 pictures eight features of a well-functioning community, which could help to ground research designed to study the 'health' of a particular community. Each feature (especially numbers 1 to 6) could be expanded to include operational indicators, and a sample of members would be invited to rate their community on these aspects. A diversity of views are to be expected, but with more agreement and more positive appraisal in a 'well' community than in a weakly functioning one. The results potentially would be useful in several ways: (1) as a preliminary step in preparing to assist a community in its functioning and problem-solving, (2) as one basis for comparison of communities, and (3) as a means to further refine the criteria and method of appraisal.

Many communities are not well functioning, but are suffering or being eroded for a diversity of reasons in a fast-moving and unsteady world. To be open to research in such situations, some members at least would need to be able to take initiatives on behalf of their community and be concerned about its well-being and development. Thus action research designed to assist the community as well as closely tracking and studying the process for knowledge advance and reporting is the most likely kind in practice. Meetings and dialogue between community members is then a vital context both for the assistive process and as an avenue of data-gathering. The data might include ratings of the kind already mentioned plus direct evidence of experienced or observed relational attitudes and feeling among members. As in the case of organizations, there would be small 'we' systems to explore, and perceptions of larger relational networks in the (struggling) community whole. Perceived change both from an earlier time and during the period of assistance would be natural foci of interest. Reduced relationship cleavage and stress, and movement toward wellness of communal process referred to above and in Chapter 7, are likely to be desired and welcomed directions of change, and their detail and just how they came about would be of particular interest in the research.

This discussion has been primarily about directions and methods of inquiry with a distinctive and largely uncharted focus as applied to the contexts of organizational life and community process. This exploratory and ground-laying quality will apply even more in the big-system context next considered.

Approaching the Study of International and Big-System Relationships

Nation states contain a vast array of relational subsystems of greatly varied dimension, kind and quality, which interact with each other directly and indirectly through other systems. As discussed in Chapters 6 and 9, the different ways that nation states come into being have implications for the way they work internally and relate externally. The inner and outer are intertwined and the study of relations between two (or more) nation states needs to closely consider their 'inner' dynamics and how these feed into their relationship. But, how is it possible to study the inner relational working of a whole nation? It would not be feasible to do this comprehensively, and the best that might be accomplished would be to take wide-ranging soundings carefully conceived as representative. A major first step in this direction would be to decide on the features and cases to take 'soundings' of.

The organization of a large nation includes major systems of government and the linked political and administrative/civil service structures (national, state/regional, and local), educational systems under various umbrellas, defence and security systems, financial systems (including banks, trust and insurance systems and the like), major commercial, manufacturing and industrial systems, information and communication systems of varied kind, systems concerned with agriculture and food production, health service systems, religious organizations, transportation systems, recreational and entertainment systems and varied others. These systems generally may be classed as organizations of varied nature that contain distinct subsystems and smaller 'working' groups – as noted in discussing organizations. Looser or informal but personally significant communities of belonging also would qualify as being important to identify and sample.

Each organized system and experienced community has its own identity (and could be separately studied, as implied) but a great part of their significance lies in the avenues and qualities of their linkages and influential interchange with other large systems. Some systems clearly have greater potency generally or in particular directions than others do. Some organizations are likely to have much more centralized control than others. Some are in constant competition with others, whereas this feature is not prominent in other cases (perhaps in the health field or in certain specialized agencies). Defence and security, for example, may have great potency and only a few masters. A national relationship audit desirably would sample all of these mentioned kinds of system and others. Relationships within each chosen system *and* the ways that members of that system see and feel about its relationship with other interacting systems would be core sources of data.

Existing census data is largely about individuals and only in small measure and usually surface ways about relationships. It would have to be radically expanded to extend into some of the areas suggested in this adventurous thought. The audit imagined here would break major new ground and require much unfolding and planning. This necessarily would include extensive consultation, brainstorming and pinning down of steps; all of this done in ways and on a scale that would enable broad political and community support. Justifications for the whole enterprise would include providing a powerful source of feedback to the population generally, to government leaders, parliaments and policy-makers on all levels 'down' to the smaller participating organizations and communities. There would be implications for needed institutional development and renewal. The audit would lend illumination to tensions 'at home' and ways that these might be constructively addressed. It would bring into much fuller view relational processes with crucial bearing on how a nation approaches relations with other nations, or with a particular nation. It could shine new light on potentialities for whole-system interaction, and be hugely informative for the United Nations and other international bodies with appropriate briefs and resources.

Conclusion

This chapter covers a broad canvas of actual and potential research – with an emphasis on 'potential' in larger systems. In those system areas I have envisaged the direction of an approach rather than trying to portray its full shape and structure. Much fleshing out needs to occur on the way to implementation. One of the advantages of a consistent focus on relationship across the great spectrum of relations is the potential for overlapping methodology and a yield of results that can be examined and combined across levels. Research methods and instruments used in studying small-group relations, for example, could be applied in gathering data from the component groups in large systems and adapted and supplemented for direct system-wide application.

Evidence from close-up study of people in their interior self-relations, from the investigation of personal relationships and/or family and group 'we' and 'I–you' systems, and from the study of community networks, could all be gathered into a single framework of multi-level interactive association. The daunting complexity of conducting a relational audit of very large systems is seen as more feasible when manageable component features are also studied in their own right. I am encouraged by the history of cases where at first a new type or level of research seemed starry-eyed to most, even threatening to the status quo of established inquiry or belief, and yet finally bore very rich fruit. The next and last chapter freshly states the perspective of this whole book and further makes the case for a virtual paradigm shift in envisioning and inquiring into the working of our human species nature.

12

Summing Up: The New Paradigm as a Way Forward

The human person is understood as an embodiment of relationship in an intricately connected living world of relation. And, we share with all other species an environmental habitat that we draw on with every breath and engage with in countless ways (Chapter 10). This wider engagement with the world of life is often overlooked in the absorption with one another and with all the things we devise and construct. However, even to say 'with one another' is a language more suited to the idea of exchange between 'you' and 'me' entities than it is with an understanding of relationships as emergent modes of being with their own nature and properties. None of us, considered individually, is ever independent of our surroundings, never removed from any inward connection with fellow humans or relationally evolved inner voices, and never without any experience of language distilled from communication and conjoint meaning. Although we move into and out of immediate engagements, we do not exist outside relationship. Moreover, present absorption in one relationship does not believably imply zero influence from all others that are outside conscious attention. These thoughts lead into a summing up of the basic stance, assumptions and approach to knowing of this book.

The Basic Understanding

A perspective that places relationship and interdependence at the core of human life processes implies a different mindset and paradigm than that which underlies more traditional individualist psychology. That discipline, as evolved in Western cultures, has devoted much and often useful effort to investigate and assess abilities, attitudes, patterns of need and motivation, learning and behaviour change, perceptual and cognitive processes and other features on which people differ and on which they can be compared with others or with themselves at different times. It is broadly assumed that discernible linkages between elements of human functioning can be found within populations or under varied conditions that will support or not support hypotheses grounded in theory or practice experience.

As already noted, 'controlled' study of change usually seeks to isolate effects of one or a few conditions on selected 'dependent' or outcome variables. In present perspective, these, effectively, are extracted from a larger dynamic context with systemic properties. Thus, the connections studied are *not* considered and treated as parts of an open field system of interwoven and interacting components in which, for example, two or more elements might easily co-vary in one group or circumstance and appear unrelated in another. When relational phenomena are examined in their systemic complexity there is no expectation of linear patterns of association between discrete variables. One kind, for example, of meaningful regularity would be to find that a certain configuration of interacting conditions unfolds, largely of itself or in describable circumstances, into another configuration. Discerning such consistencies in the working of complex patterns is an acknowledged aim in other fields, including epidemiology, weather forecasting and the study of ecological systems.

In particular, serious human difficulties need to be understood in context and broadly as disorders of relationship rather than of personality (examined in Chapter 4). The stresses and pain suffered in *personal* relations have links with strains and conflict on a community level (Chapter 7) or in organizational life (Chapter 8). They can in turn act back to exacerbate differences on these and other levels. Therapies of relationship healing and development are best suited to enabling beneficial change jointly on personal and social levels. My search pivots on the view that the life of the self is one of connection and relationship, and that relationship systems interact with each other on many levels. Though this perspective runs beyond mainstream current thought, it does appear that societal awareness of interdependence is gradually evolving. There is great need to hasten and further this evolution.

The separation, effectively, of different kinds and levels of relationship process into different specialties and disciplines, as opposed to bringing them together under one roof as in this book, works in some ways to constrain useful growth of theory and practical understanding. It also encourages enclosed 'silos' of knowledge advance. Expressed positively, the paradigm advanced here is oriented toward replacing, or at minimum complementing, more traditional perspectives. It points to another way of thinking about human life as it is lived, with direct implications for helping arts and linked scientific advance. Although people have the potential to take a considered and active stance in life, the personal consciousness resident in each person is not just produced from within looking out, but partakes of the consciousness of others connected in relationship. And, besides immediate personal engagements, our membership collectives interrelate with other group relationship entities, and these feed into relations between larger systems. The associations of groups and of peoples are forms of relationship that variably link to personal identity.

Decision-making in political, economic, educational and other systems can be seriously flawed if it is done without any long-term view of consequences.

'Long-term' to me implies decades, generations or even longer time spans, depending on the context. 'Relations' do not only exist in the present but, by extension, with future generations and the natural environment to come. It seems clear that some social attitudes and enabling structures need to change to support such awareness and the qualities of decision-making that would follow. An absence of such shifts will allow continuation of hugely destructive interventions, including resorts to war. Understanding in the sense of having deeply examined and practical knowledge of how complex relational phenomena work is crucial for human well-being. The development of such understanding requires, in addition to empathy and engagement, a certain flexibility of basic assumption along with a steady inclination to see events in context and thus in their complexity. How we construe and approach discerning the order in complex naturally occurring processes is believed crucial for understanding and practice – as previously discussed.

Human Subjectivity Within a Systemic Relational Perspective

Though people are not autonomous each of us is a *distinctively interdependent* centre of consciousness. Above all, we are feeling beings, especially in relation to each other. By feeling I mean something that includes but is broader than emotion. Feeling flows into and from perceptions in relation with each other and non-personal events, and ties in with a need to fit experiences into a frame of meaning – extending this frame if necessary. Our lives are intertwined with the working and qualities of the large people-systems we jointly create, and these connections flow into our sense of who we are and influence face-to-face relationships. It is not surprising for someone to feel that s/he is a very small entity, almost invisible and without agency, in an enormous mass. This can be a truth of experience, but also is partly a frame of mind and circumstance since people simmer with built-in energies. In our conjunctions we are contributing architects and sometimes destroyers to the shape and quality of our home, our local and planetary environment and its bounteous other interlinked living inhabitants (Chapter 10). We influence our world, effectively, by shared inactions as well as by what we do.

A person's subjective experience and consciousness is interwoven with the behaviour and inner life of others. A focus on *systems* of relationship, if it is coupled with depersonalizing language such as role interaction, may neglect the domain of inner experience and meaning. However, envisioning the complexity of human relations processes *and* searching into the life of the self and subjective meanings go hand in hand as examined here. Thinking and feeling, empathic awareness and more detached reflective comprehension are potentially strong partners in human processes. It is almost a truism that highly motivated human endeavour of almost any kind is propelled partly by passion. Creative scientific endeavour, such as the search to more deeply understand complex human relational phenomena, is an instance of this. A systematic approach that is at once system-sensitive and experiential, as in the present case, is anchored in concern for qualities and levels of *lived* relationship, these feeding into a broader and more analytic framework of understanding.

Other authors have spoken of relationship as falling in the inter-subjective realm (Trop & Stolorow, 1997, for example). I have not used this term out of concern that 'inter' implies 'between' rather than joined within a new emergent whole. My focus is on relationship as a distinct though very wide band of dynamic human systems whose existence and working has roots in subjective experience that contribute to distinctive emergent properties. The understanding advanced here reflects a long unfolding journey of experience-based reflection and more formal study. The process has been one of finding a path that opened up as I proceeded rather than that of following a given roadmap. Intuition, a sense of direction and other subjective elements have all played a vital part in informing more guided and systematic inquiry. I venture to think that some creativity has been involved and believe that scientific and knowledge advance generally results not just from narrowly cognitive engagement, but also from the use of investigators' whole relational-feeling-thinking minds. One fruit in the present context is a stance alive to the complexity of human processes generally and the field of human relations in particular – including the aspect of felt human experience. The whole outcome, in its interlocking aspects, is a distinctive perspective that amounts to a paradigm.

A View of the New Paradigm in Current Essence

The term 'paradigm' is variably applied and open to misuse. A useful meaning is taken to be broader and more general than a particular method or model, although more specific than a general cultural outlook or *Weltanschauung*. It can refer to a mindset or stance in viewing a whole field and variety of phenomena and a shift of paradigm would then imply a revision of basic assumptions about the nature of those phenomena and how to meaningfully study and theorize about them. In his classic work, Kuhn (1996) opted for a sweeping conception of paradigm, referring to the constellation of ideas that are 'thinkable' in a scientific field and the associated strategies and ways of examining phenomena. From this position, a paradigm shift ushers in a new way of seeing and studying phenomena in a broad field, asks new questions and reconfigures research inquiry. The altered vision is internalized, compelling and natural or 'native' to its proponents – as can happen even in learning a foreign language when thinking in this language no longer requires any conscious translation process. In this case 'the transition has occurred' and the person slips into the new language 'without a decision having been made' (ibid., p. 204). The process of change can of course be self-conscious and an individual might draw on the new paradigm without ever 'going native' in it.

The contrast of worldviews offered by Becvar & Becvar (2009) has in-principle resonance with the position I have advanced here. In the prevailing Western scientific tradition, which those authors trace to the philosophy of John Locke, objects exist apart from our subjective experience of them and the basic scientific challenge is to *recognize* existing order, not to create or construct it. Mind and body are two distinct though connected realms. This fits the underpinning of contemporary individualist psychology that also emphasizes objectivity and clear, mostly linear cause–effect relations. The second worldview distinguished by the Becvars centres on systems thinking, which 'directs our attention away from the individual and individual problems viewed in isolation and toward relationship and relationship issues between individuals' (ibid., p. 7). This provides for reciprocal and holistic thinking, a more subjective and perceptual position, and concern for patterns, relationships and contexts. The Becvars particularly emphasize recursive influence, using the language of cybernetics, and they look closely (pp. 65–85) at the 'paradigmatic shift' to a systems view that can accommodate both growth and equilibrium tendencies. Their book flows from a central interest in family therapy and thus the topical scope is quite different from the present volume and this also influences the way the systems/cybernetics processes are spelled out and illustrated.

The basic features of the new paradigm, as I presently distinguish them, overlap with the just-mentioned thought, although conceived independently of it. The features I discern can also be viewed as axiomatic propositions in a fresh understanding of human relational nature. The summary outline that follows of these basic features is distilled from ideas and passages throughout this book.

1. Nothing and, in particular, no person stands alone and separate. Beyond their DNA-driven biology and physical environments, people form as participants in relationship. Thus relationship is a central medium in human becoming and, in its many diverse manifestations, is the primary process of human psychosocial life.

2. People are both agents and recipients of their relationship experience and they self-evidently differ one to another in the specifics of this experience. Each person is on a *distinctively interdependent* path.

3. A principle of emergence is fundamental in this paradigm. New entities, especially human relationships, naturally emerge from the coming together and combining of components (individuals or groups) into new wholes. The new relationship 'compound' has distinctive properties and its own nature.

4. The resulting relationship also acts back to influence and sometimes to transform the identity of the persons or groups in the relationship.

5. The human self develops in the medium of relationship and is context-sensitive. Since relationship contexts differ in kind and quality a person-self normally manifests diverse modes. A psychological theory or

diagnostic system that assumes that normal personality is separate and unitary is seriously flawed (Chapters 2, 4 and 6).

6.   It is possible to discriminate and systematically map the wealth of forms and qualities of human relationship, and thus to generate a working taxonomy of relationships (Chapter 6).
7.   Living systems are dynamic self-organizing entities whose working and motion is systemic, not driven by single causes. Particular events within such systems may trigger effects but do not govern them, effects that in turn have agency (Chapter 5).
8.   Larger human systems, too, are seen to pivot on relationship. These include communities, organizations and nations conceived as human relationship systems (Chapters 7, 8 and 9).
9.   The centrality of living relationship extends to other species and the biosphere. Human–animal relationships in particular fall into distinctive groupings in function and qualities and are of great consequence for the participants and their shared natural world (Chapter 10).
10. Research uses invented approaches to reliable knowing and is vulnerable to orthodoxy. The rebalancing in this paradigm takes systemic complexity in human relations for granted and is strongly inclusive of qualitative-descriptive and 'configuration-focused' investigation (Chapter 11).

As a whole constellation these 10 features extend beyond and complement related prior thought. Together they are key elements in potentially transformative advances in knowledge, in regions of helping practice and human service, in public consciousness and social relations on many levels, and in the evolution of relational life-centred values crucial for human and environmental well-being. The conclusion to this chapter and book singles out in a few words certain key directions of change already implied.

Conclusion: What If?

What if this paradigm comes to the fore and is widely adopted? Where will this take us as a professional-scientific and general culture? What if it 'goes native' on a large scale in the thinking and outlook of people? Each reader who has kept company with me through chapters of this book may have their own picture of what the implications would be, at least in respect to the aspects they resonated to most strongly. Broad developmental consequences I see include the following:

• Humans will have broken through to a better understanding of their/our own nature and will be finding new ways to further this understanding.
• From this increased understanding we will become wiser architects and conservers of our peopled world, in the crucial wide-ranging province of relationships.

- Helping processes on psychosocial levels will be contextually person-sensitive and centrally concerned with the healing and restoration of relationship.
- Research in the human relations sphere will use inventive methodology to study process and change in its natural complexity. It thus will advance connected theoretical understanding and support practices to protect, heal and enrich life.
- Innovative developments will include multi-level study of relationships within and between nation states. New light will be thrown on ways that warring conflict is generated, its human relational costs, and how healing can happen.
- Humans will see themselves as partners with special responsibility in the great spectrum of life. A growing appreciation of other partners and active desire to see into and conserve the intricate tapestry of the living world will be widespread.

Will the paradigm pointed to in this chapter and implied earlier actually take hold? There are some encouraging signs in a mixed picture and I deeply hope so. In any case, this book itself must end here. Last words in a work of this scope, which aspires to help to move our knowing forward, are a challenge to frame. My choice is simply to remind readers of T. S. Eliot's immortal lines about returning from significant exploration to where we started and knowing the place for the first time (see, e.g., Gardner, 1972, p. 897). I invite the reader who has searched into and reflected on information and ideas in this volume to turn back and reread Chapter 1. If you find new meanings therein, ones that did not come to you from first reading, I see two implications. First, your experience demonstrates Eliot's point and, second, knowledge of your response (my email address is in the Preface) would add to my sense that the considerable odyssey of this book has been worthwhile. Much has come more distinctly into view for me through this voyage, undertaken late in my career. No such task is literally 'finished', but here I must take leave of the pondering reader.

References

This complete list of mentioned sources is long. For students or other readers who may welcome suggestions of where to start with follow-up study a 'short' selection has been singled out and identified with bold print (author name and date). Most of these selected items include a brief annotation that points inside the source and/or to where it is cited in this book. (This selection is not meant to distract attention and choice from the host of other valuable sources cited, and listed here.)

Abrams, D. (1997). *The spell of the sensuous: Perception and language in a more-than-human world.* New York: Vintage Books, Random House. (Suggest chapter 2 and pp. 261–274 of this highly original and readable work.)

Alexander, R. D. (1974). The evolution of social behaviour. *Annual Review of Ecology and Systematics, 5,* 325–383.

Allaby, M. (1989). *Guide to Gaia.* London: Macdonald.

Allport, G. (1955). *Becoming: Basic considerations for a psychology of personality.* New Haven: Yale University Press.

Altrocchi, J. (1999). Individual differences in pluralism in self-structure. In J. Rowan & M. Cooper (Eds), *The plural self: Multiplicity in everyday life* (168–182). London: Sage.

American Psychiatric Association (2000). *Diagnostic and statistical manual of mental disorders.* Washington DC. Fourth edition.

American Psychological Association (2012). *Stress in the workplace (summary).* www.apa.org/news/press/releases/phwa/workplace-survey.pdf

Anderegg, C., Archibald, K., Bailey, J., Gohern, M. J., Kaufman, S. R. & Pippin, J. J. (2006). *A critical look at animal experimentation.* Cleveland, OH: Medical Modernization Committee. www.mrmcmed.org

Anderson, D. C. (2007). *Assessing the human–animal bond: A compendium of actual measures.* West Lafayette, IN: Purdue University Press.

Asay, T. P. & Lambert, M. J. (1999). The empirical case for the common factors in therapy: Quantitative findings. In M. A. Hubble, B. L. Duncan & S. D. Miller (Eds), *The heart and soul of change: What works in therapy* (23–55). Washington DC: American Psychological Association.

Ascione, F. R. & Shapiro, K. (2009). People and animals, kindness and cruelty: Research directions and policy implications. *Journal of Social Issues, 65*(3), 569–587.

Bachelor, A. & Horvath, A. (1999). The therapeutic relationship. In M. A. Hubble, B. L. Duncan & S. D. Miller (Eds), *The heart and soul of change: What works in therapy* (133–178). Washington DC: American Psychological Association.

Baldwin, C. C., Collette, B. B., Parenti, L. R., Smith, D. G. & Springer, V. G. (1996). Collecting fishes. In M. A. Lang & C. C. Baldwin (Eds), *Methods and techniques of underwater research* (11–34). Washington DC: Proceedings of the American Academy of Underwater Sciences Scientific Diving symposium.

171

Baldwin, M. W. & Holmes, J. G. (1987). Salient private audiences and awareness of self. *Journal of Personality and Social Psychology, 52*, 1087–1098.

Barefoot Artists: The Rwanda Healing Project (undated). www.barefootartists.org/barefootartists_rwanda.html

Barlow, D. H. & Durand, V. M. (1995). *Abnormal psychology: An integrative approach.* New York and London: Brooks/Cole.

Barrett-Lennard, G. T. (1962). Dimensions of therapist response as causal factors in therapeutic change. *Psychological Monographs, 76* (43, Whole No. 562).

Barrett-Lennard, G. T. (1972). *Satisfaction in work: A critical survey of theoretical concepts, research methods and empirical findings.* Unpublished review prepared in Western Australia (1952–53) and abridged (1972) at the University of Waterloo.

Barrett-Lennard, G. T. (1979). A new model of communicational-relational systems in intensive groups. *Human Relations, 32*, 841–849.

Barrett-Lennard, G. T. (1984). The world of family relationships: A person-centered systems view. In R. F. Levant & J. M. Shlien (Eds), *Client-centered therapy and the person-centered approach: New directions in theory, research and practice* (222–242). New York: Praeger.

Barrett-Lennard, G. T. (1986). The Relationship Inventory now: Issues and advances in theory, method and use. In L. S. Greenberg & W. M. Pinsof (Eds), *The psychotherapeutic process: A research handbook* (439–476). New York: Guilford Press.

Barrett-Lennard, G. T. (1993). The phases and focus of empathy. *British Journal of Medical Psychology, 66*, 3–14.

Barrett-Lennard, G. T. (1994). Toward a person-centered theory of community. *Journal of Humanistic Psychology, 34*(3), 62–86.

Barrett-Lennard, G. T. (1998). *Carl Rogers' helping system: Journey and substance.* London, Thousand Oaks and New Delhi: Sage.

Barrett-Lennard, G. T. (2000). *The warp and weft of therapy: Relations within the self – self within relationship.* Presented in April 2000 at La Trobe University, Melbourne and at PCE 2000 in Potsdam, Germany. Also published in French (2007c listing, below).

Barrett-Lennard, G. T. (2001). Levels of loneliness and connection: Crisis and possibility. *PERSON: Zeitschrift für Klientenzentrierte Psychotherapie und Personzentrierte Ansätze, 5*(1), 58–64 (article in English, with summary in German).

Barrett-Lennard, G. T. (2003). *Steps on a mindful journey: Person-centred expressions.* Ross-on-Wye: PCCS Books.

Barrett-Lennard, G. T. (2005). *Relationship at the centre: Healing in a troubled world.* London: Whurr edition/Wiley. (Suggest Part 2 plus pp. 65–81 on family process, and pp. 83–102 on community as relationship – 'an endangered species'.)

Barrett-Lennard, G. T. (2007a). Human relationship: Linkage or life form? *Person-Centred and Experiential Psychotherapies, 6*(3), 183–195.

Barrett-Lennard, G. T. (2007b). The relational foundations of person-centred practice. In M. Cooper, P. F. Schmid, M. O'Hara & G. Wyatt (Eds), *The handbook of person-centred psychotherapy and counselling* (chapter 10, pp. 127–139). Houndmills (UK) and New York: Palgrave Macmillan.

Barrett-Lennard, G. T. (2007c). La chàine et la trame de la thérapie: Les relations à l'intérieur du soi à l'intérieur de la relation. *Approche Centrée sur la Personne – Pratique et Rechere.* No. 6.

Barrett-Lennard, G. T. (2008). The plural human self under study: Development and early results from the Contextual Selves Inventory. *Proceedings of the 43rd Annual Conference of the Australian Psychological Society.* Melbourne.

Barrett-Lennard, G. T. (2009). From personality to relationship: Path of thought and practice. *Person-Centred and Experiential Psychotherapies, 8*(2), 79–93.

Beardsley, K. & McQuinn, B. (2009). Rebel groups as predatory organizations: The political effects of the 2004 tsunami in Indonesia and Sri Lanka. *Journal of Conflict Resolution, 53*, 624–645.

Beck, A. P. (1981). Developmental characteristics of the system-forming process. In J. E. Durkin (Ed.), *Living groups: Group psychotherapy and general system theory* (316–332). New York: Brunner/Mazel.

Beck, A. P. & Lewis, C. M. (Eds) (2000). *The process of group psychotherapy: Systems for analyzing change.* Washington DC: American Psychological Association.

Beck, A. P., Dugo, J. M., Eng, A. M. & Lewis, C. M. (1986). The search for phases in group development: Designing process analysis measures of group interaction. In L. S. Greenberg & W. M. Pinsof (Eds), *The psychotherapeutic process: A research handbook* (615–705). New York: Guilford Press.

Becvar, D. S. & Becvar, R. J. (2009). *Family therapy: A systemic integration.* Boston, New York, etc.: Pearson.

Bekoff, M. (2007). *The emotional lives of animals.* Novato, CA: New World Library.

Bennett, A. (1908). *The old wives' tale.* London: Hodder & Stoughton.

Bennis, W. G., Benne, K. D. & Chin, R. (1985). *The planning of change.* New York: Holt, Rinehart and Winston. Fourth edition.

Bhattacharji, P. (2009). *Liberation Tigers of Tamil Eelam* (Sri Lanka separatists). New York: Council on Foreign Relations.

Black, A. & Hughes, P. (2001). *The identification and analysis of indicators of community strength and outcomes.* Canberra: (Australian) Department of Family and Community Services (now, Families, Housing, Community Services and Indigenous Affairs).

Blatt, S. J. (2008). *Polarities of experience: Relatedness and self-definition in personality development, psychopathology, and the therapeutic process.* Washington DC: American Psychological Association.

Blechner, M. J. (2008). Interaction of social and neurobiological factors in depression. *Contemporary Psychoanalysis, 44*, 571–580.

Block, P. (2008). *Community: The structure of belonging.* San Francisco: Berrett-Koehler.

Bohart, A. C. & Greenberg, L. S. (Eds) (1997). *Empathy reconsidered: New directions in psychotherapy.* Washington DC: American Psychological Association. (Chapters 1, 3 and 5 in this fine collection are recommended to readers seriously interested in empathy.)

Bono, J. E. & Judge, T. A. (2003). Self-concordance at work: Toward understanding the motivational effects of transformational leaders. *Academy of Management Journal, 46*(5), 554–571.

Bozarth, J. D. & Wilkins, P. (2001). *Roger's therapeutic conditions: Evolution, theory and practice. Volume 3: Unconditional positive regard.* Ross-on-Wye: PCCS Books.

Bozarth, J. D., Zimring, F. M. & Tausch, R. (2002). Client-centered therapy: The evolution of a revolution. In D. J. Cain & J. Seeman (Eds), *Humanistic psychotherapies: Handbook of research and practice* (147–188). Washington DC: American Psychological Association.

Bradley, B. J., Doran-Sheehy, D. M., Lukas, D., Boesch, C. & Vigilant, L. (2004). Dispersed male networks in Western gorillas. *Current Biology, 14*(6), 510–513.

Brandt, K. (2004). A language of their own: An interactionist approach to human–horse communication. *Society and Animals, 12*(4), 299–316.

Bregman, O. C. & White, C. M. (Eds) (2011). *Bringing systems thinking to life: Expanding the horizons for Bowen family systems theory.* East Sussex and New York: Routledge.

Brown, C. S. (2007). *Big history: From the big bang to the present.* New York: The New Press (W. W. Norton distrib.).

Brown, S. (2011). American Public Radio presentation on *Play in animals and humans*: http://onbeing.org/program/play-spirit-and-character/feature/animals-play/2080

Butler, J. M. & Haigh, G. V. (1954). Changes in the relation between self-concepts and ideal concepts consequent upon client-centered counseling. In C. R. Rogers & R. F. Dymond (Eds), *Psychotherapy and personality change* (55–75). Chicago: University of Chicago Press.

Butler, R. A. (2011). *Extinction.* http://rainforests.mongabay.com/0908.htm

Campbell, D., Draper, R. & Huffington, C. (1991). *A systemic approach to consultation.* London: Karnac Books.

Capra, F. (1996). *The web of life: A new scientific understanding of living systems.* New York and London: Anchor Books, Doubleday. (Chapters 1 and 2 are a readable and solid introduction to the book's topic, with broad relevance to this author's approach.)

Carey, P. (1988). *Oscar and Lucinda.* St Lucia: University of Queensland Press.

Cashman, G. (1993). *What causes war: An introduction to theories of international conflict.* New York: Lexington Books/Macmillan. (Chapters 1–5 have good relevance to Chapter 9 of this book.)

Castiello, U., Becchio, C., Zoia, S., Nelini, C., Sartori, L., Blason, L., D'Ottavio, G., Bulgheroni, M. & Gallese, F. (2010). Wired to be social: The ontogeny of human interaction. *PLoS One, 5*(10), e13199. [doi: 10.1371/journal.pone.0013199]

Cederman, L-E. & Gleditch, K. S. (2009). Introduction to special issue on 'Disaggregating civil war'. *Journal of Conflict Resolution, 53,* 487–495.

Chick, G. (2008). Altruism in animal play and human ritual. *World Cultures eJournal, 16*(2), Article 4.

Cholden, L. (1956). Observations on psychotherapy of schizophrenia. In F. Fromm-Reichmann & J. L. Moreno (Eds), *Progress in psychotherapy* (239–247). New York: Grune and Stratton.

Clark, J. V. & Culbert, S. A. (1965). Mutually therapeutic perception and self-awareness in a T group. *Journal of Applied Behavioral Science, 1,* 180–194.

Clark, P. & Kaufman, Z. D. (Eds) (2008). *After genocide: Transitional justice, post-conflict reconstruction and reconciliation in Rwanda and beyond.* London: Hurst & Co. (Suggest chapters 1, 2 and 8, relevant to Chapter 9 in this book.)

Connor, R. S. & Smolker, R. S. (1985). Habituated dolphins in Western Australia. *Journal of Mammalogy, 66,* 398–400.

Cooper, M., Watson, J. C. & Holldampf, D. (Eds) (2010). *Person-centered and experiential therapies work: A review of the research on counseling, psychotherapy and related practices.* Ross-on-Wye: PCCS Books.

Copeland, S. (2005). *Counselling supervision in organizations: Professional and ethical issues explored.* East Sussex and New York: Routledge.

Cox, M., Guelke, A. & Stephen, F. (2006). *A farewell to arms? Beyond the Good Friday agreement.* Manchester: Manchester University Press.

Darwin, C. (1872). *The expression of emotions in man and animals.* London: John Murray. Edition used: 2009 electronic republication by Digireads.com Publishing.

Darwin, C. (1874). *The descent of man, and selection in relation to sex.* London: John Murray. Second edition.

Deacon, T. W. (2007). Three levels of emergent phenomena. In N. Murphy & W. R. Stoeger (Eds), *Evolution and emergence: Systems, organisms, persons* (88–110). New York: Oxford University Press.

De Waal, F. B. M. (2007). Commiserating mice. In 'Mind Matters' on the topic *Do animals feel empathy? Scientific American*, 24 July. www.scientificamerican.com/article.cfm? id=do-animals-feel-empathy

De Waal, F. B. M. (2009). *The age of empathy: Nature's lessons for a kinder society.* New York: Crown Publishers (Random House).

Diamond, M. A. & Allcorn, S. (2009). *Private selves in public organizations.* New York: Palgrave Macmillan. (See, e.g., chapter 4, as follow-up to the referencing passage in Chapter 8 of this book.)

Dickson, W. J. & Roethlisberger, F. J. (1966). *Counseling in an organization: A sequel to the Hawthorne researches.* Boston: Harvard University (Division of Research, Graduate School of Business Administration).

Dimaggio, G., Hermans, J. M. & Lysaker, P. H. (2010). Health and adaptation in a multiple self: The role of absence of dialogue and poor metacommunication in clinical populations. *Theory and Psychology, 20*(3), 379–399.

Doidge, N. (2008). *The brain that changes itself.* Melbourne: Scribe (also Viking-Penguin Group [USA]: 2007). (This book, cited here in Chapter 2, is engaging as well as substantial on its topic. Suggest chapters 2 and 3, and reader-selection from Doidge's index under 'brain' and 'neurons'.)

Dostoevsky, F. (1866). *Crime and punishment.* Trans. by Constance Garnett and republished in Cleveland by Fine Editions Press: 1947.

Dupré, J. (2008). *Climate change and microbes: Influence in numbers.* Environmental research-web – Talking Point, 10 December 2008.

Ellis, G. F. R. (2007). Science, complexity, and the natures of human existence. In N. Murphy & W. M. Stoeger (Eds), *Evolution and emergence: Systems, organisms, persons* (113–140). New York: Oxford University Press. (An interesting, useful article – cited in Chapter 5, this volume – within an interesting collection.)

Ends, E. J. & Page, C. W. (1959). Group psychotherapy and concomitant psychological change. *Psychological Monographs, 73* (10, Whole No. 480).

Erikson, K. & Peek, L. (2009). *Hurricane Katrina research bibliography.* New York: Social Science Research Council (USA).

Etzioni, A. (1968). *The active society: A theory of societal and political processes.* New York: The Free Press (and London: Collier-Macmillan).

European Circus Association (undated). *Animals in the circus: Telling the truth – facts and figures.*

Farace, R. V., Monge, P. R. & Russell, H. M. (1977). *Communicating and organizing.* Reading, MA: Addison-Wesley.

Farber, B. A., Brink, D. C. & Raskin, P. M. (Eds) (1996). *The psychotherapy of Carl Rogers: Cases and commentary.* New York and London: Guilford Press. (Suggest that therapy-interested readers consult chapters 1–4, at least.)

Fenton, K. (2011). *Self variability: A qualitative investigation of participant responses motivated by the Contextual Selves Inventory.* Unpublished BPsych thesis, Murdoch University, Perth.

Finlay, L. & Evans, K. (2009). *Relational-centred research for psychotherapists: Exploring meanings and experience.* Oxford and Chichester: Wiley-Blackwell.

Fossey, D. (1983/2000). *Gorillas in the mist.* New York: Houghton Mifflin Harcourt (1983); Mariner Books edition (2000).

Francis, D. & Hewlett, G. (2007). *Operation Orca: Springer, Luna and the struggle to save West Coast killer whales.* Madeira Park, British Columbia: Harbour Publishing.

Fraser, D. (2008). *Understanding animal welfare: The science and its cultural context.* Oxford and Chichester: Wiley-Blackwell. (Early chapters would be one good follow-up to Chapter 10 of this book.)

Furness, J. B. (2006). *The enteric nervous system.* Oxford: Blackwell Publishing, Inc.

Gardner, H. (1972). *The new Oxford book of English verse: 1250–1950.* New York and Oxford: Oxford University Press.

Gasana, S. N. (2008). Confronting conflict and poverty through trauma healing: Integrating peace-building and development processes in Rwanda. In P. Clark & Z. D. Kaufman (Eds), *After genocide: Transitional justice, post-conflict reconstruction and reconciliation in Rwanda and beyond* (145–169). London: Hurst & Co.

Gaylin, N. L. (2001). *Family, self and psychotherapy: A person-centred perspective.* Ross-on-Wye: PCCS Books.

Gergen, K. J. (1994). *Realities and relationships: Soundings in social construction.* Cambridge, MA and London: Harvard University Press.

Gergen, K. J. (2000). *The saturated self: Dilemmas of identity in contemporary life.* New York: Basic Books. Second Edition (First published 1991).

Gergen, K. J. (2009). *Relational being: Beyond self and community.* New York and Oxford: Oxford University Press. (Chapters 2 and 3 recommended as follow-up to prominent mentions in Chapter 3, this book.)

Gergen, K. J. & Gergen, M. M. (1988). Narrative and the self as relationship. In L. Berkowitz (Ed.), *Advances in experimental social psychology, 21* (17–56). New York: Academic Press.

Gibb, J. R. (1978). *Trust: A new view of personal and organizational development.* Los Angeles: Guild of Tutors Press.

Gomes, W. B. (1981). *The communicational-relational system in two forms of family group composition.* Unpublished Masters thesis, Southern Illinois University.

Goodman, G. & Easterly, G. (1988). *The talk book: The intimate science of communicating in close relationships.* Pennsylvania: Rodale Press.

Gozdz, K. (Ed.) (1995). *Community building: Renewing spirit and learning in business.* San Francisco: NewLeadersPress (Sterling & Stone).

Grandin, T. (1993). Teaching principles of behaviour and equipment design for handling livestock. *Journal of Animal Science, 71,* 1065–1070. www.grandin.com/behaviour/principles/teach.html

Grandin, T. (1995). *Thinking in pictures, and other reports from my life with autism.* New York: Doubleday.

Grisogono, A-M., Batten, D., Abbot, R. & Davies, P. [Co-chairs] (2010). *Causal and influence networks in complex systems:* TTCP Technical Report DOC-AG14-C&IN #4-2010. (Contact: Anne-Marie.Grisogono@defence.gov.au)

Harlow, H. F., Dodsworth, R. O. & Harlow, M. K. (1965). Total social isolation in monkeys. *Proceedings National Academy of Science (U S A), 54*(1), 90–97.

Hawe, P., Shiell, A. & Riley, T. (2009). Theorising interventions as events in systems. *American Journal of Community Psychology, 43,* 267–276.

Henig, R. (2002). *The origins of the First World War.* London and New York: Routledge. (Also, Taylor & Francis, e-Library, 2003.)

Hermans, H. J. M. & Hermans-Konopka, A. (2010). *Dialogical self-theory: Positioning and counter-positioning in a globalizing society.* New York: Cambridge University Press.

(The authors' generous Introduction spells out the essence of their innovative thought, introduced here in Chapter 3.)

Herriot, P. (2001). *The employment relationship: A psychological perspective.* East Sussex: Routledge; and Philadelphia: Taylor & Francis.

Hill, C. E. (2012). *Consensual qualitative research: A practical resource for investigating social science phenomena.* Washington DC: American Psychological Association. (Chapters 1–3 of this original new work are a good beginning – cited here in Chapter 11.)

Hodgkinson, P. E. & Stewart, M. (1998). *Coping with catastrophe: A handbook of post-disaster psychosocial aftercare.* London and New York: Routledge. Second edition.

Jacobs, D. H. & Cohen, D. (2010). Does 'psychological dysfunction' mean anything? A critical essay on pathology versus agency. *Journal of Humanistic Psychology, 50,* 312–334.

Jahoda, M. (1958). *Current concepts of positive mental health.* New York: Basic Books.

James, W. (1890/1950). *The principles of psychology. Volume 1.* New York: Henry Holt & Co. (1890). (1950 unabridged reprint [Vols 1 and 2 together]. Mineola, New York: Dover Publications Inc.)

Jewish Virtual Library (2012). Sourced from *Encyclopaedia Judaica* [2006 edition]: Macmillan Reference USA.

Joll, J. & Martel, G. (2007). *The origins of the First World War.* London, New York, etc.: Pearson Longman. Third edition.

Kelly, M. *Top five causes of World War 1.* In About.com: American History –http://americanhistory.about.com/od/worldwari/tp/causes-of-world-war-1.htm

Kennedy, S. E. (2005). *More than man's best friend: A look at attachment between humans and their canine companions.* Scholar Commons: Theses and dissertations, Paper 719. http://scholarcommons.usf.edu/etd/719

Kenny, S. (2006). *Developing communities for the future.* Melbourne: Thompson. Third edition.

King, D. & Cottrell, A. (2007). *Communities living with hazards.* Townsville: Centre for Disaster Studies, James Cook University.

King, R. (2010). *Evaluating a community-based mental health model in post-genocide Rwanda.* Presented to the Faculty of Social Work, University of Toronto. (Author is from Rwanda, working on action research for her PhD at the University of Toronto.)

Kirschner, S. A. (2010). Knowing your enemy: Information and commitment problems in civil wars. *Journal of Conflict Resolution, 54,* 745–770.

Koch, E. J. & Shepperd, J. A. (2004). Is self-complexity linked to better coping? A review of the literature. *Journal of Personality, 72,* 727–760.

Kolb, B. & Whishaw, I. Q. (2005). *An introduction to brain and behavior.* New York: Worth. Second edition.

Kovjanic, S., Schuh, S., Jonas, K., Van Quaquebeke, N., Jonas, K. & Van Dick, R. (2012). How do transformational leaders foster positive employee outcomes? A self-determination-based analysis of employees' needs as mediating links. *Journal of Organizational Behavior, 33,* 1031–1052.

Kreger, N. (2003). Putting sea mammals to work: Dolphins help coalition forces in Iraq. *Journal of Mine Action, 7*(2). (Publication name now *Journal of ERW and Mine Action.*)

Kreitzer, L. & Jou, M. K. (2008). *Healing from genocide in Rwanda: Alternatives to violence.* www.docstoc.com/docs/33101277/Healing-from-genocide-in-Rwanda

Kriz, J. (1985, rev. 1989). *Grundkonzepte der Psychotherapie [Fundamental concepts in psychotherapy* – reference here is to the final chapter]. Munich: Urban & Schwarzenberg.

Kriz, J. (2008). *Self-actualization: Person-centred approach and systems theory.* Ross-on-Wye: PCCS Books.

Kuhn, T. (1996). *The structure of scientific revolutions.* Chicago: University of Chicago Press. Third edition. (First published 1962, University of Chicago Press.)

Lang, M. & McCallum, P. (2000). *The answer within: A family in therapy re-examined.* Melbourne: ACER Press. (Whole book includes generous transcript information and narration of events. Recommended for all readers with therapy interest.)

Leray-Meyer, T. (2005). Review of Pape, 2005, *Dying to win: The strategic logic of suicide terrorism. Defender.* Canberra: Australian Defence Association.

Lynn, J. (2007). *Racing 'strain' on animal welfare.* UK: BBC report. http://news.bbc.co.uk/2/hi/uk_news/england/wear/6457425.stm

Mackay, H. (2010). Untitled *inaugural oration.* Melbourne: Australian Psychological Society.

MacMillan, M. & Lago, C. (1996). The facilitation of large groups: Participants' experiences of facilitative moments. In R. Hutterer, G. Pawlowsky, P. F. Schmid & R. Stipsits (Eds), *Client-centered and experiential psychotherapy: A paradigm in motion* (599–609). Frankfurt am Main: Peter Lang.

Mader, S. S. (2002). *Human biology.* New York: McGraw-Hill. Seventh edition.

Malouf, D. (1993). *Remembering Babylon.* London: Chatto & Windus; Vintage, 1994.

Mancinelli, I., Comparelli, A., Girardi, P. & Tatarelli, R. (2002). Mass suicide: Historical and psychodynamic considerations. *Suicide and Life-Threatening Behavior, 32*(1), 91–100.

Martin, S. (2007). Stop the genocide. *Monitor on Psychology, 38*(9), 26–27. (Washington DC: American Psychological Association.)

Maslow, A. H. (1970). *Motivation and personality.* New York: Harper & Row. Second edition.

Masson, J. M. & McCarthy, S. (1995). *When elephants weep: The emotional lives of animals.* New York: Dell Publishing (Delta book).

May, L. (2010). *Genocide: A normative account.* Cambridge, UK, etc.: Cambridge University Press.

McGoldrick, M. (Ed.) (1998). *Re-visioning family therapy: Race, culture and gender in clinical practice.* New York and London: Guilford Press.

McGoldrick, M. & Carter, B. (1999). Self in context: The individual life cycle in systemic perspective. In M. McGoldrick & B. Carter (Eds), *The expanded family life cycle: Individual, family and social perspectives* (27–46). Boston: Allyn and Bacon. Third edition.

McMurray, A. (2007). *Community health and wellness: A socio-ecological perspective.* Sydney, London, New York, etc.: Mosby-Elsevier. Third edition. (Especially chapter 1.)

McReynolds, P. & Altrocchi, J. (2000). Self-pluralism: Assessment and relations to adjustment, life changes, and age. *Journal of Personality, 62*(2), 347–381.

Mearns, D. (1999). Person-centred therapy with configurations of self. *Counselling, 10,* 125–130.

Miller, J. B. & Stiver, I. P. (1997). *The healing connection.* Boston: Beacon Press.

Milton, M., Craven, M. & Coyle, A. (2010). Understanding human distress: Moving beyond the concept of 'psychopathology'. In M. Milton (Ed.), *Therapy and beyond: Counselling psychology contributions to therapeutic and social issues* (57–72). Chichester (UK): Wiley-Blackwell.

Morgan, G. (1986). *Images of organization.* Beverly Hills/Thousand Oaks, London and New Delhi: Sage.

Morris, M. (2007). A collaborative inquiry between a person-centered therapist and a client: Working with an emerging dissociated 'self'. Part one: Adult Mary/Young Mary – one self, two parts. *Person-Centered and Experiential Psychotherapies, 6,* 81–91.

Motschnig-Pitrik, R. & Barrett-Lennard, G. T. (2010). Co-actualization: A new construct in understanding well-functioning relationships. *Journal of Humanistic Psychology, 50*(3), 374–398.

Nantulya, P., Alexander, K., Kanyugu, D., Rwamamara, S. & Mzungu, G. (2005). *Evaluation and impact assessment of the National Unity and Re-conciliation Commission [NURC, Rwanda]: Executive Summary.* Cape Town: Institute for Justice and Reconciliation.

National Hazards Center (2006). *Learning from catastrophe: Quick response research in the wake of Hurricane Katrina.* Boulder: University of Colorado.

Neville, B. & Dalmau, T. (2008). *Olympus, Inc.: Intervening for cultural change in organizations.* Greensborough, Victoria: Flat Chat Press (NMIT). (Suggest chapters 1–3. Book is original, readable and valuable, especially in relation to Chapter 8, this book.)

Nobel Prize in Literature (1949). William Faulkner acceptance speech. www.nobel prize.org/nobel_prizes/literature/laureates/1949/faulkner-speech.html

Nuffield Council on Bioethics (1996). *Animal-to-human transplants: The ethics of xenotransplantation.* London: Working party report – Chair: Prof A. Wheale. http://www. nuffieldbioethics.org/sites/default/files/xenotransplantation.pdf

Öberg, M., Möller, F. & Wallensteen, P. (2009). Early conflict prevention in ethnic crises, 1990–98. *Conflict Management and Peace Science, 26*(1), 67–91.

O'Leary, C. J. (2011). *The practice of person-centred couple and family therapy.* Houndmills (UK) and New York: Palgrave Macmillan.

Oliver, D. W. (1976). *Education and community: A radical critique of innovative schooling.* Berkeley: McCutchan Publishing.

Osborn, L. (2010). Number of species identified on earth. *Current Results: Research News and Science Facts.* www.currentresults.com/Environment-Facts/Plants-Animals/ number-species.php

Pacelle, W. (2011). *The bond: Our kinship with animals, our call to defend them.* New York: William Morrow/imprint of Harper Collins.

Palmer, I. (2006). *Managing organizational change: A multiple perspectives approach.* Boston: McGraw-Hill/Irwin.

Pape, R. (2005). *Dying to win: The strategic logic of suicide terrorism.* Melbourne: Scribe.

Pidwirny, M. & Jones, S. (2010). *Fundamentals of physical geography.* Second edition. Online e-book: www.physicalgeography.net/fundamentals/contents.html

Pinsof, W. M. (1986). The process of family therapy: The development of the family therapist coding system. In L. S. Greenberg & W. M. Pinsof (Eds), *The psychotherapeutic process: A research handbook* (201–284). New York: Guilford Press.

Piontelli, A. (2002). *Twins: From fetus to child.* London and New York: Routledge.

Polster, E. (1995/2005). *A population of selves: A therapeutic exploration of personal diversity.* San Francisco: Jossey-Bass (1995); Gouldsboro: Gestalt Journal Press (2005).

Pape, R. (2005). *Dying to win: The strategic logic of suicide terrorism.* Melbourne: Scribe. (Recommend the short chapters 1–4. Chapter 7, 'Demystifying Al-Qaeda', is suggested also, according to the reader's interest. Cited in Chapter 9, this book.)

Pope, J. (2006). *Indicators of community strength: A framework and evidence.* Melbourne: Department of Victorian Communities (Strategic Policy and Research Division). (Contact: Jeanette.pope@dvc.vic.gov.au)

Preece, R. (Ed.) (2002). *Awe for the tiger, love for the lamb: A chronicle of sensibility to animals.* London and New York: Routledge.

Prinn, R., Paltsev, S., Sokolov, A., Sarofim, M., Reilly, J. & Jacoby, H. (2008). *The influence on climate change of differing scenarios for future development.* Cambridge, MA: Report No. 163 of the MIT Joint Program on the Science and Policy of Global Change.

Prouty, G. F. (1994). *Theoretical evolutions in person-centered/experiential therapy: Applications to schizophrenic and retarded psychoses*. Westport: Praeger.

Pryor, K., Lindbergh, J., Lindbergh, S. & Milano, R. (1990). A dolphin–human fishing cooperative in Brazil. *Marine Mammal Science, 6*(1), 11–82.

Quarantelli, E. L. & Dynes, R. R. (1977). Response to social crisis and disaster. *Annual Review of Sociology, 3*, 23–49.

Rains, G. D. (2002). *Principles of human neuropsychology*. Boston, etc.: McGraw-Hill.

Rajewski, G. (2011). Navy dolphins are safeguarding national security and advancing human medicine. *Tufts Veterinary Medicine, 12*(2).

Ramiah, D. A. & Fonseka, D. (2006). *Reconciliation and the peace process in Sri Lanka: Frameworks, challenges and ways forward*. Stockholm: International Institute for Democracy and Electoral Assistance.

Raskin, N. J. (1996). The case of Loretta: A psychiatric inpatient. In B. A. Farber, D. C. Brink & P. M. Raskin (Eds), *The psychotherapy of Carl Rogers: Cases and commentary* (44–56 [transcript, 33–43]). New York and London: Guilford Press.

Raven, P. H., Johnson, J. B., Mason, K. A., Losos, J. B. & Singer, S. R. (2008). *Biology*. Boston: McGraw-Hill Higher Education. Eighth edition.

Reid, C. (2013). Developing a research framework to inform an evidence base for person-centered medicine: Keeping the person at the centre. *International Journal of Person Centered Medicine, 3*(2).

Reves, E. (1947). *The anatomy of peace*. London: Penguin Books. (First published 1945, Harper, New York.)

Roethlisberger, F. J. & Dickson, W. J. (1967). *Management and the worker*. New York: Wiley.

Rogers, C. R. (1954). The case of Mrs. Oak: A research analysis. In C. R. Rogers & R. F. Dymond (Eds), *Psychotherapy and personality change* (259–348). Chicago: University of Chicago Press.

Rogers, C. R. (1959). A theory of therapy, personality, and interpersonal relationships as developed in the client-centered framework. In S. Koch (Ed.), *Psychology: A study of a science. Volume 3: Formulations of the person and the social context* (184–256). New York: McGraw-Hill.

Rogers, C. R. (1961). *On becoming a person: A therapist's view of psychotherapy*. Boston: Houghton Mifflin.

Rogers, C. R. (1964). Toward a modern approach to values: The valuing process in the mature person. *Journal of Abnormal and Social Psychology, 68*, 160–167.

Rogers, C. R. (1967). A silent young man. In C. R. Rogers, E. T. Gendlin, D. J. Kiesler & C. B. Truax (Eds), *The therapeutic relationship and its impact: A study of psychotherapy with schizophrenics* (401–416). Madison: University of Wisconsin Press.

Rogers, C. R. (1977). A person-centered workshop: Its planning and fruition. In *Carl Rogers on personal power* (143–185). New York: Delacorte Press.

Rogers, C. R., Gendlin, E. T., Kiesler, D. J. & Truax, C. B. (Eds) (1967). *The therapeutic relationship and its impact: A study of psychotherapy with schizophrenics*. Madison: University of Wisconsin Press.

Rose, G. (2010). *How wars end: Why we always fight the last battle*. New York: Simon & Schuster.

Rosenzweig, D. A. (1996). The case of Gloria: Summary. In B. A. Farber, D. C. Brink & P. M. Raskin (Eds), *The psychotherapy of Carl Rogers: Cases and commentary* (57–64). New York and London: Guilford Press.

Rowan, J. & Cooper M. (1999). *The plural self: Multiplicity in everyday life*. London: Sage.

Rowe, S. (2000). An earth-based ethic for humanity. Prepared in English and translated for *Natur und Kultur: Transdisziplinäre Zeitschrift für ökologische Natchhaltigkeit*, 1(2), 106–120. www.ecospherics.net/pages/RoweEarthEthics.html

Rwanda profile, *Timeline* (February 2013 update). BBC News.

Sanders, C. R. (2003). Actions speak louder than words: Close relationships between humans and nonhumans. *Symbolic Interaction, 26*(3), 405–426. (This article, cited in my Chapter 9, is worth tracking down for the light it casts on the potential depth of the human–animal bond.)

Sanders, P. (2007). Schizophrenia is not an illness. *Person-Centered and Experiential Psychotherapies, 6*, 112–128. (Recommend tracking the journal down for this valuable article, and others the reader may find of equal interest.)

Schein, E. H. (2009). Helping leaders and organizational clients. In E. H. Schein, *Helping: How to offer, give and receive help* (128–143). San Francisco: Berrett-Koehler. (Schein is well known for his texts on organizational processes and development. The selected chapter in this more popular book stands out and connects with Chapter 8, this book.)

Schluter, M. & Lee, D. J. (2009). *The relational manager: Transform your workplace and your life.* Oxford: Lion Hudson.

Sears, C. L. (2005). A dynamic partnership: Celebrating our gut flora. *Anaerobe, 11*(5), 247–251.

Shlien, J. M. (1961). A client-centered approach to schizophrenia: First approximation. In A. Burton (Ed.), *Psychotherapy of the psychoses* (285–317). New York: Basic Books. (Also in Sanders, P. [Ed. 2003]. *To lead an honorable life: Invitations to think about client-centered therapy and the person-centered approach* (30–59). Ross-on-Wye: PCCS Books.)

Spiro, M. E. (1970). *Kibbutz: Venture in utopia.* New York: Schocken Books. Augmented edition.

Stanley, E. A. & Sawyer, J. P. (2009). The equifinality of war termination: Multiple paths to ending war. *Journal of Conflict Resolution, 53*, 651–676.

Starik, M. & Sharma, S. (Eds) (2005). *New horizons in research on sustainable organisations: Emerging ideas, approaches and tools for practitioners and researchers.* Sheffield: Greenleaf Publishers.

Staub, E., Pearlman, L. A., Gubin, A. & Hagengimama, A. (2005). Healing, reconciliation, forgiving and the prevention of violence after genocide or mass killing: An intervention and its experimental evaluation in Rwanda. *Journal of Social and Clinical Psychology, 24*(3), 297–334.

Sullivan, H. S. (1961). *Schizophrenia as a human process.* New York: W. W. Norton.

Teibel, A. (2010). *Marking centenary, the kibbutz reinvents itself.* Associated Press and Yahoo! News, 12 November.

Thompson, P. & McHugh, D. (1995). *Work organizations: A critical introduction.* Houndmills (UK) and London: Macmillan. Second edition.

Titelman, P. (Ed.) (2008). *Triangles: Bowen family systems theory perspectives.* New York and London: Haworth Press (Taylor & Francis).

Trenberth, K. E., Miller, K., Mearns, L. & Rhodes, S. (2000). *Effects of changing climate on weather and human activities.* Sausalito: University Science Books.

Trop, J. L. & Stolorow, R. D. (1997). Therapeutic empathy: An intersubjective perspective. In A. C. Bohart & L. S. Greenberg (Eds), *Empathy reconsidered: New directions in psychotherapy* (279–291). Washington DC: APA Books.

Turner, R. (2007). A collaborative inquiry between a person-centered therapist and a client: Working with an emerging dissociated 'self'. Part two: The therapist's perspective. *Person-Centered and Experiential Psychotherapies, 6*, 92–106.

Twigg, J. (2009). *Characteristics of a disaster-resilient community: A guidance note* (version 2). London: Report commissioned by the Interagency Group on Disaster Risk Reduction, funded by the UK Department for International Development. (Contact: j.twigg@ucl.ac.uk)

US Department of Health and Human Services (1999). *Mental health: A report of the Surgeon General*. Rockville, MD: US Department of Health and Human Services.

US-Canada Power System Outage Task Force (4/2004). *Final report on the August 14, 2003 blackout in the United States and Canada: Causes and recommendations*. https://reports. energy.gov

Wachtel, P. L. (2008). *Relational theory and the practice of psychotherapy*. New York and London: Guilford Press.

Walker, M. & Rosen, W. B. (Eds) (2004). *How connections heal: Stories from relational-cultural therapy*. New York and London: Guilford Press.

Warner, M. (2000). Person-centred therapy at the difficult edge: A developmentally based model of fragile and dissociated process. In D. Mearns & B. Thorne (Eds), *Person-centred therapy today: New frontiers in theory and practice* (144–171). London: Sage.

Webb, J. (2006). *Organisations, identities and the self*. Houndmills (UK) and New York: Palgrave Macmillan. (Suggest the Introduction and chapters 1 and 7 in this accessible and integrative work.)

Wenner, M. (2009). The serious need for play. *Scientific American Mind, 20*, 22–29.

Wikipedia (2010). http://en.wikipedia.org/wiki/Northeast_Blackout_of_2003

Wilson, T. D. (2002). *Strangers to ourselves: Discovering the adaptive unconscious*. Cambridge, MA and London: Harvard University Press.

Wood, J. K. (1984). Communities for learning: A person-centered approach. In R. F. Levant & J. M. Shlien (Eds), *Client-centered therapy and the person-centered approach: New directions in theory, research and practice* (297–336). New York: Praeger.

Wyatt, G. (Ed.) (2001). *Rogers' therapeutic conditions: Evolution, theory and practice. Volume 1: Congruence*. Ross-on-Wye: PCCS Books.

Yalom, I. D. (2001). Fat lady. In D. Wedding & R. J. Corsini (Eds), *Case studies in psychotherapy*. Itasca, IL: Peacock Publishers. Third edition.

Yalom, I. D. (2005). *The Schopenhauer cure*. Melbourne: Scribe. (This book is a work of 'fiction', but is founded on long professional experience and thought, and singled out as engaging and usefully illuminating regarding intensive helping groups.)

Yalom, I. D. & Lescz, M. (2005). *The theory and practice of group psychotherapy*. New York: Basic Books. Fifth edition.

Zec, C. (2011). *Multiple selves and the ideal: Variability in the self-concept and its implications for female self-esteem*. Unpublished BPsych thesis, Murdoch University, Perth.

Zimring, F. (1996). Rogers and Gloria: Commentary. In B. A. Farber, D. C. Brink & P. M. Raskin (Eds), *The psychotherapy of Carl Rogers: Cases and commentary* (65–73). New York and London: Guilford Press.

Zorbas, E. (2004). Reconciliation in post-genocide Rwanda. *African Journal of Legal Studies, 1*(1), 29–52

Name Index

Subject Index

Note: 'n' after a page reference refers to a note on that page; 'ref(s)' after a page reference refers to the References section.

Printed in China